YIELD MANAGEMENT

The Leadership Alternative for Performance and Net Profit Improvement

YIELD MANAGEMENT

The Leadership Alternative for Performance and Net Profit Improvement

Jeffrey L. Magee, CMC, PDM

$S{_L^t}$

St. Lucie Press

Boca Raton   Boston   London   New York   Washington, D.C.

HD
57.7
.M34
1998

Library of Congress Cataloging-in-Publication Data

Magee, Jeffrey L.
    Yield management : the leadership alternative for performance and
net profit improvement / Jeffry L. Magee.
            p.   cm.
    Includes bibliographical references and index.
    ISBN 1-57444-206-6 (alk. paper)
    1. Leadership. 2. Corporate profits.   I. Title.
HD57.7.M34 1998
658.4′092—dc21   97-45717
                                                                                     CIP

No claim to original U.S. Government works
International Standard Book Number 1-57444-206-6
Library of Congress Card Number   97-45717
Printed in the United States of America   1 2 3 4 5 6 7 8 9 0
Printed on acid-free paper

FOREWORD

Over the past thirty years it has been my good fortune to live a life mixed with the excitement of managing within a global multi-business organization and a mid-sized financial services business as well as sharing my experiences with students of business.

During that time, many have joined in the dialogue of untangling the elemental differences between what it takes to become a capable manager and what it takes to become an effective leader. If there is a difference which favors leadership, just how do leaders get people to do things they don't want to do and, moreover, how do they get them to like it? Is the seed of motivation within the manager or does motivation come from within the worker? How does the successful manager adapt his leadership style to varying situations yet maintain a sense of credibility among his followers? Is Taylor right? Or does the thinking of Maslow and McGregor make more sense in the new work environment of this century and beyond? What is a transformational leader and how is one developed? Is it possible to empower workers to become self-managers, let alone have them develop the traits of self-leaders?

Jeff Magee has found a way to meld broader concepts based on accepted and emergent management theory into practical demonstrations of "how-to" become a successful leader. Magee's work provides a practitioner's approach to development of the tools required to lead people.

Yield Management holds the key to why one manager may be thought of as a productive leader while another is capable but ranks lower on the succession chart. The answer may be contained in the thought that effective leading requires significant understanding of the "people challenges" of the new work environment.

Yield Management makes a strong contribution to defining the differences between **managing** and **leading** in a very readable format. For managers and leaders who have yet to embrace the notion of "corporate culture" as other than a soft ivory-tower issue, this book presents a practical and personal approach to identification of key people issues. In Section One Magee's approach embraces the accepted thought that there is no best leadership style for all situations. Thus, there is a continual sensitivity to drawing upon a learned skill of adapting to the leadership style which will result in the successful achievement of the management task at hand.

Section Two presents straightforward methods for transforming the practice of management to leadership styles tailored to meet the challenges of the new work environment in a very personal way. Magee has captured the power of the sentiment that adaptive leadership styles seek to match strategic intent to workers' abilities and personal needs.

If there is a "best" leadership style, it is one built on recognition of the nature of the tasks to be performed and the relationship one has with those involved in successful completion of the tasks. **Yield Management**© will empower you to reach the levels of management and leadership success you desire.

Anthony Marshall, Ph.D.
Dean, Business School
Columbia College

PREFACE

Gaining a marketable and manageable advantage in today's place of business is critical to both survival and growth. How individuals within organizations manage their resources and develop leadership skills to lead the people on their teams is the focus of *"Yield Management: The Leadership Alternative for Performance and Net Profit Improvement"*.

Sadly enough, though, many business schools and graduate level courses in management still profess the ways of days gone by. This may be due in part to the fact that many college professors teaching today have never held any sort of professional position within the communities they teach except that of professor! And in some cases, there are even some professors teaching at the college and university level who don't have the credentials they profess to have.

Gaining a better understanding of what does and what doesn't work requires neither an advanced degree nor some high profile celebrity consultant with top selling pop-science books. What it does take is minds and eyes open to the successes and failures around you. Model your development and behavior after the successes you see and experience and avoid repetitive patterns that have led others to failure and bankruptcy. In fact, look at the stewardship of leading businesses around your community and across the nation. Notice that in the first four years of the 1990s there were more displaced CEOs of Fortune 500 firms than in the previous twenty-five years.

Some firms and some managers and leaders, though, are very stead-fast in changing their ways and expect others to change to fit and meet their styles and needs. This compounds stress, anxiety and failures within the work environments which could have been otherwise avoided. Consider some large firms and their styles of management and the executive level influences which mentally support the negative behaviors that ultimately lead to the collapse of institutional leaders - witness the migration of some of the fired CEOs of Fortune 500 firms. Many serve on one another's Board of Directors!

So how can you identify signs of a decaying organizational structure and leadership? How can you initiate change patterns and institute winning alternative management ways? The answer is not as difficult as some would have you believe! Consider some of the following warning signs and note which ones sound like your environment:

✓   **Warning Signs of Decaying Management**
• Only senior management can call meetings. • Only senior management initiates new policies, procedures and directives. • Only senior management initiates training and educational development ideas, curriculum, sessions. • Senior management initiates training programs for staff and doesn't participate themselves. • A tendency to deny problems or unpleasant situations exist. • Excessive need for controls. • A tendency toward secrecy and mid-level manager controls on information and access to materials necessary for successful development unless managers are involved. • Compulsive behavior. • Autocratic leadership and thinking. • Inconsistent moods (mood swings) and emotions. • An overriding loyalty to the organization that leads to maintaining the status quo at all costs. • Inability to successfully address critical issues. • Overriding tendency to involve emotions in issues. • A protective attitude that guards against discussing certain topics. • Strict lines of authority and power. Little vertical movement. • Defined lines of bureaucracy and layers of management that may outweigh workers on the staff. • Layers of mid-level managers that may equal one manager for as few as 20 to 50 rank-and-file workers.

Total number of responses that match your environment,
= _____ !

As you worked through the questions in the "*Warning Signs of Decaying Management Inventory*" (previous page), did you feel your emotions become involved in the questions? Did you have several signs which were present in your environment?

Whether your management style resembles the previous chart or not, there are alternative management styles that can be utilized at every level of management to instill self-confidence among your organization's players, allowing them to become proactive and to attain higher levels of success.

Reflect upon the changing environment that you live and work in. Consider the *chaos* the market stimulates and you, in turn, have to operate in. With changing markets, increased competition (locally, regionally, nationally and internationally) and changing needs among the players on your team, your ability to manage with alternative styles and techniques is fundamental to your success and ability to provide world-class _____ (your product or service) to your internal and external customers.

Why this book? The answer is easy! Today there are literally dozens of management and leadership books populating the market, yet not one of these new gospels arms individuals with the ideas, techniques, formulas and tools necessary to attain peak performance. Many books by some of today's leading authors don't even tell the educated reader anything more than the current litany of existing leading business names and a profile of what they are either doing or have done - no step-by-step tools. It doesn't take a rocket scientist to search for, identify and profile today's excellent companies!

Yield Management looks at organizational dynamics unlike previously seen. **SECTION ONE** will focus energies on ideas, methodologies and those strategies that will impact *Strategic Planning (SP)* activities and efforts. With **SECTION TWO**, the foundations of leadership will illustrate the immediate application techniques necessary for *Organizational Development (OD)*. The design of these two sections requires that successful leaders and management personnel incorporate ideas from the two sections into individual efforts. **SECTION THREE** then takes the material presented one step further and illustrates how many organizations around you serve as effective successful role models to effective stewardship of organizational dynamics as presented throughout this book. Being competitive in your marketplace requires alternative styles of management and leadership.

Compounding this further is an emphasis on organizational and *Corporate Cultures (CC)* and the evolutionary changes which they are experiencing today. In an attempt to design environments which foster, promote and which are conducive to dynamic interactions and growth, this publication will explore numerous ways in which success and effective interactions can be attained. *We are no longer in a professional marketplace of "Heads" versus "Hands" management mentality* !

To be successful, today's management leader must encharge, empower and enforce people to feel powerful, rather than helpless - become a "value-added leader" with alternative management skills (and ultimately lead you and those around you to attaining the "BETA" Factor ©!).

> As Aristotle said, "We are what we repeatedly do. Excellence, then, is not an act, but a habit."

Now! Learn "how-to" utilize alternative styles of management with each interaction to attain maximum results and stimulate maximum performance from each person you come into contact with. Here is your *step-by-step management-to-leadership users' guide* to serve as the skill development map for emerging leaders - become a change manager and leader for tomorrow, today!

Jeffrey L. Magee, *PDM*

"What lies in front of you and what lies behind you, pales in significance when compared to that which lies within you ... unless you try to do something beyond what you have already mastered, you will never grow!"
• Ralph Waldo Emerson

About The Author

Jeffrey L. Magee, CMC / PDM, is a recognized authority with explosive ideas, a style that captivates audiences, and an energy level that is contagious. He presents more than 200 keynote and educational seminars each year internationally. He is also one of the most requested business speakers in America presenting repeatedly throughout all 50 states. In addition to all this activity he started JEFF MAGEE INTERNATIONAL® in 1990 (a management consulting and training firm), has written five best-selling books, produced two personal success-oriented audio tapes series and anchored a team building supervisory video series - audios and video through CareerTrack® Seminars and SkillPath® Seminars. And, he serves as publisher of Performance magazine. Jeff is also a Certified Management Consultant through the Institute of Management Consultants, the only recognized US-based member of the International Council of Management Consulting Institutes. Jeff is also a member of Who's Who In Business.

His tenure includes ten years as business reporter, a top nationally ranked sales person with a Fortune 500 firm, management positions within the Fortune 500 and as the chief operating officer for a national publishing and marketing business.

Contents

SECTION THREE

SECTION ONE

Chapter 1

Ground Zero -
All Factors Being Equal

"Management today is reactive behavior.
You put your hand on a hot stove and yank
it off. A cat would know to do as much."
• W. Edwards Deming

"The operational mind-set of "Heads" versus "Hands"
in an organization can no longer be allowed to exist.
Every "Hand" within an organization has a "Head" and
every player has to be cultivated and empowered to
take ownership and use their head while using their
hands to make things happen!"
• Jeff Magee

GROUND ZERO -
ALL FACTORS BEING EQUAL

Traditional business school doctrine for decades in America was one which professed lines of authority, lines of responsibility and account-ability. Upper management layers were reserved for analysis and direction. Lower levels of management needed the hand and guidance of upper management; likewise rank-and-file workers needed the hand and guidance of middle managers for productivity and success. This style of management actually stifles growth and productivity in workers. There are even studies on traditional management styles and hierarchies ("Heads" versus "Hands") which show them doing more damage to the overall organizational growth in the long term.

Traditional and old school management styles resemble a pyramid in structure. In fact, does your organization resemble this?

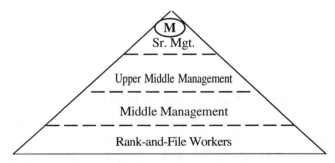

The Wharton School of Business studied this traditional format and organizational structure and found the awareness levels of the individuals within the various levels ranged dramatically in being able to pinpoint the challenges and problems facing an organization!

They found that the *Rank-and-File* workers could identify roughly 44 percent of the challenges and problems facing an organization on a regular daily basis.

The upper layers of management break down dramatically. *Mid and Upper levels of Management* could identify roughly 14 percent of the challenges and problems facing an organization. *Senior Management* could identify roughly four percent of the challenges and problems facing an organization on a regular daily basis.

Traditional organizational structure breeds contempt, apathy and lower levels of participation. It also stifles communication of upward ideas and concerns.

There are ways to turn this flow of percentages around and stimulate inner activity among players for greater success and rewards. Consider the new view of organizational dynamics. Consider what this visual implies to others and how this changes the performance of management and rank-and-file workers alike.

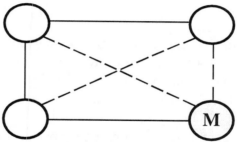

What the *new view* of organizational structure (whether called teams, work groups, self directed work groups, etc.) advocates is an image of team and player equality. This image sends the visual message of player equality, whereas the traditional diagram of organizational structure (on the previous page) sends the message that an individual is equal to his level of colleagues only and is subordinate to those players above him.

In essence the new view allows for an equally sized circle for each player. Notice that the "**M**" for management is still present, only now you are telling members that "**Management**" has the job of ensuring results and that a manager will assist a player in performing his functions. However, management will not be ultimately responsible for a player's position. Old and traditional management sent that message which is why many times at the end of the day, workers would be gone and management would still be there - completing others' jobs!

The *new view* of management sends the signal that all players in a winning and thriving organization are both accountable and responsible for their own actions and responsible for the performance of the team overall!

If the team wins, then each player wins, and, if the team loses, then ultimately each player loses! Characteristics of the *new view* organization imply some of the following ingredients are present in an organization:

> • Each player is accountable to one another, with ultimate authority still going to one player who is responsible and leads the team or unit in a mutually agreed upon direction.

> • Cross-training and functional awareness are both initiated at all levels and fostered among all flattened hierarchical layers and players.

> • Interactive and non-confrontational communication occur among players, teams (departments, units, layers, regions and geographies, vendors, customers, and players), both internally and externally in an organization.

> • Interdependence develops among players to become proactive and not reactive.

> • Vertical and horizontal movement and advancement occur between the players and management team within the organization.

> • Lateral, vertical and horizontal synergy and development occur on a regular basis!

Ultimate advancement of an organization and *Yield Management* focus on management ground zeros. Today an organization can not afford to feel that its marketable advantages rest on traditional business school organizational resources: Structure, Financial Budgets, Products/Resources. Management by these three sole factors alone will lead to "dead zones" far more often than any other single factor!

As Peter Drucker warned in his 1973 classic *MANAGEMENT: Tasks• Responsibilities•Practices,* in a ground zero market, any of these three major resources can be attained, refined and even expanded upon by your organization. Yet a competitor can, and many times will, attain and deliver better on these three than you. Many times a traditional management structure works to protect these three factors at the expense of the customers - the people on the team on the inside and the people on the outside that make your existence possible.

Therefore, your only truly marketable and lasting advantage points are your *people. Yield Management* focuses upon developing and maximizing that resource - the *people* factor!

Given the need for flexibility in the midst of the chaos and professional challenges facing you daily, having immediate alternatives for improved people interactions will lead to greater efficiency, effectiveness and profitability. Using staff cuts and gradual quality improvements as a business map to greater profitability and growth is a dangerous map to travel on. The IBM Way is a great example of how this doctrine can make an organization look solid and strong on the surface. Yet underneath all these cosmetics the organization still flounders. For example, in the 1970s IBM experienced financial problems due to its inability to meet market needs as fast as the competition - which supports the need for the new view exactly. Compare the 1970s IBM to the 1990s IBM (both eras found the firm in tough financial times and facing dramatic business and cultural changes):

> • To meet the tough financial times of the 1970s IBM moved on three immediate fronts to position itself for survival. First, it froze the hiring line, thus addressing staff and labor costs. Then, it moved to consolidate some of its divisions and research/development activities, thus reducing physical costs. And, finally, it sold off real estate to acquire immediate liquid cash to make its stockholders happy.

> • In the 1990s Big Blue again found itself in tough financial times.

What did Big Blue do to secure survival? First, it addressed labor costs by downsizing to the tune of tens of thousands of staff eliminated! Then it sold off, eliminated and reduced activities within several of its divisions. Finally, it sold massive chunks of real estate to obtain liquid cash to make itself look good again to its stockholders.

• What key factor did upper management not pay attention to? The people factor. The wave of the world was away from IBM's massive systems and main frames to more mobile systems and user friendly systems. And who was grabbing this market? The laptoppers - such as Bell, Apple, Zenith, etc... More importantly, where did these new organizations find this technology?

• The technology was developed by the same giants who were experiencing trouble, in the back research and development rooms by their people. Yet their upper management did not reflect upon and listen to what the market wanted or what their own players were developing. It would seem evident that someone should have noticed that smaller systems were showing up with other business names stamped on them.

The IBM Way illustrates the need for players at every level within organizations to be able to interact with one another, professionally challenge one another and to stimulate peak performance from one another. This requires alternative techniques for people interaction, and management must evolve into leadership and guidance roles in the future - away from frenzied control junkies running around with their hands in everyone's activities.

The ability to strike when opportunity knocks is critical to management and organizational successes. To empower oneself and those within an organization to take calculated initiative and advance causes, the front leaders within an organization (managers, supervisors, team leaders, work group facilitators, executive staffers, owners, etc...) have to understand what it is that the organization is about and how the players fit into that picture. Individuals placed in leadership and management positions need to realize there are a lot of techniques and strategies to be incorporated in people management.

Traditional management focused upon the effective and efficient use of resources in one's environment to accomplish desired results. In order for management to accomplish this there has to be new vitality within the leadership personnel of an organization. Traditional management and traditional management school ideology have taught that management's function in an organization is to maintain primary participation in *five key areas*:

From the traditional five key management responsibilities, management today must focus on additional factors and must empower those around them to assume responsibility and accountability for the five areas above, and other directional maps. Among these interaction maps (habits, styles, techniques, strategies) is the need to have developed and understood mission statements. The fastest way to growth and productivity is a well-defined mission statement. Within organizations today there needs to be several different, yet interlinked mission statements. The *new view* of management incorporates a flexibility, willingness and ability to make adjustments in how one interacts, motivates and thus manages the only true management advantage - your people.

The starting point for managing winning teams is to gain a better understanding of how people interact with one another and how mission statements impact this factor.

Sidney Yoshida, a guidance quality expert in Japan, studies the structure of business organizations and the interaction abilities of players within them. Mr. Yoshida's studies also include the awareness of players at all levels within an organization of problems, customer concerns, growth concerns and the overall challenges which players and organizations face.

Startling statistics have been measured from focus groups as to the level of awareness of players within these organizations and at differing levels (from rank-and-file through senior management) as to what is happening around them. In many cases a culture has been created whereby many players hide the problems they experience from senior management. Yoshida found:

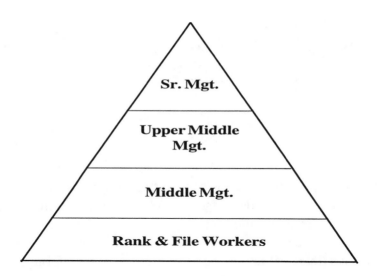

• **Senior Management** was aware of roughly *4* percent of problems.

• **Upper Middle Management** was aware of roughly *9* percent of problems.

• **Middle Management** was aware of roughly *74* percent of daily problems.

• **Rank & File Workers** could identify and were aware of roughly *100* percent of the daily problems facing an organization and its related customers.

All factors being equal in the global marketplace of today, business leaders, managers and individuals operating within business markets have to empower themselves and others to obtain maximum results and peak operational performance on a daily basis!

To meet the complexities of organizational growth and maintaining one's competitiveness for future market placement, the traditional hierarchy and organizational charts of the first part of the 1900s will have to evolve into a more team focused environment. Organizations are facing a new change pattern - every year organizations face tighter budgets, leaner staffs, while at the same time the work loads increase. The human machine is a dynamic and fascinating one. Given these three factors, most every department and organization not only meets this new demand for performance, but in many cases sets new performance records. How do groups of people facing these three factors make this happen? Teaming!

Whether you call your group of people a department, work group, quality focus group, independent work team, self-directed work group, self-directed team - they are all exhibiting various dynamics of being part of a team!

The performance of people in a peak performing relationship is dependent upon players being able to interact successfully with one another and to share with and interact with one another without apprehension. When a player fears the outcome of interacting with another (whether that interaction is a lateral or vertical interaction), the dynamics of a team will break down as Yoshida found in his studies of many organizations.

Focusing the efforts and energies of all players, while reducing the actual interaction and hand-holding time by management, is the thrust of the next chapter. Whether your position is that of performing independently from others or with others, success comes from clear vision and leadership of what each step in the business operation is, does, and should be.

Explore alternative ways for managing the resources around you and for leading the people that will be a part of these interactions and successes in both your professional and personal life!

Sheldon's earlier studies parallel the reality to business today. The post war business philosophy of the 1950s and 1960s - "make it and they will buy it" doesn't apply today. The need today is for organizations to take into account the people factor as the marketable growth and success factor. For this reason management and leadership must look for and apply alternative management and leadership techniques and methodologies for survivability!

This transference is seen throughout this text with the multitude of techniques and ideas applicable to the global approach to organizational development in today's most successful teams and organizations. Witness the new approaches to management and leadership across America today!

Here are just some of the teams from across America who are successfully incorporating *Yield Management* points:

> • *Arthur Andersen*, a major accounting and consulting firm, has successfully implemented in their Sarasota, Florida, computer software division a powerful **MENTOR**ing program (see Chapter Four) whereby senior personnel are paired (voluntarily) with younger members of the team as alternative points of contact, along with traditional management personnel.
> • *American Express Travel Related Services* division in Scottsdale, Arizona, has undergone a major management change, in which departments have been designed into teams responsible for seeking out and coordinating on-site, on-going, educational training programs to meet the teams' (departments') respective growth needs.
> • *TUV Rheinland of North America*, located in Newtown, Connecticut, empowers and provides the resources and training for its engineering and technical team to provide a full-service approach to customers. Engineers and technical support team personnel who know customers and customer needs better than anyone are now charged with giving a customer the entire service needs they know each deserves - consulting, customer service, sales, negotiation, engineering, etc...

Chapter 2

Five Mission Statements For Ultimate "New View" Success

"Mission Statements are like maps. With a map
you can navigate your actions toward a goal and success.
Without a map, you are always guessing and taking
short-cuts, which always become long-cuts and lead toward
confusion, stagnation and ultimately failure."
• Jeff Magee

Five Mission Statements
(or vision/purpose statements) For
Ultimate *"NewView"* Success

Identifying all of the objectives and goals of the people involved in every organization is not easy - yet it is not impossible! Understanding these varying objectives or missions and how each ties into the other is critical to management success and to understanding how the management alternative styles of leadership come together. While many consultants speak of mission statements and assist in the strategic development of them, there are still a shocking number of failures and bankruptcies in the business world today from organizations which had mission statements.

Tom Peters has widely quoted a statistic that "only one in every ten organizations which undergo management changes of Total Quality, Total Quality Management, Continuous Quality Improvement, etc... will survive!"

How can this be? The answer is really fairly easy to recognize. Start by evaluating the *"Warning Signs of a Decaying Management Inventory"* in the PREFACE. Then proceed to recognize that for people to interact and integrate for success, each level of an organization must understand the other and how each player, department, team, committee, etc... impacts the big picture - called success, quality and profitable results.

In order to maximize each player's abilities within an organization, consider these five mission statements in the following order. Which statements do you have in place and which statements still need to be completed for your future success?

Understand that these five mission statements need to be developed in this order for maximum success, and in the following participation sequence to avoid confusion and chaos. Consider the following five mission statements and decide how many of these you already have identified and which ones need to be developed. Also, decide how many of these mission statements are not addressed by some of today's more popular consultants and then you'll understand why so many followers of these doctrine-espousing gurus are out of business today! You understand the nuances of your industry and you understand your people better than any consultant, therefore you must take the ideas presented and merge them with your common sense prior to initiating any action.

The *"Five Mission Statements"* necessary for ultimate organizational development, productivity and success are:

I.	**Organizational**
II.	**Departmental/Team/Work Group**
III.	**Player(s)/Colleagues**
IV.	**Customers (internal & external)**
V.	**Yourself (professional & personal)**
=	**Greater "Yield Management©" Results**

Let's take each mission statement individually and break it down as to what it is to focus on and ways in which you design each mission statement for maximum participant involvement, buy-in and thus ownership!

The **Organizational Mission Statement** should be designed by an organization's key players only. All members of an organization should never be involved in designing the foundational mission statement, unless they have vested financial interest! This mission statement serves as the foundation against which all decisions and actions can be measured to determine if a possible action or decision is consistent with the purpose and direction of said organization, or, if a decision or action about to be taken is in conflict with the foundational mission statement.

View the Organizational Mission Statement as that posted statement which can be easily remembered, written down and against which all other decisions and actions can be gauged.

The Organizational Mission Statement serves as a formal and official document by which a company is communicating to its members and the outside world what it is all about. This statement communicates what its purpose is and what the company or organization sees as important (beliefs, values, goals, vision, etc.).

Consider some of the following key statements from some recognizable organizational statements as guideposts toward higher levels of success:

> • First, *General Electric*, the only organization which could be considered to be a Fortune 500 firm in 1901 and is still among that list in 1995 - "Boundaryless...Speed...Stretch."

> • Second, aviation giant *Delta Airlines* maintains focus with - "Throughout the world, we face innovative competitors and alliances. There is unrelenting pressure to control costs while providing excellent, high value service. Our established ways of doing business which served us well in the past will not sustain us in the future."

> • Third, health care leader and home care partners to families for decades, *Johnson & Johnson* marches on with - "We believe our first responsibility is to the doctors, nurses and patients, to mothers and fathers and all others who use our products and services."

> • Fourth, the explosive success and growth of *Carl Sewell* and his automotive dealerships across America, support the power behind these mission statements as maps. Carl Sewell has grown a small automobile dealership in 1968 from $10 million in business to a chain of dealerships in 1995 doing more than $250 million dollars in annual sales, making Sewell the single largest General Motors dealer in America! Sewell's take on them - "There are only three reasons for having a sign: to name your business, to describe your product, or to give directions... Signs, in a subtle way, tell the world what your values are and what kind of business you are running. Since that's true, do them right."

The **Departmental Mission Statement** is the second map to be developed. Once the overall organization has developed its map - Organizational Mission Statement - then each department, work unit, team needs to set aside time to review this foundational mission statement and design its independent statement. Each department, for example, cannot and will not be able to make the overall Organizational Mission Statement happen. Each department only contributes a piece toward that big picture.

The Departmental Mission Statement should be designed by all members of a department, work unit, team, etc.... When members within a department or on a team participate in designing this one, then ownership and synergy will occur. Have players assist in establishing the "how" in the plan of how your department will go about contributing to the organization's goal and how it will be accomplished. To increase the impact of the Departmental Mission Statement, once created, have each player sign the statement and post it proudly within the department for all players and visitors to see. This regular reminder of the department's map will further foster energy and team interaction!

Understanding the **Players' Mission Statement** is the third step. Every person has (to some degree or another) a professional intention or map as to where they are aiming in life. Once you have a glimpse into other people and, especially on a team (as a manager), have gained that understanding as to what a Player's Mission Statement is, then you will better understand what is important to them. You will develop a better understanding of how to best interact, motivate, communicate, delegate and develop players for the overall team to be successful!

Players' Mission Statements are derived from their values, principles, goals and desires in life. Each person on your team has different needs in life and seeks different goals, therefore a better understanding of the people within your department is necessary for your management success.

The fourth mission statement to be developed or understood for management and organizational success is the **Customer Mission Statement**.

The Customer Mission Statement is the map which customers follow in making their business decisions. Always remember that a basic psychological point of reference for people is, "what is in it for me!"

By understanding what your customers' needs are and what they are striving for, you can then gauge your decisions to consider these points. You will recognize multiple ways to assist customers to obtain greater levels of success and growth through your position once you know what your core customers' base needs are. Another reason for gaining some perspective on what your Customers' Mission Statements are, is that this insight will impact your decisions and change your growth in future Organizational, Departmental and Player advancement Mission Statements!

As Stephen Covey reflects in *Seven Habits of Highly Effective People* and *Principal Centered Leadership*, "seek first to understand, then to be understood." The purpose of the five core mission statements is to guide you toward understanding the forces around you which you must draw upon for ultimate success within an organization and within a competitive marketplace today!

The final mission statement to be designed is **Your (Self/Professional) Mission Statement** (as a manager, supervisor, leader or business owner)! Until you have gained some degree of understanding of the initial four mission statements, it is difficult to effectively develop Your (own) Mission Statement and have it integrate with the other four.

By understanding the first four statements, you can ensure maximum integration and thus you will be spending energy toward both Your Mission Statement and the others' objectives / statements. If you were to have Your Mission Statement established prior to giving consideration to the other four statements, you would find that Your Mission Statement (also known as your agenda) would more than likely not parallel the other four mission statements (or known otherwise as other agendas). When you have insight to other mission statements, then all five mission statements come together and the team synergy takes over.

Designing the **Organizational** and **Departmental Mission Statements** (or purpose statements) is an involved process. Each statement should be able to address and/or identify several key issues. When designing your statements consider how each statement answers or incorporates the following guideposts. Consider:

> • *Six Key Letters:* W, W, W, W, W, H. Every mission statement should identify: Who, What, When, Where, Why, and How.
>
> • *30 Words or less:* Every statement should be condensed to a few lines; a short paragraph. The longer and more involved your statements become the more you increase the likelihood that you and others won't be able to remember the statement and that means your map becomes confusing.
>
> • *Design Time*: The appropriate players should come together for this strategy and brain storming session either off-site or in an area where limited (or no) distractions will cause participants to lose focus on the purpose of the mission statement development session.
>
> • *Involvement*: All players critical to the design and implementation of a statement must participate in the creation of the core elements of the statement. The more active participation by appropriate players at each statement development level, the greater the ownership level becomes and, thus, increased participation, productivity and success will take place.
>
> • *Signatures*: Once a statement is developed, it needs to be signed by all participating players and posted as a sign of will!
>
> • *Ultimate Objective*: The final analysis of a statement is that it should serve as a clear, non-debatable map of an organization's aim. It should help players to focus their efforts, provide a measurement system, and allow for celebrations of success!

You can obtain additional information for use in designing mission statements or in determining others' statements (**Player** and **Customer Mission Statements**) via these same steps and through *profiling* the appropriate parties. Provide information to vested parties, design a questionnaire and gather *questionnaires* from these parties to attain the desired information and their respective insights!

Finally, the ultimate reasoning for the design and implementation of these sequential **Mission Statements** (as minimums within an organization) is to empower members to focus their energies upon the same points of reference and the same goals. These statements serve as mental *maps* (MAPs©: Mental Action Plans) or models for individual and team effort. They serve as a guiding point for activities, energy, commitment and where resources are to be applied and in what order.

Individual hesitance to commit energy in many cases is due to unclear direction and an uneasiness about whether or not senior management (leaders) is really committed, or whether they are merely paying "lip service," to a cause!

These are the factors that can threaten any well-managed and well-intentioned organization and company. Another major factor in designing these statements, both individually and as a team, is to pull those empowered players together. To empower individuals within an unaligned organization (one without these statements developed and in place) can be counterproductive.

People must share a common vision (mission) for success. Otherwise an organization will experience increased stress, anxiety and tension among its players. Management will carry an increased burden to maintain controls and productivity and a slow (in some cases, fast) demise will fall upon the organization.

To facilitate the design of a personal, departmental or organizational statement and to aid in vision-making among players and leaders, consider the following chart as a planning tool. This chart can be used as a planning work sheet for individual or group interaction.

You may want to weigh this planning chart against any existing *mission statements* to determine if the critical elements have been addressed and accountability is assigned or whether or not a present *mission statement* is so esoteric that it actually threatens long-term survivability and success!

MISSION STATEMENT PLANNING SHEET ©

(Editorial Explanation of Purpose or Intent:) To,_____
_____
_____
_____ !

W: _____
_____

W:_____
_____

W: _____
_____

W: _____
_____

W: _____
_____

H (Action Plan-One=Short Term/immediately need to do's)**:** _____
_____
_____
_____

H (Action Plan-Two=Medium Term): _____
_____
_____
_____

H (Action Plan-Three=Long Term): _____
_____
_____
_____

Reminder: Now transfer the above into a single coherent statement that can
be seen and signed by applicable participants!

Three Subgroups In Life
"Rule 80/10/10©"

Three subgroups in life impact your mission statement development and implementation. The three subgroups also impact your people influencing ability on a daily basis!

In order to design effective and applicable mission statements and thus to gain a better working perspective of how an organization will develop, foster and ultimately avoid the traps of stagnation, procrastination, apathy and bankruptcy, consider how people come together and interact with one another.

Sociology looks at groups of people and has determined that whenever you interact with a group of people (your organization, department, another department, a client, vendor, your family, a social gathering, a civic organization you participate in, etc...), the group as a whole can be further broken down into three subgroups. *Yield Management* breaks down 100 percent of a group into three manageable subgroups.

RULE 80/10/10©

• **80% = Transmitters** of the norms and status quo. They work and perform based upon what the influencers have conditioned them to do. These people are also known as *followers*. The influencers are members of the next two subgroups.

• **10% = Transformers** of change and action. These are often seen as the proactive and positive members of a group with strong convictions and are carriers of high levels of self-esteem.

• **10% = Terrorists** of change and positive energies. These people are often seen as the negativists, complainers or devil's advocates and fight change for no real reason. They just don't like the idea because the idea wasn't theirs.

Your final statement for each mission statement will reflect your influence among and how you have been conditioned by these subgroups. You can also increase your ability to persuade and influence others by by expanding the *"Rule 80/10/10 ©"* further into your own management realm. Determine if your team is reflective as a group of all three subgroups, or does it resemble only one or two subgroups. If so, think about how many times you feel as though you're interacting with (and trying to motivate) a team of Terrorists!

Management techniques for dealing with the three subgroups will be presented later in the text and multiple techniques will be presented for turning your Terrorists into Transformers, for converting your Transmitters into proactive Transformers!

An immediate way of stimulating significant organizational growth and for dealing with these three subgroups comes from making a major personal management *paradigm shift*. Consider your normal daily office procedures. For many it resembles:

> • **First:** Enter office with mental plan of action established (nothing in writing) and get caught off guard by multiple urgencies, emergencies and problem player situations (terrorists).
> • **Second:** Immediately get caught up in dealing with a problem player situation (terrorist) that preoccupies a major portion of time - crises management. Attitude becomes negative and stressed from this person and interaction.
> • **Third:** When you finish this encounter and leave to interact with others, you notice they are not being productive. Several individuals who have been put off ("Just one minute," or "Wait a second.") when they tried to see you, have been converted from Transformers into Transmitters!

Increase your organization's productivity and overall attitude by as much as 25 percent by changing your morning routine from the nightmare above to something new!

Whether it is ten minutes, one hour, or even more time intense, the first group of people that you have to interact with every morning are your Transformers! Then interact with your Transmitters in route to deal with problems and Terrorists!

Think about how this paradigm shift will impact management's attitude and productivity, as well as the attitude and productivity of the players on a team. There are many reasons for making the conscious change in daily activity. Consider:

> • By making your first interaction at the beginning of a working shift/day with a proactive, positive Transformer, you ensure and reinforce your positive attitude and energies. You can empower these individuals to carry your message through the day to fellow Transformers, and, more importantly, they can assist management in motivating the Transmitters with positive energies.

> • Your second interaction should always be with the Transmitter. Also, note why a person may become a Transmitter? There are three types of Transmitters: First, if one does not know what to do or how to do something, then he is a *legitimate* Transmitter. Second, if a person has been given feedback in a non-productive manner, he will be less proactive than expected, therefore becoming a *forced* Transmitter. Third, others have learned how to play clueless or otherwise are *learned* Transmitters. Each of these three require a different management interaction approach!

> • Your third daily interaction should be with the Terrorist(s), unless a life is at stake. By making this your third interaction, you will find that you have more energy, a better perspective, more control and that others on the team are working to move the team forward while you are dealing with the Terrorist(s)!

Otherwise, if management interacts with Terrorist(s) at the beginning of a shift/day the management attitude is immediately zapped. Meanwhile, others on the team who need to interact with management are delayed due to management's interaction with a Terrorist(s). This, in effect, neutralizes the Transformers. Management is then responsible for converting a Transformer into a Transmitter. Nothing gets accomplished, and tension goes upward. Change management habits and change organizational effectiveness!

Chapter 3

The
FIST FACTOR©:
Your Board of Directors

"Birds of a feather flock together!"
• Mrs. Murphy's Law

"Your *Law of Attraction* impacts your circle
of influence and your capacity to lead from
within your outward actions."
• Jeff Magee

THE FIST FACTOR©
Your Mental Board of Directors

(reinforces your leadership abilities)

To create an immediate and lasting positive impact in your personal and professional life, think about the centers of influence in your life. The conditioning factors that hold the greatest impact and shaping power over you and your potential are tied directly to your hand - your **FIST FACTOR©**.

Make a fist and shake it. Close your eyes and visualize and feel that fist. Feel the weight of your fist and the power that your hand can make when those fingers close tightly upon one another!

Did you do this? If you have, then continue reading.

Research indicates that most people have a nucleus of five core people in their life that they confide in, do things with, talk, share, and laugh with. Now look at your fist. From your fist you see four fingers and one thumb. For sake of this concept and exercise, consider this to be five fingers. As you look at each finger, individually, associate a name with each finger from your nucleus. You may visualize a few less than five or a few more than five names. For most people, however, there are five fingers and there will be just about five core key names!

Affix the core names of your **FIST FACTOR©** to each finger below, and shake your fist one more time. Now feel the weight of those individuals upon your body!

The fastest way to evoke a change in your behavior pattern is to adjust your **FIST FACTOR©**!

What is the connection of your fist with *Yield Management?* The connection is a direct connection. Think of the concept this way:

Organizations and businesses have *Boards of Directors*. The purpose of a Board of Directors is to guide and influence the direction of that organization or business. The Board is charged with making sure that the organization or business is on track with its mission statements (another word for mission is goals) and when it loses focus or needs assistance, the Board is there to do so. Each Board of Directors is also designed to be a certain number strong. Do you agree with these two generalities?

Well, that Board of Directors is the same as your **FIST FACTOR** ©. Your fist is only a certain number of fingers strong, and each member you affixed to your fist (you chose consciously) has the same role and influence upon you (subconsciously) as the Board does on that organization and business. When a Board member no longer is serving a viable and valuable role in its respective group, the member is asked to leave or is fired.

To create a positive environment, condition an organization or direct business toward success, the fastest solution is to assure that the right members make up the Board. Your **FIST FACTOR©** is the same as saying you hold your own personal Board of Directors within your FIST. If you don't like what you see and feel, then fire a board member and replace him with someone who deserves to take up your mental space!

So, who should be on your Board of Directors? Think about someone who would best serve as a Board member by looking into these five diverse segments. Name only one person from each segment to your Board! After all, another name for your **FIST FACTOR©** is - *MENTOR(s)* !

FIST FACTOR© - CANDIDATES/MEMBERS

FAMILY: _____

FRIEND: _____

COLLEAGUE: _____

SUPER SUCCESS: _____

UNDER-DOG: _____

Upon reflection, this is a very diverse group of individuals and will allow you the luxury of being able to confidently and assertively interact with any one individual when the need rises. These core people have more to do with who you are and where you will go than any other single factor in life!

If your nucleus is unhealthy then you have a negative influence close to your psyche and any outside conditioning factors can only be received negatively. Does your Board make (internal) statements to you like:

- Go for it!
- You can do that!
- Make sure that is correct, before you...
- Is there anything I can do...
- I once did that and I found that...
- Why can't you...?

Or does your **FIST FACTOR©** scream out (internal mental) statements at the other extreme of the attitude line of life like:

- Don't even try that...
- Who do you think you are?
- That is way out of your league!
- Last time you did...you screwed up...You'll ...
- Wait for... before you try...
- That is not your job description!

Design a working **FIST FACTOR©**, mentally hold regular Board meetings to assess the state of your Board and then hold on for ultimate success!

FIST FACTOR© members impact how you interact with others and how you will go about designing the five core mission statements detailed in the previous chapter. These personal Board members also impact how effective you will be in management as detailed in coming chapters. You can test the validity of this concept by considering the following map.

Has your (subconscious/mental) Board changed recently? You can test the validity of the **FIST FACTOR**© and whether or not members of this very personal motivational and attitude Board have changed in recent memory. Consider the following three questions as a point of reference, and as you reflect upon them, ask yourself whether or not any of your members changed within each set of questions.

"Memory Set Questions"

1. Where do you shop for groceries on a regular basis?
2. What is your professional title?
3. Where do you live?

Question One: As you reflect upon your **FIST FACTOR**© members, have any members changed in the last three months?

Question Two: Go back one year ago in your memory. Ask yourself if any of the members of your **FIST FACTOR**© have changed as you use the three Memory Set questions above.

Question Three: Now, go back three years ago in your memory. As you reflect upon the three "Memory Set Questions" above, have any of the members of your **FIST FACTOR**© changed?

Most people will find change in the names of their nucleus of the **FIST FACTOR**© on the first question. Others will start to see some of the names change as they reflect backward one to three years ago. When did you start to see the names change?

By using the three measurement questions within the "Memory Set" as a point of reference, you can see that changing some environmental factors, sometimes changes your (mental influencers) **FIST FACTOR**©. More importantly, these people influence you positively or negatively.

To evoke a powerful change in yourself, your colleagues, among teams and departments, make sure that everyone has the right **FIST FACTOR**© (mentors) member make-up!

With the **FIST FACTOR**© in mind, you can begin to see that there are certain individuals within your life who hold a guiding light position. As you look inwardly upon who comprises this select group of people, you must always pose a question as to whether these people are positive influences upon your life - Transformers; or, are the members of your select group neutralizing factors on you - Transmitters. Even worse yet, are these members a negative influence on you - Terrorists!

To maintain a positive and healthy perspective, consider a Board of Directors for both your professional and personal life.

Having these groups provides you with opportunities to mentally reference what you have learned from them and what they might do if placed in situations similar to what you might encounter in the future. And, a Board of Directors also affords you opportunities to physically interact with them (or at least mentally reference) for guidance, suggestions and valuable input in professional and personal matters.

These people will also assist in shaping your overall perspectives on management and effectively discharging the four core alternate management styles in the next Chapter!

> **Remember:** You consciously picked these people for some reason important to you at some time in your past. Once picked, they then occupy subconscious space within you and thus influence every decision and action made as a leader manager for the future!
>
> How does this concept work? Simply. There are specific influencers within us which impact our thoughts. Our thoughts impact our self image. Our self image impacts our self view and inner mirror. Our inner mirror reflects to us, who and what we are. That signal then gets projected outwardly to others. What gets projected to others is, therefore, directly influenced by our *"Mental Board Of Directors"* or what we have labeled here as your **"FIST FACTOR©"**.
>
> Of all your Board Members, it is typically the Family category members which have the most power and influence on who we are, as they are the most deeply rooted and weigh in the most on our conscious and subconscious mind!

Chapter 4

Four Alternative
Leadership Styles

"See, Say, Do -
When they *see*, then that means we are doing it.
When they *say* they understand, that typically
means we are doing it. And, when they *do* it, then
we *see* and can *say* they know how to *do* it!"
• Jeff Magee

Four Alternative
Leadership Styles

For many managers, management deals with knowing what results need to be attained and then focusing energies on available resources to make this magic act happen.   In the course of working toward short and medium-term results, management focuses upon who is most effective at barking out directions, giving orders and maintaining significant degrees of power by controlling resources.

In order to truly attain peak performance, personally and professionally, *management in the future needs to recognize there are four completely different ways in which one can interact with others to facilitate the directional growth and production needed on a daily basis*. A better understanding of the four core management (or coaching approaches) styles will lead a management member to an understanding of how to alternate the styles to obtain optimum results (from a team, individual players, and oneself), thereby becoming an effective leader!

The four alternative management styles are profiled on the following pages and a successful management player in a winning organization must recognize only one style of management can be efficiently utilized at any one time.

Think of the management styles as *hats* on a hat rack inside your organizational walls. *You must first take off your personal hat* when you come in the door each morning and then assess the environment continually *to determine which management hat to take from the hat rack and place on your head.* Remember, only one hat can be on your head at a time. To maximize your management capabilities, you will therefore be continuously taking hats off and putting them on. In doing so, you will be able to reduce interaction time with players, stimulate greater interactions and ultimately you will see a significant increase in team productivity and positive attitude. This means less management stress and increased management productivity during the traditional daily working hours - less pre-AM and post-PM work to maintain the status quo!

Breaking management down into four subcategories is easy when you recognize that each day management personnel participate in only four activities. If management doesn't recognize its four basic alternatives, then, no matter how hard management works, it will feel as if it is holding on for a fall (and frustration) every day.

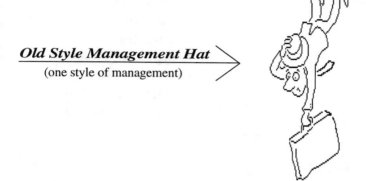

Old Style Management Hat
(one style of management)

The job of effective management is knowing when to put on the correct management hat. The four alternate management styles (or *hats*) are: **Manager, Mentor, Counselor,** and **Coach**.

Consider the traditional dictionary definition of management prior to analyzing the four alternate management styles. Traditional and old style management closely resemble the following definition.

> • **Management** *v.* **1.** To direct or control the use of. **2.** To make submissive. *n.* **3.** The act, practice, or process of managing. **4.** Executive skill. **5.** To direct or administer. **6.** To succeed in accomplishing one's purpose.

To better understand the roles and responsibilities of each management style, the following chart has been designed. Notice the traits common to some of the styles of management and the differing traits as well. Based on the leadership alternatives, you can assess the whys of some recent interactions and why those management interactions were less productive than desired.

Reduce your interaction work and increase results via less autocratic methods of management. Consider the following four alternative styles!

Four Alternative Management Styles

Management Style (hat)	Responsibilities/Traits
MANAGER	• *Hands-On* • Training • Education • Appraisal Evaluator • Policy Enforcer • Rule(s) Regulator • Procedure Driven
MENTOR	• *Hands-On* • Educator/Influencer • Encourager • Compatibility • Guides & Navigates
COUNSELOR	• *Hands-On* • 1-on-1 In Private • Serious Approach • Pain Factor Motivator • Educator • Solution Oriented • Disciplinarian
COACH	• *Hands-Off* • Attitude Adjuster • Encourager/Focuser • Calming Factor • Personal Cheerleader • Education Reminder

The power of management rests on one's ability to realize what role needs to be assumed at any given time to obtain organizational results and success. There are actually four core management styles which a person can assume in managing his interaction with others. It is more critical to the success, productivity and development of the players that a member at the management level understands that the four core management styles are defined and distinguishably different from one another.

For an organization to attain peak performance, management needs to assess daily environments and the players within those environments to determine how much time needs to be invested in any one specific management style.

For management to be truly effective, it needs to assume all four core management styles and alternate them routinely to obtain results. Those players vested with the four responsibilities must understand the essence of each. Explore in greater detail the thrust of each management style within your environment and let the following four management subsections serve as a guide to effective leadership alternatives.

MANAGER. The **Manager** is the person who watches out to ensure that organizational rules, policies and guidelines are being followed and addressed. Within this management style, structured training and education of the players are established and executed.

The enforcement of these standards is the primary responsibility of the MANAGER. This position is the most time consuming. When the MANAGER style (or hat) is being worn, the MANAGER is tied down with interaction(s) with very specific players. Therefore, he has limited time(s) available for interfacing with other players on the team or for focusing energies on the tasks charged specifically to the MANAGER. Traditional management focuses (and is followed up with academic disciplines which focus) efforts on a MANAGER being merely a MANAGER. Organizations which desire to survive and grow in the future need more than MANAGERS! Other styles of management are required.

As long as a member of the management team focuses his energies on solely being a MANAGER, the ultimate result is a team being held back from attaining peak performance, increased player tension, organizational frustration and higher levels of employee turnover than necessary.

In management, the role of MANAGER is the most labor intensive role a player can assume. As long as management players focus on being MANAGERS there will be players on the team (Transformers and even more positive Transmitters) who are being ignored, while management is tied down with problem players (Terrorists) or engaged in micromanaging everyone's activities.

Another major drawback to the traditional MANAGER style is that these players are charged by the organization with ensuring that things are getting done. This philosophy is inherent to holding organizations and players back. Most MANAGERS focus their efforts on "**how**" things are being worked on, addressed, completed and done. This is a dangerous word (and management concern) for the future. Focusing on the word "**how**" in today's business world is a self-destruction route. Every time a MANAGER uses the word "**how**" with another player, he automatically provokes a mental fight with that player. With some players this mental challenge is seen in an external outburst, tension, conflict, anger or hostility in the workplace.

The reason for this is simple. Society has been conditioned (especially via the media for fifty years!) that it is acceptable to challenge another's intellectual position and opinion on issues and things in general. When you use the word "**how**," you are challenging another person's intellectual position and asserting that your intellectual position is better and more sound than theirs - instant mental challenge and conflict!

There may be times when something needs to be done a certain way ("how"). Successful management realizes that the best (and least threatening) way to communicate this message is to replace "how" with words like, "*what*" and "*why*!" The word "how" sounds very threatening to another person's ear. Even if management doesn't intend for it to be a threat, it still is! Consider:

- "That is not how I asked you to ...."
- "We don't do it that way, here is how I ..."
- "Let me show you how..."

All of these statements are offered hundreds of times daily and more than likely are not intended to be negative or confrontational. Yet to the listener they are very threatening (see *Improving Interactive Communication*, Chapter Ten).

To communicate the "**what**" and "**why**" requires that management flex its style and alternate management styles as necessary to accomplish objectives!

Whether you are practicing the management alternative styles outlined to be a MANAGER, MENTOR, COUNSELOR or COACH, you can make the same statement above and substitute another word for the "how," changing potentially negative interaction into an educational player interaction. Consider:

- "I can appreciate what you have done here. What we need to focus on is..."
- "Here is why we need to complete the project according to these specifications..."
- "To save you time, let me show you what I need..."

Other alternative management styles to adapt and adopt are: MENTOR, COUNSELOR and COACH!

MENTOR. Another management style is that of Mentor. While this is also a hands-on style and labor intensive position, it does not mean that management actually serves (although they can) as the Mentor. Key players on the team at any level can augment the MANAGER'S efforts by serving in this valuable position. There are some basic requirements for an effective MENTOR to develop within an organization to have a successful interaction and professional relationship with another colleague or team player.

Management needs to assess the ability of each player individually (via the **"SA Model©"** to be presented later in this chapter and techniques that will be presented in Chapter Six). A primary function of MANAGERS is to determine which players can be assisted to greater levels of productivity by assigning them a MENTOR. Players on a team that could be tapped to serve as MENTORS would be Transformers of any age and capacity within an organization!

Mentors need to be patient, sage people who are willing to share their learned experiences and knowledge freely with wanting individuals. An effective MENTOR divorces emotions from the situation and serves to educate and expand a player's ability and knowledge base through both hands-on interaction (based upon their success and failure experiences) and through simple compatibility and show-n-tell with the mentee. The players on the team need to know there is someone they can turn to, confide in and gain direction and support from, in the absence of their MANAGER and COACH!

Developing players into MENTORS is also a powerful way to stimulate valuable interaction from senior level players on a team who may be burning out and slowing down. Older players can serve as great organizational champions if utilized genuinely and strategically within the management structure overall.

MENTORS must understand the five mission (vision, purpose) statements as outlined in Chapter Two. The role of MENTOR is actually very powerful. The MENTOR is, in essence, shaping a life and building security for the future of an organization. Choose your MENTORS wisely and empower them with the resources and support to accomplish your objectives.

Five Different Mentor Styles/Types: The Mentor LifeCycle©

Elementary Mentor: A mentor who serves as an educator and teacher to the mentee. They provide the mentee with the basics and "how-to". *Secondary Mentor:* The mentee has graduated and knows the "how-to's" and now needs a motivator, encourager, coach. *Post-Secondary Mentor:* The mentee now knows and is performing. Now the mentee needs someone to bring him along and serve as his champion and keep building and reinforcing his confidence level(s). *Master Mentor:* This mentor serves as the mentee's sponsor, promotes his abilities to others. They serve as your PR representative. The mentor finishes polishing off the mentee here and prepares him for the next level or mentor type. *Reverse Mentoring:* Now the mentee returns the deeds to someone else as his mentee. The mentee now becomes the mentor and starts the cycle, process all over!

COUNSELOR. Not as glamorous a management position, yet critical to an organization's ultimate success and team attitude, is the style known as the COUNSELOR.

The management cliche of "out of sight, out of mind" unfortunately does not apply here. As long as management tries to ignore a difficult and unpleasant situation or player, everyone else on that team will know exactly what is going on, and more importantly who is getting away with what. Consequently, when management does decide that it is time to deal with the negativity, there will be more than just the initial problem at hand. There will always be additional challenges that have developed as a result of the management inaction!

When a problem surfaces or there is a difficult player on a team (as the **"SA Model"** © will illustrate later in this chapter), and management has exhausted all pleasantries and niceties ... only one management option is left. That is to assume the role of COUNSELOR!

The COUNSELOR role is a most unpleasant style as this position is where management stands and must hold its ground. While there may be limited give-and-take negotiation allowed, when a relationship has advanced to this position and management has assumed the style of COUNSELOR, the worst-case scenario has already been prepared for. Management must go one-on-one with the problem player (and his or her representative if your environment is conditioned for such instances).

Things are serious at this point and the player with the challenging or negative behavior or attitude is becoming counterproductive to the team and organization and <u>must</u> be dealt with.

Refer to Chapter Nine for a detailed approach to dealing with a difficult and challenging player. Should the situation dictate a one-on-one interaction or a formal counseling session, refer to the section in Chapter Nine on counseling the difficult player for a step-by-step approach to structure a win/win session.

COACH. The ultimate goal of management is to assist players to reach peak performance and to position themselves in the management style of COACH; there when players need them and off to the side otherwise, navigating the team!

It is when management is acting as COACH that management can focus energies on developing the team, meeting needs and budgeting energies for future successes. It is also when management players are acting as COACHES that they are able to concentrate on the responsibilities of management and not worry about what the players are doing or "how" they are doing it. Management at this level realizes that players are assuming accountability for their own actions. They are acting as if the organization is their organization and not that they are merely a part of some sort of large machinery.

It is when management arrives at COACH that they are actually practicing a hands-off approach to management and leadership. The players here realize that they are accountable for their player responsibilities and that management has its own unique responsibilities and doing a player's job is not one of them.

The primary focus of the COACH is to help players maintain mental and physical perspective and focus on goals. The COACH is charged with maintaining the proper attitudes for a healthy, happy and productive environment to develop and sustain productivity.

As management learns from the **"SA Model©"**, the ultimate objective is to advance each player in his own way to the quadrant which puts each player in a MENTOR position for future growth and daily effectiveness. In this position the management player can assume the position of COACH. He can strategically interact as needed to assist each player individually for ultimate growth and success!

Reduce your management workload by COACHING the team to success and not worrying about needing to be a hands-on MANAGER. By being able to determine what management style (or hat) is required at any given time, you can substantially reduce your interaction time and work loads.

Recognizing what position a player, colleague or customer is in at any given time will determine which management style is required and how to increase your level of interaction effectiveness. One technique or model you can utilize to determine where a player is, and therefore, which management style (or hat) you need to put on, is the **"SA Model©"**.

Every player is operating professionally within a need level; he is always in need of something in order to maximize his potential. As you review the four alternative management styles from the previous chart (mentally or physically), recognize that only one style (or hat) should be used at a time. By identifying what need level a person has you can more quickly identify which style to use, reducing your interaction time while increasing your interaction effectiveness.

To determine the need level of another person, review the following **"SA Model"** © chart and plot a few players mentally on the chart. Once you have plotted a few players (Transmitters, Transformers, Terrorists), then recognize the need level or management style at which they have appeared!

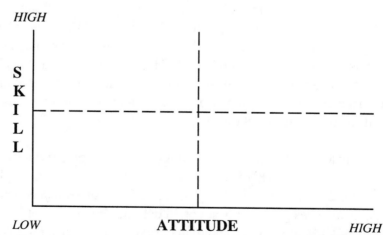

Question One: Plot high to low on the vertical axis line the **SKILL** ability of the player in your mind as associated with an issue in your mind.

Question Two: Plot left to right on the horizontal axis line the **ATTITUDE** level of the player in your mind as associated with that issue and in relationship to you on this specific issue. Now put their initials in the appropriate quadrant (box)!

Now, based upon which quadrants you have your players plotted on (and you may want to visualize or plot on the chart an additional Terrorist, Transmitter and Transformer from your team), you now know which management style to take.

"SA Model©" Management/Player Index:

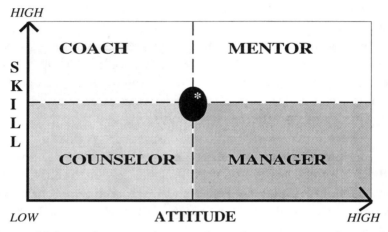

Based on which quadrant you have a player in, you must take on the responsibilities of that specific management style (and nothing more or less). Remember, the management cliche of *"out of sight, out of mind"* may make sense to you with a problem player on occasion, but once this player is identified in the **COUNSELOR** quadrant, you must deal with him! The longer you allow this situation to continue, the longer everyone else on the team is aware of what is going on and, more importantly, who is getting away with what on any given day!

The ultimate objective of the **"SA Model©"** is to recognize which players are operating in the **MENTOR** quadrant (noted with an *). Those players are your peak performers and may be viewed as your *Transformers.* The model is also designed to assist you in determining your best course of action (BCOA) to motivate and manage every player to the **MENTOR** quadrant eventually. And, remember that you don't have to serve as the **MENTOR**. It would probably best be left to another player to serve in this valuable role, thus freeing up one of your hands for something else!

Based on the quadrant in which you (mentally or physically) plot players, colleagues and superiors, you will gain the needed insight for successful interaction and increased persuasive ability.

For example, you have two alternatives for moving a player in the **COUNSELOR** quadrant toward **MENTOR**. One option is for you to move him from **COUNSELOR** to **MANAGER** and then ultimately to **MENTOR**. The problem with option one is that it becomes labor intensive for you as a **MANAGEMENT** option, as **MANAGER** means hands-on. On the other hand, a second alternative would be to move that player from **COUNSELOR** to **MENTOR** through the **COACH** quadrant, as **COACH** means hands-off! Every decision brings with it another set of decisions and questions, each unique and impacting the ultimate productivity, attitude and performance levels of you and your organization's team!

Consider the reasons a player may appear in one quadrant on one day and in a different quadrant on the next. There are a multitude of management explanations for why players appear in the various **"SA Model©"** quadrants.

> • A player who lacks proper knowledge or education on an issue, task, project or subject may procrastinate. Fear factors set in and cause delays in productivity. The player becomes a Transmitter waiting for influence and direction. Your role then becomes that of *MANAGER*!
> • A player who has lost enthusiasm for issues, tasks and projects may need a subtle push of encouragement. Your role becomes that of *COACH*!
> • A player who appears on-site as an over-eager and power-charged individual can become a loose cannon on the team. While you want to maintain that energy level, it is critical to ensure that their energies are directed in the right direction. The role you take on, or empower someone else to assume, in relation to this player, is that of *MENTOR!*

• A player who resists activities that lead to productivity, team interaction and success, or spreads rumors about others, serves as your Terrorist behind the scenes and has to be dealt with immediately. This player typically has low levels of *skill* and/or asserts a low (and thus poor) *attitude* toward you and management in general. When you can mentally or physically plot a player into the lower left quadrant of the **"SA Model©,"** then the role you must assume is that of *COUNSELOR!*

What are some of the variables that lead players toward or away from any specific quadrant? Consider how the following environmental stimulants impact actions, feelings and human motivation:

• Mergers of organizations
• Merging markets and competition
• Decreased customer demand for specific products or services
• Management change (personnel or styles)
• Retiring and/or firings of peers or superiors
• New product or service introductions into one of your markets
• Increased organizational profits
• Decreased organizational profits
• Increased training and educational opportunities on-site
• Decreased on-site educational and training opportunities
• Introduction of a new Transformer to the team
• Introduction of a new player to the team, who turns out to be a Terrorist
• On-the-job traumas of some degree
• Off-site traumas (in the personal life, at home, with family members, etc...) to some degree

Always remember that players are not static and will appear in differing **"SA Model©" Management/Player Index** quadrants!

In **SECTION TWO** you will explore very specific ways in which you can facilitate the four management alternatives. Techniques will be presented that have immediate application within your organization!

A strong reason for utilizing the four management alternatives is to stimulate greater individual participation and growth and to infuse energy in a team (or department) with minimal effort on behalf of management personnel. Traditional management techniques and policy demanded close interaction with players and placed the burden of accountability on the shoulders of management and not on the players on a team - where it should be.

The new ideologies, methodologies and doctrine of *Yield Management* suggest that accountability be equally shared by all players on a team. And, for an organization to attain peak levels of performance and productivity, the management players need to empower players to a level of "take charge attitude and performance " not witnessed before. Therefore, management needs to pull away from traditional interactions and their "doing" behaviors and allow players to explore, do, fail and succeed for ultimate growth and prosperity themselves. The more management is involved, the less player (team) interaction there is and the less management participates, the more the player (and team) participates and accomplishes!

View traditional management and the proposed transition to this new concept (as outlined in Chapter One) through the following diagram.

Management/Team Control Model:

Traditional Management Doctrine and Protocol

(Unilateral Decision Making/ low employee participation)

span of control

Team Infused Doctrine

(Employees attain higher levels of freedom and participation)

The team approach adds increased participation, player ownership, quality and value to efforts. It also reduces the degree of responsibility and accountability on management personnel. The more opportunity that management affords players to interact with one another, the greater the management and organizational yield will be. Yield in terms of:

> • *Significantly increased synergy and higher quality solutions.* The ability to ask questions and interact to determine what is best - people interaction.

> • *Increased player ownership will develop.* By allowing players to interact and by reducing the volume of management hand-holding, players will learn that they need one another to be successful both individually and as a team, unit, department and organization.

> • *Increased awareness, cooperation, cohesion, commitment and productivity.* By empowering management to back off and let go and thus allow the players (that constitute the team) to make educated decisions which impact their productivity by them-selves, (note that this is all impacted by an understanding and participation of the players in the mission statement princi-ples set forth in Chapter Two), the organization benefits in two ways. First, by placing each player in an organization at a level of optimal performance, negativity goes down. Second, man-agement is now maximizing all resources - including the most valuable of all, its people!

The more management works to let go and the more that the players on a team recognize that they are in greater control of their destiny, the greater the level of organizational accomplishment will be. As you make the transition from your present management style, start with small team interactions. Work specifically from that point to strategically assigned *self-directed work team* environments - you have to initiate one step at a time. Gain small team or unit wins and build from these smaller, more obtainable victories and work outward toward larger and more involved tasks and projects.

The ultimate management and team empowerment grid may look more like the following grid than it does the grid on the previous page.

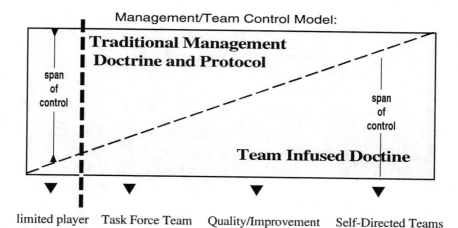

Management/Team Control Model:

limited player   Task Force Team   Quality/Improvement   Self-Directed Teams
participation   (Decision Making Teams
                                                            as noted in Chapter Nine)

The greater the team involvement becomes the greater that team's level of participation will be in taking control and managing change effectively and the higher their level of accountability and authority will be!

The more management releases controls, decision making abilities and access, the greater the need for teaming will be - **distribute the power** to the individual. This leads as a progression toward greater interacting teams and unity. In reverse the greater the management role of authority and control is, the lower the level of player participation will become. As an alternative interaction style, consider the four management alternatives as guideposts toward interaction in future situations and work to involve others and not alienate them from activities and productivity!

Another way to review this management model is to overlay the four management alternative styles and determine at what level of management participation an organization experiences what levels of player participation and effectiveness. Consider what level of player participation and ownership management would receive from players with each alternative management style utilized by management personnel and as a basic interpersonal skill style with one-on-one interactions, regardless of the authority or seniority issues of the players involved. There is a parallel with these four management styles and that of parenting - change your interaction style to attain differing net results.

The four specific management alternatives or styles would fall into alignment with this management model in the following manner:

Management/Team Control Model:

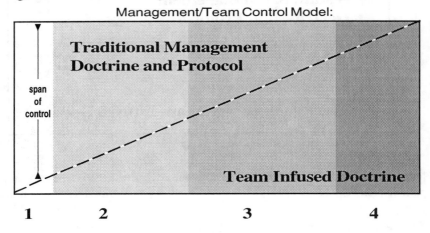

The four core management styles impact player and team performance in direct proportion to the management role in interactions. The four management styles on the above management model are:

- **1** = *Counselor* style as management role (or hat).
- **2** = *Manager* style as management role (or hat).
- **3** = *Mentor* style as management role (or hat).
- **4** = *Coach* style as management role (or hat).

With each style management personnel utilize, increased player participation will occur and team effectiveness develops. With each management style you deploy, different net results are possible and with differing players on a team you may need to fluctuate between the four styles to effectively utilize the correct style of management given the player and circumstances that you are faced with - always working to keep mentally focused on what the immediate management goals are and how those interface with the medium- and long-term goals.

With an understanding that there are alternative styles of interaction, management styles that individuals can exhibit and work from to attain desired results, the next management objective is to realize how the daily operations of an organization evolve and how the management alternatives can be further utilized.

As you explore the five organizational dynamics and operational levels in the next chapter, consider first how much time you presently spend as a MANAGER, MENTOR, COUNSELOR, and COACH. When you interact with players in your organization and in working to motivate and empower those around you to greater levels of participation and owner-ship (as outlined in the previous *"Management/Team Control Models"*), determine just how much time is consumed at stages one, two, three and four from the previous chart.

For most managers working in traditional management and organiza-tional structures (see Chapter One), the greatest amount of time is spent acting as a COUNSELOR and MANAGER. This is also where the organization realizes the lowest player participation, creativity, owner-ship and proactiveness. Only when management begins to let go, trust, educate and support the players does an organization experience true successes - and this typically occurs when management lets go and takes on the management styles of MENTOR and COACH (a more hands-off perspective as outlined in the beginning of this chapter).

You can see how this is impacted in terms of how much time organiza-tions and management spend when it comes to the five differing and always present organizational structures or levels (as outlined in the next chapter - Chapter Six). Most organizations invest significantly too much time maintaining the status quo and dealing with challenges, problems, wildfires, conflicts, confrontations, in-fighting among players, and nega-tivity. This can typically be traced back to the same management players not having spent adequate time in the foundational organizational struc-tures or levels (see levels one and five in the next chapter).

If MANAGERS can train themselves to invest equal amounts of time in the five different levels, then everyone on the team will experience greater rewards and accomplishments!

At the Regents Park HILTON Hotel in London, customers experience a finely tuned team, which emulates these ideas. While on a tour of the United Kingdom presenting "Customer Service" conferences, one of my venues was the HILTON facility in London. The meetings facility manager and his team were consistent in reaching and surpassing expectations. Nothing was beyond their capability. Any request made was immediately addressed and never were customers or I ever made to feel as if a request was unreasonable, undoable or   unattainable. Never did a member of the meeting facility team have to check with someone for permission, every player was made to be a significant member of the team and was able to make command decisions on the spot - no matter what the subject matter!

Beyond making independent decisions, the members of the team were vested with the power to make the difference and give others a powerful reason to want more and want to come back to them when a need developed *(EMPOWERMENT = Knowledgement + Ability + Authority + Attitude* [willingness])!

What makes the "Management/Team Control Model©" so powerful is that when you experience an encounter like this one, you then have a point of reference to measure future interactions by; and now it becomes very clear when you experience peak performing teams and those teams that are bogged down by sabotaging mid-management players demanding tight controls which stifles creativity and success.

Chapter 5

Five Differing Organizational Structures And Levels:
Stepping Stones Toward Greater Success, Productivity And Profitability!

"The task of the leader is to get his (her) people from where they are to where they have not been."
• Henry Kissinger

"For it remains true that our only sure guides to the present which so often seems so bewildering are the lessons - the often terrible lessons - of the past."
• Henry Cabot Lodge

Five Differing Organizational Structures And Levels

In order to truly maximize your time and management abilities and to maximize the resources at your management disposal, you must realize and accept that every organization is in a constant state of fluctuation. No player within an organization (including yourself) nor any layer within an organization is ever at a static position or level. New stimulants may cause a player or department to evolve from any specific level into another without warning.

Understanding the fundamentals of each level will enable you to navigate that level more efficiently and will mentally empower you to guide players and situations from one level to the next for peak performance and optimum results!

Management experts, consultants and lecturers for decades have called the five organizational transformational layers by many names. We can focus our energies on the five organizational structures as stages which we grow in and out of depending on the circumstances about us. The five levels range from a start-up or beginning stage/level and progress to a conclusion or ending stage/level. This chapter will focus on the five levels as a sequence of steps which players and organizations migrate from and toward on a regular basis - as if we are operating in autopilot mode.

Tom Peters called some of these organizational operational levels *CHAOS* in his classic work *Thriving On Chaos*. His premise is that nothing is a constant and things about us are always causing change, conflict, confrontation and new evolving challenges. In his work, *Liberation Management*, Peters changes his perspective as he analyzes change about us. No matter how you view it, the premise still goes back to minds like W. Edwards Deming and Peter Drucker.

The five levels are: Begin, Defend, Blend, Transcend, and End!

LEVEL	CHARACTERISTICS
BEGIN	• formation or start-up stage, expectations developed • introduction of new policies, ground rules, procedures, memos, products, services, meetings, beginning of the day or week, etc... • hiring of a new player, interviews, etc... • transfer of a player and the receipt of that new person into your area, department, team, work unit, etc... • brainstorming session, designing mission statements, setting objectives and goals into motion
DEFEND	• conflict in meeting, someone challenges a new policy, procedure, idea, rule or etc... • Terrorist on the loose in your organization • delegation disaster • break down in interactions and communication • tension among players calls for patience • lack of commitment among players toward something and a feeling of forced defense of positions
BLEND	• things begin to come together and get done, norms • players are falling into a flow, pacing • decisions take less time to make • your Transformers are taking the lead and the Transmitters are falling in behind them • productivity is maintaining your status quo and routine expectations are met
TRANSCEND	• some players attain peak performance, rise above • your results and expectations are exceedingly high • players are interacting with low stress, little tension, effective communication and decisions are being made jointly among the players at this level • commitment to decisions is attained • players perform outside boundaries to attain results with no complaints • players assume responsibility and accountability and the team is moving ahead of competition and beyond status quo
END	• analysis is allowed to take place at conclusions for better planning of future actions • you are able to monitor and modify for tomorrow • final analysis activities

The significance of these five operational levels is critical to your assessment needs, both in terms of which developmental level each player is at any given time, and in identifying which operational level your organization is at with respect to a given issue, project, problem, customer or vendor relationship or the alliances which you are forging with others. Being able to mentally put your finger on the level you are in will assist in directing your future responses - from reactionary management (autopilot) to response and proactive (logic driven) management!

These five core, organizational structures or levels will guide your management style and assist you in putting the proper management style (or hat) into action. The five core levels also give you perspective in designing team focus, organizational mission statements, assist in strategic planning and enabling leaders to gain momentum.

> "An organization that is not capable of perpetuating itself has failed. An organization, therefore, has to provide today the people who can run it tomorrow. It has to review its human capital. It should steadily upgrade its human resources.
>
> "An organization which just perpetuates today's level of vision, excellence and accomplishment has lost the capacity to adapt. And since the one and only thing certain in human affairs is change, it will not be capable of survival in a changed tomorrow."
>
> • Peter Drucker
> *The Effective Executive*

As a management alternative, a successful manager has to realize that there are many different styles or roles one assumes in the quest for success and in search of being the best!

Why do so many authorities on the subject of organizational management miss the core issue and why have so many organizations which have followed these popular doctrines failed so miserably? Lack of common sense has a lot to do with it. Lack of immediate application of people-oriented skills could be another!

Ken Blanchard, of <u>*One Minute Manager*</u> fame, asserts a concept in management and in people development that proposes a major reason for organizations not spending adequate time in each of the five organizational levels. Becoming side-tracked into spending disproportionate amounts of time in only a few is a concept called the "*Grief Cycle©*". The "*Grief Cycle©*" says that for most players (Transmitters and Terrorists), the reason it takes so long to get to the BLEND, and ultimately to some degree of a TRANSCEND level, is that many players get caught up in opposing anything out of the norms of the organizational flow and society - regardless of the merits.

"Grief Cycle©"

today   future

• denial	*• commitment*
• resistance	*• exploration/investigation*

If management could become more efficient in the early stages or levels of management (BEGIN, DEFEND), then it would actually be able to reduce everyone's *grief* and pain (thus reducing DEFEND) and enable players and teams to reach operational levels and productivity faster (BLEND, TRANSCEND). This would also allow management more time to plan, organize, strategize, foresee needs and market patterns, etc... (END)!

The better one's understanding becomes concerning the five organizational levels and the four management alternative styles, the faster a manager of people can move from *denial* to *commitment* and thus reduce the down time spent in *resistance* and *exploration.*

Most organizations, however, live in the grief area of the *"Grief Cycle ©"* by spending major amounts of time in denial and resistance (BEGIN and DEFEND). That orientation makes the organization look like an inverted bell curve when plotted on a *"Grief Cycle ©"*.

As a manager, how would your immediate team (department) plot on the chart? How would your organization as a whole plot on the chart?

Manager (Vocabulary) Style Changes

Management must also realize that a major transformation (*paradigm shift*) must take place mentally and verbally when management (especially MANAGERS) interacts with players. Traditional management focuses on and uses words like *"how"* when interacting with a player, especially if that player has done something either wrong or not as management wanted. When you interact with someone and use a word like *"how"* (i.e., "that is not how I want it done;" "that's not how we do it;" " let me explain how I want this done..."), you are directly challenging his intellectual capacity. This can lead to tension, and, with a Terrorist, it can lead to a conflict and confrontation!

The management mind set and vocabulary should be to move from the use of words like *"how,"* toward the *"what"* and *"why's"* (see Chapter Ten for more communication ideas)!

In order to determine how best to merge the four management alternative styles into the five organizational structures and levels, first analyze your team.

To gain a better objective insight of each player on your team (as a direct report or an indirect report), consider the following chapter. With a better idea of each player's strengths and weaknesses, a better perspective on a player's attributes and detriments, managers will be able to determine a player's capabilities, and, thus, what level of results can be expected from each player. This analysis and insight of each player will give a valuable and powerful position to the organization or team overall.

Chapter 6

Analyzing Players
And Prospects
For Team Success

"Don't tell people how to do things,
tell them what you want and expect.
Then, let them surprise you with their
abilities and ingenuity!"
• General George Patton

Analyzing Players And Prospects For Team Success

The most overlooked component of people management today, both in the academic halls of America's colleges and universities and the class-rooms of today's management and team building seminars, is the element of "how-to" assess the abilities and capabilities of the players on a team! Why else could we have such staggering figures for high employee turnover within certain industries. Consider that in 1993 United States Department of Labor statistics associate the highest level of job displace-ments (after downsizing, mergers and bankruptcies) to people interaction problems. In March of 1996, then Labor Secretary Robert Reich attrib-uted the highest number of job displacements and lower income receiving positions to those individuals with the least amount of education!

Imagine an athletic team where the coach is given players to perform results, but the coach is given an empty employee personnel performance file and the coach is not allowed to observe the players in pregame warm-ups or during weekly practices. Imagine a baseball season where coaches were unable to have any spring season workouts or games, yet are expected to produce a winning team come game time in the active season!

The comparison is very close to how many Managers operate and how many Managers have been trained to interact with their teams.

In order to maximize your time and strategically utilize the resources at your disposal, consider a few basic objective analysis concepts for identifying and more thoroughly profiling the players on the teams you interact with. In order to analyze those around you, let's start with some self-analysis and see how objectively you can analyze yourself!

On the following page you will be invited to participate in a very difficult self-profiling exercise. Mentally, if not physically, fill out this inventory!

Time yourself for sixty seconds. Focus your attention on the right column and for sixty seconds fill in any responses that come to you in connection with the question posed. After that sixty seconds is up, stop writing in the right column and do the same drill for the left column. Don't read the next paragraph until this exercise has been completed!

2-Minute "Self Analysis Inventory"	
Attributes/Strengths/Positive Traits	Detriments/Weaknesses/Negative Traits

Go back to the preceding inventory and add up your entries for each column. Write that score at the bottom of the appropriate columns. As you look at your score, which column has more entries? Most people will find it easier to respond to the negative and critical analysis side (the right) and there will be fewer entries for the positive (left column) side.

Where did you find yourself? Ultimately, there should be three-to-five times the number of positive entries as there are negatives. Are you there or is there some homework ahead for you?

Take this same concept one step further. You should conduct a profiling page like this one on every player on your team. The responses to the questions will give you insight as to what you know and what you don't know professionally about those around you. If you expect to motivate and manage others you must first know who they are. Know who they are and what is important to them, and the secret to personal motivation will be clear with every player on your team!

There are some valuable insights which come from this first analyzing technique. How you see yourself, for example, on the *"Self Analysis Inventory"* will give you a clue as to how others see you and treat you. If you have more initial negative entries than positive entries, this may be an indicator of low personal self-esteem, self-worth, self-confidence and an overall low self-image. This impacts your inner motivation and team interaction skills. Imagine a coach with a low self-image trying to manage a World Series Baseball team.

There are studies which connect personal performance to one's self-image. Consider how you fare against these studies and let that be an indicator to why we observe player performance to the degree or lack of degree which we do. Consider:

> • Robert Schuler in 1990 commissioned a survey through the Gallup Organization. Gallup found that 80 percent of adult Americans view themselves as having a low self-esteem level!
> • Stanford University polled incoming freshmen and found that those students, among the top in the world, could identify six negatives within themselves for every one positive!

There are six ultimate models that can be presented to you for profiling those on your team and those that you may consider in the future. These techniques and models will allow you to objectively assess the players' potentials and abilities. Consider each independent of each other. They are:

- The "SA Model © Management/Player Index" *
- The "Self Analysis Inventory" *
- The "TE Factor ©"
- The "Personal Mission Statement" *
- The "Player Capability Results©" Index *
- The "Upside-down to Right side-up" Identifier

By efficiently analyzing the players around you, you can reduce your interaction times and more effectively place players in positions which draw upon their strengths and not positions which play upon their weaknesses (mentally or physically).

A very effective technique for objectively analyzing a player on your team or a prospective player for your team, is the *"Player Capability Results Index©,"* a player analysis formula. You need to take one variable at a time and identify it in its entirety. With each variable identified and placed together in a sequence, a clear picture develops with respect to a player and your next step becomes obvious with that player. This formula is also valuable, as it will assist a manager/team leader in identifying which management style (hat) to utilize to manage a player.

The "Player Capability Results" Index©

$$\text{CAPABILITY} \quad \frac{\text{Training}/2 + \text{Attitude} + \text{Performance}}{\text{Expectations}/2} \quad = \quad \text{RESULTS}$$

1. The *RESULTS* a player is capable of producing for you is dependent upon their *CAPABILITY*.
2. Their *CAPABILITY* is based upon: (a) their *Training* to date, merged with any *Training* they may still need; (b) their *Attitude*; and, (c) their *Performance* to date. This is divided by (d) their *Expectations* of you and the organization, along with your *Expectation* of them!

---

* Ideas and techniques presented herein *THE LEADERSHIP ALTERNATIVE.*

The *"Player Capability Results Index©"* affords you valuable insight as to a player's status in terms of his/her knowledge and training and his/her abilities via the performance to date as witnessed from his/her personnel file and performance which you immediately observe. This is enhanced further through his personal expectations of their position, his/her colleagues, supervisors, the organization and in general terms his/her overall expectations period. When you merge the findings of each variable from the preceding analysis chart, you gain a valuable and powerful picture of the player on your team to TAP into.

At any variable along the way in this diagram you can analyze which management style (hat) you need to assume to interact with a given player to help him grow and to move toward your management goals and objectives - so as to produce the results required of you in management. Another reason for this analysis diagram is that most human problems and errors occur due to a breakdown in one of the variables presented: The Ability becomes shadowed due to a problem or overburdened "P" or "T" or "E."

By understanding the *Expectation* level of each player individually you can then move on to another player and team analysis technique, the *"TE Factor ©"* . By understanding the expectations of every player professionally, and if appropriate personally, then you will be able as a Manager to identify that common thread that holds the team together. Once you have identified the commonalities among the individual players on your team, you can draw upon that commonality and pull the players collectively together as a cohesive team and synergy develops! This collective commonality becomes the *Team Expectation* (the *"TE Factor©"*).

"TE FACTOR©"

Team Expectation = A+B+C+D+E+......

Team Expectations are arrived upon by identifying the individual expectations of each player on the team (as represented via letters A, B, C, D, E,...) and then taking the common expectation trait and using that to bring the players together and create a cohesive unit.

Another technique which can be utilized to arrive at both individual player expectation levels and the team's expectation level, as well as identifying the real need level of the organizational overall is the *"Upside-down to Right side-up" Identifier* ©. This technique is a little like connect-the-dot!

The first step is to list all the primary functions, roles and responsibilities required in facilitating your organization's business - a list of job functions in essence without identifying anyone's name on the team. Either list those job functions, duties, responsibilities, skills, etc... on a piece of paper or write one entry per index card. When you have identified all of the above entries, place that list or stack to the side. The second step is to write every player on your team on a separate piece of paper or on individual index cards as well. When you have completed these two steps you will have two stacks or piles.

The third step is to set out side-by-side all of the cards or paper pieces which have the players names on them. With the players names separated, take the stack of organizational duties, tasks, responsibilities, functions, skill requirements, etc... and place one entry at a time on the person's name (stack) who is realistically most qualified to deal with it - regardless of whether that is the player currently taking care of it.

Once this fourth step is completed you will notice several positions which you have placed yourself in, and, along with each position you will notice which management style (hat) needs to be assumed!

For every item left over in the unmatched stack, you have to assume the position of MANAGER and train someone to facilitate that item.

With any items which have been attributed to a non-traditional player of that item, you can decide if that is where it really should be (delegated, tasked, assigned, flowed, etc...) or if you need to entrust that player to train and motivate other players to rise to a new level of organizational ability and enable others to perform at the level of expectation at which you are trusting them to perform.

Other items will fall to players that you had not thought of assigning to them before. This will help you to realize that many times in management MANAGERS become habit-bound and assign items to players out of habit with little regard to whether or not that player is the most qualified to perform or facilitate that item!

Finally, you will have items left over that don't make sense for this team to be addressing or there are players left over who have no items on their name. In this case, either training needs to take place with a player to get him up to speed on facilitating those leftover items, or horizontal or vertical movement with respect to that player needs to take place.

This last technique is perhaps the most powerful, objective way to go about shaking up an entire organization (including you), to arrive at a new organization which has been realigned for greater success and productivity for the future!

> • Think of it this way. It is like taking the names of all of the players in your organization and putting them on the reverse side of jigsaw puzzle pieces. Then taking each individual piece and putting them in a paper sack. You shake that sack up and let all of the names fall out of the sack. Now put the puzzle back together the right way, instead of how it was thrown together initially!

If you have the luxury of responsibility and the power or flexibility to utilize a technique like this last one (after you have determined each player's strengths, weaknesses, abilities, expectations), you will find significant organizational growth, productivity and team spirit will develop.

Looking from within also helps to answer what you need to look at from the outside to complement your team for future growth and success. Consider the number of personal experiences which you have had in your professional career when interviewing a prospect for your team (or interviewing by team a candidate for a team you are a part of), extending an offer to the prospect, and having him turn out to be a Terrorist after you have hired him and he is on the team. It seems while we work hard to develop current players in an organization, management keeps on hiring more nightmares to the team - Terrorists and Transmitters!

Many of the same organizations which experience the pain of misguided interviews, as seen in high turnover statistics nationally, actually have scripted interviews. The players in an organization which conduct the interviews are not even trusted by their organization to conduct fact-finding interviews and are relegated to asking a series of predesigned questions to which the prospect's responses are then graded against a score sheet. Candidates and prospects who reach certain numerical levels are taken to another level in the interview, while candidates and prospects who score below certain levels are declined further interviews. In the attempt to find the *right* candidate who fits an organization's needs (technically, intellectually, academically, skill level wise, etc...), many of these right players are hired, and they are the very players that actually hold an organization back from actualizing true success!

Why? The answer is so obvious that it will make you laugh and cry at the same time!

Organizations and MANAGERS have been conditioned through years of want-to-be managers and consultants (people who want to be managers and want to be consultants, but don't deserve to be if you look at their long-term track record...) to look for candidates and prospects that fit a certain organizational profile - technically qualified for the organization's needs.

In fact, what organizations are really looking for in a potentially success-ful candidate or prospect has very little to do with what you might initially feel is what you are looking for. So how do we make sense out of this last statement? Consider the following exercise and you will see the answer!

This exercise is a way in which you can identify what you are really looking for in an ideal new player for an organization. Then we will identify ways to find this in a candidate or prospect. This is a powerful self-awareness activity and you may also want to duplicate the activity with colleagues entrusted to growing an organization to get their involvement and ownership in a plan of action afterward.

The question is simple. On the following chart write in any response to the question given. There are no right or wrong responses, merely responses. Once you have listed several ideas (five or more) proceed to the next paragraph!

Mentally, if not physically, write in your responses below.

WINNING PLAYER TRAITS

• If you were interviewing a player for consideration on your team, what are the traits that you would be looking for in him, and if he possessed these traits or characteristics would you feel he would be a winning player in your organization?

Measuring Key: A =   **S =**

With those responses filled in on the preceding chart, go back and qualify each entry individually with the following measuring key. You can now label the measuring key on the bottom of the preceding chart with these two categories. The "A" is for *Attitude* and "S" is for *Skill.*

Place one letter adjacent to each entry. No entry can have both letters, so pick between the two letters if you feel an entry could have both. Place either a letter "A" or a letter "S" directly on top of each entry in your chart.

Notice from your entries what makes for a winning player in your organization. Which letter comes up the most?

What you will find as you do this exercise individually or as a team effort with your colleagues, is that the dominant response for what you and everyone is really looking for is a *winning attitude.* As with a positive attitude, practically all training and education of a player can occur, and with a negative or bad attitude, training and education is an uphill challenge.

In conducting this exact exercise with MANAGERS (manager is defined here as anyone in any position that has responsibility for other players and/ or other players report to him) across the world, the collective responses have always taken people back to the bottom line measuring key response. What people are really looking for are *attitude traits* and not *skill/knowledge traits* when a choice has to be made between the two!

So how do you find these attitude traits in candidates and prospects? That answer is really easier than you might expect. First, recognize the nuances of your organization, industry and geography, as in many places there are rules, regulations and even laws which prohibit you in the interview stage from asking the legitimate questions management should be able to ask for the development of a truly cohesive winning team. In spite of the very mediocre individuals (Terrorists) that legislate what can be asked, you can still be successful!

The bottom line of any interview situation for management is to determine two answers:

1 • How can this player help the organization make money?

2 • How can this player help the organization save money?

Every position in any organization ultimately comes down to those two variables. If a player does neither, then what purpose does the player serve. And in tight economic situations the players that management typically turns to first to reduce work time or eliminate from the team are those players who answer the question(s) the least!

In your attempt to find candidates and prospects who answer those two questions most effectively, remember what it was you identified earlier as desired traits for a winning player. In every interview situation and with the questions you pose to the player in front of you in your search for answers to the above two questions, listen to the responses to identify two answers which come from every question in life anyway!

Every question you pose to players already on your team and to those individuals that you consider adding to your team affords you two insights or two actual responses.

You ask and they will tell you through their responses:

1 • *Skill* aspect of the question/answer you seek. This comes *from the actual words* out of their mouths. The words give the technical answers.

2 • *Attitude* aspect of the question/answer you seek. Listen to the *tone of their voices* in the responses they give you. This tone will give you an insight to their attitude and thus the attitude they may have if made an active player on your team!

Identifying the attitude level of a player is critical to effective management - both in the players on your team now and for those individuals whom you may consider adding to your team in the future!

With the proper and thorough analysis of the players who constitute your team comes the aggressive development of the players on that team. When organizations invest in their players to develop them, the return on that investment will always be greater than any losses!

Player development is critical to organizational success and to the overall effectiveness and success of the winning MANAGER/COACH today.

Being committed to the development of all the players on your team(s) is critical. Consider just how much time you and your colleagues actually spend annually on educational training and development programming (in both the hard skill and soft skill enhancement areas). Guess-timate how much time your direct competition invests in the employee development areas outlined herein; and compare these two figures against how much time is invested into player development programming in foreign countries (specifically in Japan and Europe).

> • 1993 CNN/Gallup Poll profiled workers in three geographical power centers throughout the world to determine what percentage of workers' time each year is spent in on-going training and educational programming (as it relates directly and indirectly to job/position expectations/needs). The results were alarming!
>
> Workers in Japan, on average, received and invested roughly 22 percent of their working time each year in these educational environments.
>
> Workers in Europe, on average, received and invested roughly 20 percent of their working time each year in these educational environments.
>
> Workers in the United States, on average, received and invested roughly 2 percent of their working time each year in these educational environments.

Reflecting on this study/poll response, consider how your team adds up with these international statistics and how much time you invest?

In designing the appropriate educational training development program for your team - the players on your team who have been analyzed and the players to be added to your team in the future - consider what constitutes correct training. Traditional training today focuses on reactive needs. A winning approach taken by the MANAGER seeking alternative management success patterns *focuses efforts on or in three areas*:

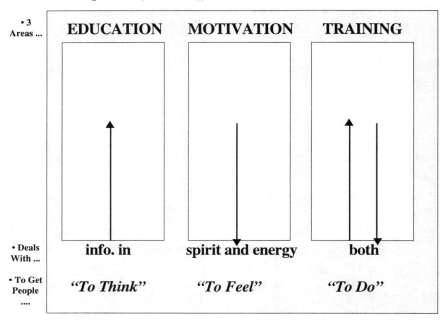

Proactive versus reactive, the overall objective of *training* is to attain a behavior change. By incorporating all *three areas* from the above **"E.M.T." Factor ® (Education, Motivation, Training)** into your organizational training and development programming, as a MANAGER you will attain greater results from your players and team. More importantly, you will be working toward sustaining your success quotients! Focus on all three:

- Get better understanding of something - that's knowledge need or Education centered!
- Get a better inspired team - that's Motivation centered!
- Get better results, build higher goals - that's Training centered!

By utilizing the models presented in this chapter, management can more fully and objectively analyze players' abilities, attributes, strengths and their weaknesses or shortcomings for a better understanding of the team overall. Armed with this new perspective, management (and teamed environments) can now approach training and organizational development from a more wholistic approach.

With this new assessment of the players on a team and those players which may be added in the future, management now has the advantage of designing or adjusting training and educational programs or agendas to meet the need levels of the players in order to meet the organization's developmental needs for survival and success.

With the design of existing and future training programs, maintain as a minimum the **"E.M.T." Factor** © from the previous chart - all training needs to be based upon:

> • **One** - *Educational* quality and content of information inbound to meet the needs of both the player and management.
>
> • **Two** - *Motivation*-based and full of energy transfusion to stimulate the player to outwardly expand both spirit and energy toward others.
>
> • **Three** -*Training* is a two-way activity whereby management trains and monitors that players are receiving and understanding what is being presented; and, whereby players train management as to how to adjust materials so they do receive and understand what is being presented.

When training is presented it needs to be interactive and meet the immediate needs of the players you have analyzed and set the foundation for future training programs to be presented as well. Continued development of the players on your teams will impact the overall success which management experiences and can budget upon.

Examples of individuals and organizations that exemplify the ideas and technologies presented in these first six chapters abound in the last decade of the Twentieth Century. One such organizational manager who exceeds the definition of a leader would be Al Dunlap. Known to some as a "success" and others as a "scare," his record speaks loudest in capitalist circles of the Twentieth Century.

Dunlap is known for taking more than a dozen Fortune 500 type corporations from the brink of bankruptcy and moving them back to major market player status (Among them: Crown-Zellerbach, Diamond International, Sterling Pulp & Paper, American Can, Australia National Industries, Consolidate Press Holdings, Scott Paper Company). His formula for success is easy and very straightforward.

In an interview with Joshua Shapiro, Dunlap laid forth his plan of action for making a winning environment. Consider:

• **First,** have the right management team with the right abilities, skills, and capabilities who are willing to act aggressively on matters.

• **Second,** initiate an aggressive one-time restructuring on everything to address/reduce costs and bring them into line with what you're best at doing.

• **Third,** focus efforts on what you do best and eliminate and sell off all aspects of a business that don't play to your core purpose for being (Mission).

• **Fourth,** and finally. Design, create and implement a set of mission and visions to address both the immediate and long-term growth and development of the organization.

Editor's Note: These four strategies, while controversial, have proven successful every time. *The Leadership Alternative* equips management and organizational players with the necessary skills and tools to accomplish these very business strategies.

This book and the above business glimpses provided by Al Dunlap always beg the question in management today, "What is our purpose and how best do we get there?"

Chapter 7

Sustaining Your Professional Success Quotient

"Always bear in mind that your own resolution to succeed is more important than any one thing."
· Abraham Lincoln

Sustaining Your
Professional Success Quotient

To maintain perspective and keep the management flame within you burning, you must sustain your success levels through a definite mental perspective that allows you to Focus-Focus-Focus!

There are several ways you can go about maintaining a focus and sustaining both the personal and professional success levels which you desire. You can maintain your success level and quotient several ways: By developing a personal, professional mission statement and referencing it regularly to ensure that you are on track (developed in Chapter Two). By developing and associating with a powerful positive center of influences - **FIST FACTOR** © (presented in Chapter Three). By developing positive nuclei - **FIST FACTOR** © - for your team players (presented in Chapter Three). By focusing your energies and efforts around those strengths (knowledge, skill, attitudes, etc...) you possess (presented in Chapter Six). By designing down times or recharging time for you and your fellow MANAGERS; and, through the use of organizational management systems, you can maintain a balance among all of these elements!

On a daily operational basis as a MANAGER and member of the management structure, you need some sort of a system to manage yourself and, most importantly, your work load in light of the demands that others around you will place upon you - colleagues, players on your teams and the people that you report to as well. One technique that affords you the objective ability to prioritize your *important* or *urgent* work items and gives you daily professional control is a time management technique called the **"Quadrant Manager©"**. This technique can be developed on a blank piece of scrap paper, on a note card system and directly into a day-planner device, if you utilize one.

Let's develop the **"Quadrant Manager©"** tool for your immediate use and design ways by which you can implement it today!

As you reflect upon all of the time management techniques and systems you have seen professionally and possibly even utilized, you will notice there is a behavior pattern that all people have in common when it comes to using these systems. No system on the market today fully addresses the behavior pattern, because if a system did, it would have a monopoly on the day-planner market. The core problem with most systems and why people become frustrated trying to use them is that a human element is missing.

Consider how you as a person or management player process work items in your mind. As you look at a paper stack or work responsibilities (especially if have ever used a *To Do List*), you sort through each item mentally categorizing it into one of four categories - as everything you do professionally falls into one of four categories and it will always fall into one of these four categories. If you establish the four categories first, then mentally or physically log the *to do's* in the appropriate category, you will be able to scan the entries in these four categories. You will be able to prioritize the work within the categories accordingly. Thus productivity on the important items in your professional environment will increase substantially!

What are the four core areas in which we concentrate our working time daily and into which all work-related items can be categorized. The **"Quadrant Manager©"** system allows you to focus visually on your most important responsibilities, which are one of the following four categories: **TO DO, TO SEE, TO CALL, TO WRITE!** Every day we have items which we have *to do*. Every day we have items which dictate that *we see* other individuals. Every day we have people whom *we have to contact/call* in order to facilitate work. Every day we also have things *we need to write, finish, draft, authorize and review.*

To utilize the **"Quadrant Manager©"** system to sustain your success quotient, consider adapting this technique in your current day-planner system (whatever brand system you now use), where there may be some typically unused space, so that this becomes a standard adaptation to your system. If you don't have a system and are unable to make that personal professional investment, you can use this system on any blank piece of paper at your disposal!

(NAME)
_____

"QUADRANT MANAGER© "
_____

(DATE)

TO DO LIST	**TO SEE LIST**
TO CALL LIST	**TO WRITE LIST**

To maximize the use of a **"Quadrant Manager©"** system you should follow the following four steps for peak performance!

> • **First:** Identify the four categories that comprise the system, mentally or physically - DO, SEE, CALL and WRITE!
> • **Second:** Enter items in each category as they come to you without numbering the entries. Merely log in the appropriate entries via dash, dot, line, star, etc... no numbers!
> • **Third:** Once you have your items listed in the appropriate categories, go back and look at each entry. Number the entries in order of importance with a number one, two and three only (you may realize that an entry that is written in a category first may not end up with the number one next to it). If you have more than three entries in any one category, leave entries number three onward unnumbered. Place a number one next to the entry that is the most critical and important entry in that respective category to be taken care of either today or in preparing for tomorrow's work, then the number one for tomorrow. In essence you will have four number ones on this chart, one number one in each category - DO, SEE, CALL, WRITE!
> • **Fourth:** Start on your number ones and don't allow yourself or anyone else to sidetrack you to any other numbered item on your chart until you have completed your four number ones - or have progressed as far as you can on a specific number one due to other reasons. As long as you are working the number ones, and then working on your number twos, you are working on the most important items. Maintain your success quotient by maintaining focus!

Another way you can utilize the **"Quadrant Manager"** © system is to enter your items into the four core categories. Then go to each of the four categories and realize that sometimes one category of work may take priority over another category; in those situations you may also want to prioritize the categories themselves by entering 1, 2, 3, 4 in the center shaded zone. This directs you to focus on the entries in category 1 before proceeding on to the next three categories.

This is truly the most powerful day-planner and day-organizer system you can utilize, as this is how your brain categorizes your daily work anyway!

Keeping your own professional flame burning has a lot to do with sustaining your success quotient. Consider your management behavior pattern, for example, in terms of how you typically start your day off. For many MANAGERS a day starts off by immediately being cornered by a Terrorist when you walk in the office door in the morning. Or the first items on your daily "to do" list are the problem issues or problem players. If this sounds familiar, ask yourself if you are immediately interacting with these people and situations at the beginning of your work day, what does this interaction and person do to your attitude? For most, the management attitude gets zapped and goes downward, which is directly linked to one's productivity - high attitude equals high productivity and low attitude equals low productivity, for us and the players we interact with!

Sustain your daily success quotient by changing this behavior pattern - make a behavior paradigm shift - toward a different standard morning behavior pattern interaction. Unless a life is critically attached to your immediate interaction, you should never walk in the door in the morning and immediately interact with a problem, challenge and especially with a Terrorist. The first people for you to interact with each day (whether this is a ten-second, ten-minute or one-hour affair doesn't matter) are your Transformers! Then interact with the Transmitters on your team, as they are waiting for someone to influence their daily actions and this better be you or a fellow Transformer and not left up to the Terrorists! Then when you have a controlled positive interaction, thus reinforcing your positive attitude and behavior, go and interact with challenges, problems and Terrorists.

By seeing a Transformer first every day you are given a mental and physical tune-up for that day and, as management, it is critical to remember that our players look to us for a hint as to what attitude and performance to have each day. If we are down, then they are down and if we are up, they are typically up! Surround yourself with other positive influences and those influences will consciously and subconsciously help you sustain your success quotients!

Another paradigm shift that management needs to experience to sustain personal and professional success is that of one's *belief* system!

For decades psychology modeled a path of human behavior pattern changes via the focus on one's own behavior. That behavior is what others are then responding to, which is either creating a positive or negative atmosphere. In management, then, MANAGERS were taught that to stimulate a change in a player's behavior, first change your own behavior. While this variable is factual there should be another perspective added to the *ABC Model Of Human Behavior* designed in 1943 by psychologist, Albert Ellis.

The *ABC Model* offered an explanation for human behavior and how to best influence and interact with another person by asserting that each letter of the *A-B-C Model* represented the following:

A	B	C
A + B = C		
Activating Event(s) + Behavior = Consequence(s) (your)		

The point of the *Model* is that in life there are and will be <u>activating events</u> which you have no control over and all of the energy expanded in the world won't change what has happened. Yet, many people (MANAGERS) will spend time trying to redo and undo what has been done with total failure. In life there will be <u>consequences</u> and those also cannot be changed. However, it is your own <u>behavior</u> in response to those <u>activating events</u> which causes the <u>consequences</u>. Address and change your own <u>behavior</u> first (which is the only factor you truly have 100 percent control over in life) and the <u>consequences</u> will begin to change as well!

<u>Behavior</u> is influenced by one's "beliefs" and "belief system." By understanding what your true "beliefs" are and what shapes those "beliefs," you will gain a better understanding of your <u>behaviors</u> and

why those behaviors come about. It is your "beliefs" about circumstances, people, and your expectation "beliefs" which trigger your
behaviors!

By becoming more aware of what your "beliefs" are and how they trigger
certain behavioral responses, then as a MANAGER you can identify
which "beliefs" are accurate and which "beliefs" are erroneous - thus
enabling you to modify behaviors for differing consequences (outcomes)
in life!

Understanding the linkage between "beliefs" and behaviors and their
respective impact upon B.F. Skinner's *ABC Model Of Human Behavior*
will allow you to maintain and sustain your success quotient and to
stimulate energy in the teams you interact with in life!

Many times management personnel will find themselves being mentally
zapped of energy and motivation when anger, hostility, conflict, stress
and confrontations take place within the professional workplace. The
ability to maintain personal controls over these situations will also greatly
impact your success ratios and will impact your ability to sustain lasting
personal and professional success.

Several techniques can be instantly utilized to gain or regain control over
your emotions and challenged behavior patterns to allow your logic to
reign superior. Management, of all organizational players, has to be able
to maintain a public face of focus, stability and concentration if
management's expectation of its players is to do the same - remember that
players typically reflect the actions and attitudes around them.

To energize your cells and to maintain management control in challenged
situations, consider the following techniques for **"Powering Down"** for
a more efficient start up. Just as one does when faced with a problem with
a computer, you power it down and start back up anew; the same paradigm
applies to managing people and organizations. Sometimes what serves an
individual and organization best is to focus energies away from what may
have a person challenged and stressed for a period of time and onto
something different. By re-addressing the stimulant a new view and
approach will result in greater successes. Consider the following

techniques for **"Powering Down"** and refocusing mental energies for a greater end result:

• *Breathing Pattern Adjustments* - take a period of time (sixty seconds or more) and adjust your breathing pattern sequences. Typically, when one becomes threatened or stressed the breathing pattern becomes hurried and draws upon one of the two breathing passages (in and out through only one's mouth or nose). With breathing pattern adjustments, you are going to force yourself to consciously inhale each breath (slowly/gradually) through your nose and hold for a few seconds and then gradually exhale through your mouth. Repeat this gradual pattern for the entire period of time you have dedicated (sixty seconds or more). By changing the typical breathing pattern, this inhale and exhale sequence will slow down your heart rate, mental rate and thus, physiologically your metabolism will slow down and the new state of calm will afford you clearer thinking abilities.

• *Mental Imagery* - take an extended period of time (two, three or even five minutes) and close your eyes in a quiet place. Reflect upon a different environment that reminds you of a more pleasing experience. For example, if you have recently been on a vacation, then vividly remind yourself through your mental imagery (turn your mental VCR on to play) of those experiences. Get very vivid and remind yourself of the sights you saw, the smells you smelled, the sounds you heard, the tastes you tasted and the things you felt. By conscious stimulation of the five core body sensors you can stimulate self-relaxation.

• *Countdown* - to gain control over emotionally peaked anger, pick a number (100) and begin counting down backwards toward zero. By immediately and consciously focusing your mind off a challenged stimulant and toward something else, by the time you reach zero you will more often than not have calmed yourself down and gained needed self and management control for a more efficient interaction with others.

• *60-Second Power Vacation* © - a powerful technique and form of self-meditation - you are and will be in complete control of yourself throughout the entire duration of this exercise. This is one of the most powerful ways to refocus your mind and body for greater energy and sustained success in professional (and personal) environments. To initiate this technique there are only three requirements. You can also expand the concept of this technique and the manner in which you utilize it to gain greater self-rewards.

To evoke this technique consider these steps for implementation success: <u>FIRST</u>, secure an environment where you will not be disturbed and where it is as quiet as you can possibly find for a period of only a few minutes (sixty seconds for the actual length of the exercise). <u>SECOND</u>, give yourself a period of sixty seconds or so on a clock (timer/buzzer...). <u>THIRD</u>, close your eyes and recall mental imagery of a great vacation or experience in your past. Put yourself back into the mental imagery that you are recalling and experience all of the positive and pleasure experiences that you experienced earlier. This will begin to psychologically calm and relax you. <u>FOURTH</u>, adjust your breathing pattern sequence for the entire duration of this exercise. This will begin to physically relax you. <u>FIFTH</u>, establish a slow return from this vacation and back to your immediate environment, where you must return and regain interaction with others for success.

This is also a very disarming technique and relaxing stimulant at the end of the day in a hot bath prior to going to sleep. Put your mind and body into a state which is conducive for relaxation and sleep and you will experience a more restful night of sleep, which in turn gives you greater energy!

• *Diet & Meals* - in the workplace especially, maintain awareness of what you eat and drink, as much of the intake during the day directly relates to how one acts and reacts. For example, in high stress environments maintain control and minimize stimulants like caffeine, nicotine and sugars.

Common sense needs to reign here so watch your habit patterns. You can fall victim to adding additional stress and inner stress through what you eat and drink during the day.

• *Forced Tensors* © - another powerful physical technique for realigning your energies away from stress and toward success, away from anger and exhaustion and toward control and vigor are forced tensors. This is a powerfully refreshing technique which can be utilized during the day anywhere one might be (sitting at a desk, sitting in a meeting, standing in a hall way, in an elevator, waiting in a line, sitting in traffic while in a car, ...).

The purpose of this technique is to stimulate maximum energy toward one physical activity and, through a repetitive sequence, you conclude the activity with a new mental and physical view. This activity allows you to draw upon the energy of the body's muscles and at the same time this stimulant activity serves as a pseudo exercise workout.

Start by adjusting your breathing pattern to a ten count; whereby, as you mentally count to five you are inhaling and at the same time tensing up your body and every muscle within it (tighten your legs, arms, and make a fist). At the count of five hold your breath and the tense muscle state you have attained, then as you resume the count toward ten start to gradually relax as you exhale from the hold to ten. Repeat this pattern a minimum of ten times. At the conclusion, you will feel a different kind of tiredness and at the same time a different kind of energy level.

• *Private Isolation Time* - every key manager knows the value of isolation time. Whether this time is used for work, brainstorming, reflection or merely self-time; invest regular time for yourself each day to enable you to maintain control and focus.

Management needs to ensure that it allows self-time for focusing and regaining self-control when pressed into challenging situations. When balancing the four primary management styles with the five organizational levels (Chapter Eight) these techniques will help!

SECTION TWO

Chapter 8

Management Styles Meet Organizational Levels: Which Of The Four Styles Of Management To Utilize And *"How To"* Utilize Them For Leadership Success

"The difference between success and failure is the amount of energy. You decide whether to channel that energy toward a positive or negative point!"
• Jeff Magee

Management Styles Meet Organizational Levels:
Which Of The Four Styles Of Management To Utilize And *"How To"* Utilize Them For Leadership Success

With the tenents presented in Chapters Five and Six detailing effective management, tomorrow's management and organizational leaders must know which management style (or hat) to utilize given the organizational structure or level they are currently operating within. In essence, an effective and successful MANAGER has to be able to flex the four core management styles (hats) together to attain desired results at any given time for the optimal growth and operational successes of a team!

SECTION TWO will focus efforts on actual application techniques for maximizing interactions among players (colleague-to-colleague) and within structures (player-to-superior - COACH). Depending upon which of the following levels you find yourself within at any given time, you are limited by what you have control over and what you merely have influence over. **Start with *level one - BEGIN* equals MANAGER !**

FIVE ORGANIZATIONAL LEVELS				
BEGIN	DEFEND	BLEND	TRANSCEND	END

Remember, the more involvement you have with your team, the more you increase the likelihood you will be maintaining too much control and that you will be participating significantly more in the actual work processes than you need to be or should be. The more you release controls to the players on the team, the more ownership players will assume in their work and the overall organization.

The more ownership players assume, the greater the player participation becomes, the greater results will be attained, and the more a team develops from the traditional work organization. The more a team develops, the more interaction and synergy will take place, and that will ultimately lead to greater efficiency and effectiveness - increased profitability, increased growth and decreased down times!

As you flex your management styles within the five organizational levels always keep an eye open to your three subgroups of people (Transmitters - Transformers - Terrorists). In order to maximize your time and the efficient use of your players, especially in level one, interact accordingly with your three subgroups to establish the pre-group dynamics you need.

You can evaluate the five organizational levels. Match each level where the four quadrants of the "Grief Cycle" © match up and this gives you an indicator as to which players you will be able to cultivate (Transmitters), which players to empower and have lead the team (Transformers), and which players (Terrorists) to isolate, eliminate, terminate or interact with (as a COUNSELOR) for behavior and team dynamic changes!

Typically the 80 percent subgroup - Transmitters - will fall within the first three levels of the previous organizational level's chart. They never really get up to complete, independent speed of the *TRANSCEND* level. The ten percent subgroup which challenges and slows down the processes - Terrorists - typically get tied down in levels two and three, *DEFEND* and *BLEND*. The remaining ten percent subgroup - your Transformers - typically become irritated when tied down in levels two and three and typically operate at levels four and five!

Typically, no one really likes level one, *BEGIN*. This level usually means the beginning and that implies something new. When you bring a team or players together for a meeting, briefing, to present new policies/procedures/forms and paper work flows, etc... or send out a memo, it means a change from the status quo and most players don't have the capacity to independently determine whether that change is going to be pleasure or pain. In level one, the Terrorists become energized and they become management's biggest challenge when confronted. Terrorist interaction then immediately leads you into level two, *DEFEND*!

To avoid this negativity and *DEFENSIVE* interaction and meltdown, focus your energies on designing a winning structure for the interactions within level one. Continue your planning processes into each organizational level to ensure peak performance within any level. Most MANAGERS typically rush into *BEGINNING* activities. This instant interaction due to pressing deadlines and heavy work loads is exactly what contributes to a less than 100 percent success attainment on the activities and projects which grow out of the start-up stage.

View the *BEGINNING* stage as the foundation upon which you plan to erect a skyscraper. With the proper foundation you can build to the stars, and with a poor foundation the smallest factor can cause the structure to tumble downward.

To start off any organization, there are times when the management style (or hat) you must wear is that of MANAGER! Examples of level one and your style of management, being a MANAGER, would be:

- The beginning of a day, week or in a meeting
- A new player onto a team (hiring, transfer, promotion)
- A new client/customer/vendor relationship
- A new project or work assignment
- Etc...

In essence, when you have your first interaction or relationship with someone or something, you will find yourself at level one, *BEGIN*.

Second stage or *level two* **is** *DEFEND***!** Level two is the *DEFEND* that typically sets in when *BEGINNING* has been hurriedly attempted and no solid structure has been established. Terrorists quickly assess when they have a fighting chance at derailing a MANAGER and when their agendas can be presented to an entire group (Transmitters-Transformers-fellow Terrorists) of people at management's expense. They will take any opportunity to do so - until someone makes them accountable for their challenges in a non-confrontational and non-personal manner!

FIVE ORGANIZATIONAL LEVELS				
BEGIN	**DEFEND**	BLEND	TRANSCEND	END

In level two management, focus efforts on limiting the confrontations (especially public confrontations with a colleague where there may be witnesses to the feud...), and shortening the typical "Grief Cycles©" so as to move interactions on to productivity modes; which means levels three and four of the organizational management and operational levels.

In level two, the management styles which afford the maximum control and leverage over players and with players would be MANAGER and COUNSELOR! When a conflict or breakdown develops, you can't afford to be passive and believe that you can out wait the *DEFENDING*. This does not happen! The longer a *DEFENDING* process takes place, the more players become emotionally involved, the greater the problems may be long-term and the deeper the scars will become.

For MANAGER and COUNSELOR of difficult situations and difficult people, the following chapter will outline techniques and strategies for handling these challenges and increasing success quotients!

Third stage or *level three* **is** *BLEND*! Level three is where most players live (Transmitters) and is where you need to move your challenging players (Terrorists) toward. This is the level where most organizations, unfortunately, spend the disproportionate amount of player and team time.

FIVE ORGANIZATIONAL LEVELS				
BEGIN	DEFEND	**BLEND**	TRANSCEND	END

In level three, your management style (the hat you wear) is primarily that of MANAGER and COACH. Through these two styles of management you can motivate, lead, educate and inspire others to productivity and result attainment. You, as MANAGER, will have already (and will continue to) evaluate the players who are on your team and with whom you interact to identify whether or not you have the right players on the right tasks - player analysis as developed in Chapter Six.

Other means to ensure productivity, while you are present and when you are absent, from the team is through the use of MENTORS. You will want to develop and cultivate others to become MENTORS for those players you identify as possible candidates (Transmitters and Transformers) so that they have a point of contact professionally to confide in and look toward during the day, allowing them to attain higher levels of success without your direct interactions!

Creating work teams and designing decision teams will allow for greater levels of productivity and growth. Ideas, techniques and strategies for maintaining operational flow will be designed in the following chapter as well.

The ultimate goal of management is to grow players and a team to the level where players understand what needs to be done, take the initiative to do so and are entrusted with the tools, knowledge and authority to do so. This fourth level of organizational structure is very uncomfortable for many traditional managers and is a primary reason why many organizations stay in level three. Many organizations ultimately either remain at lower levels of capacity and success or some organizations that start off with successes burnout from within.

> "One in every ten organizations which undertake the management changes and growth of Total Quality Management (TQM), or any variation thereof, to compete in the coming of the Global Economy will actually succeed!"
> • Tom Peters

The *fourth level* is *TRANSCEND*! In this fourth level the management style necessary for growth and success is that of COACH and MENTOR (whether you or someone else serves as the MENTOR doesn't matter).

FIVE ORGANIZATIONAL LEVELS				
BEGIN	DEFEND	BLEND	**TRANSCEND**	END

In the fourth level the primary function of management is to ensure that all players have the resources, support and encouragement they need to interact and function at peak performance. Peak performance means that the players within this level are operating up to, or exceeding, their potentials and therefore they, the team, and the overall organization all win!

At this level it is critical that management maintains distance between the Terrorists and the Transformers who live within this level!

In order to attain *TRANSCEND* levels, players have to be treated with respect, expected to perform up to individual potentials (and not up to someone else's potentials), entrusted with resources, knowledge and access to whatever they need to function. Players, within reason, should not become bogged down in attaining signatures and authorization for every move they make.

In level four players need to have properly assigned tasks and be placed in positions which will allow them to draw upon their strengths (refer to Chapter Six). They should not be challenged with activities that play upon their weaknesses and place them outside their comfort zones. When players have properly assigned work and responsibilities, their attitudes go up and so does performance!

The final level of organizational management, and the level at which most players and management spend the least amount of time, is the *END* or analysis and conclusion stage. It is amazing how many cases of hindsight there are on this business level --- repetitive, costly mistakes by employees/players, management and organizations operating themselves directly out of business.

The *fifth level* is *END*! The management style to be assumed here is that of MENTOR with other players, MANAGER and COACH with the entire team and with oneself, and COUNSELOR in a one-on-one interaction with a challenging player.

FIVE ORGANIZATIONAL LEVELS				
BEGIN	DEFEND	BLEND	TRANSCEND	**END**

It is at this *END* level that analysis, benchmarking, review, comparison, analysis, etc... should take place. Here players and management need to have ample time to reflect on past actions and activities, to analyze the positives and successes for future similar courses of actions. Likewise, analysis needs to take place so improvements can be made for future actions and to identify any specific actions which could be eliminated in the future to avoid difficulties which may have been experienced in an activity or project.

It is interesting to analyze these five organizational levels of operation and especially to reflect upon this last level. In the daily professional environment, players tend to spend the least amount of time here, yet when adults were younger they had perfected the fifth level and the "why" of spending time in this fifth level. Consider when you were a child. If you had older brothers or sisters, you were always monitoring what they were doing and whether or not they were getting away with something. If you observed and analyzed how they got away with something, you emulated that behavior. If that older brother or sister got caught at something, then your analysis told you what modifications to make for a more efficient use of your time; and, thus, how to avoid a similar disaster!

Therefore, the fifth level can be considered the level at which you invest time in monitoring what happened and making any necessary modifications for the future to ensure equal or greater levels of productivity, efficiency, profitability and growth.

In Chapter Twelve, techniques and strategies will be presented for an effective *ENDING* process!

Now, with a better understanding of the *"Five Organizational Levels"* and which management style to assume given your relationship to these five levels, the following chapters will arm you with immediate interaction application techniques for success at each level and with each management style (hat) you assume!

> **Remember:** In studies of high-growth organizations with ownership-assumed traits among employees and management out of direct control (hence a wider span-of-control as noted in Chapter Four),

it is noted that effective leaders within management invest more of their direct time on Organizational Operating Levels One, Four and Five! Within peak performing environments (teams, work groups, self-directed work groups, etc...), the peak performing leaders have opportunities to invest mental and physical time within Organizational Operating Level Five, thus reviewing after-the-fact facts and planning better for next time.

Weigh these findings against where you and members of your team spend significant amounts of actual daily time.

Nine Steps To High Impact Leadership: Empowering Others Through Leadership/Management Interaction Techniques

"Freedom is man's capacity to take a hand
in his own development. It is our capacity
to mold ourselves and empower others."
• Rollo May

"A basic definition of *Empowerment*:
Knowledge + Ability + Willingness + Positive
Attitude + Authority = Empowerment"
• Jeff Magee

Nine Steps To High Impact Leadership: Empowering Others Through Leadership/Management Interaction Techniques

The role of management is to provide structure and direction for the members within the organization. Management need not "hold hands" with the players. Management needs to facilitate the growth of each player independently within the organization. Over the decades, management has taken on a lot of characteristics similar to parenting. Unfortunately for most managers, they have not realized the parallel and thus have not realized that many of the organization's players have learned how to manipulate them (just as children learn how to manipulate parents)!

Consider the parallel that most adults learned and perfected their behavior patterns in childhood. If a baby learns that by crying the parent will give attention to them, then the baby continues to cry. As that baby grows older and yells and screams, it becomes more difficult for it to gain attention. If this is so, then the negative behavior will continue. This is the child that grows into a rebellious adolescent. This problem teenager becomes the difficult colleague on your team. In order to change someone else's behavior, and in order to foster someone else's behavior in management, first observe your behavior and what it is you do which others are either acting on or reacting to.

As Albert Ellis (behavioral psychologist and famous for his 1943 *ABC Model To Human Behavior*) noted, the only thing in life that we have 100 percent control over is our own behavior (our attitude influences that behavior). To attain a change in someone else's behavior, start with yours.

Go back to parenting. If you stroke positive child behavior, you typically receive more positive child behavior. If your attention only goes to the negative child behavior, you will typically receive more of it. If you typically pay no attention to either extreme behavior, then it is left to the make-up of the child to decide for himself (based upon other factors) which behavior he will assume! Consider where these learned behaviors in childhood lead if no one ever interacts to stimulate a change:

- The cry baby child becomes the whiner!
- The temper tantrum child becomes the colleague pouter!
- The class bully becomes the aggressive colleague!
- The unresponsive child becomes the unresponsive and ignoring colleague who never volunteers, speaks out or offers assistance. As he has learned, if he maintains a low profile everyone else does the work because everyone else gets frustrated trying to interact with him which wastes time!
- The teacher's pet becomes the political player.
- The tattlers become players who talk behind others' backs and spread rumors to incite tension and trouble.

To stimulate a change, there are parallels from parenting that have application in designing a winning team. In management, just as in parenting, you have to eventually let go of the child's (and player's) hands if you are ever to see them accomplish things for themselves and thus increase productivity. To empower fellow players within an organization, there are many facets which need to be explored. Personality is the starting point for improved interaction. You must realize that people have a primary personality style which directs their behavior on a regular basis. However, people also have a multitude of secondary personality styles which surface and take over temporary navigation of their personality depending upon environmental conditioning factors (as outlined in greater detail in *THE "P" FACTOR: The "Personality Jumpstart" Advantage* - see the "Suggested Reading" list in back of this text and the special offer section).

All mankind is motivated by differing factors with some similarities among all. In management, if the human motivator variable can be identified for any given player at any given time, then management has a powerful insight as to how to best interact with an individual player or team!

This chapter is designed to give you immediate application skills for emerging leaders by empowering them with the tools for increased interaction with your team for increased effectiveness.

Consult the outline on the first page of the CONTENTS to identify any immediate subsections to read, reference or make copies of any of the specific page(s) to facilitate growth and success with fellow management colleagues.

How To Utilize The Empowerment Impact Section: The following pages outline the specific abilities of effective leaders and have been designed with a three-part approach. Each concept is presented and laid out:

- **First:** Editorial text appears presenting the premise and ideas.

- **Second:** A log chart of ideas, step-by-step techniques and/or specific tools for immediate application with your team.

- **Third:** Mental or physical exercise grids to consider prior to utilization with a player or with your team overall.

- *Note:* Each empowerment idea is presented with a team *routing grid* in the upper corner. In some situations you may want to make a copy of that idea and pass it along to others.

The following nine subsections explore detailed *"how-to"* interactive techniques, strategies and tactics for increased team dynamics. The subsections are: *Ego Gratification, Motivating The Player And Team, Delegation Dynamics, Designing Decision Making Teams, Effective Meeting Management Skills, Managing The Difficult And Challenging Person, Counseling The Difficult Player, Dealing With Procrastination And Burn-Out,* and *Dealing With Time Wasters*.

Consider each subsection, one section at a time, for personal advancement and in assisting the success levels of those around you!

Ego Gratification

```
┌─────────────────────────────┐
│ Team Route List             │
│ Return To: _____  │
│            _____  │
│            _____  │
│            _____  │
│            _____  │
│            _____  │
└─────────────────────────────┘
```

Management needs to realize that what may motivate one player may do the opposite with another player. In order to stimulate growth and productive participation among players on a team, management needs to realize how to feed the human ego!

Some people are hungry and need their egos fed on a regular basis to operate at peak performance, while others seldom need ego feeding and have low levels of outward ego gratification needs to operate on a professional basis. When it comes to *"Ego Gratification"* consider the wide range of perspectives of what constitutes this need for ego gratification. Compare the professional application to feeding the ego of individual players on your team. When management looks at ego needs, that which is being addressed is what unique motivators are required by individual players to keep them content, happy, motivated, make players feel needed, appreciated and what factors stimulate greater levels of participation and ownership from players. By identifying the ego needs and stimulators for players, management can gain a better perspective of how to motivate and manage the team overall.

From this insight, management can then develop techniques and the means by which incentives and motivators can be designed to gain maximum benefit for players. Remember, when push comes to shove in life, it's one's ego (emotional psychology) that feeds one's physical actions!

The following chart is presented as a thought provoker for what may be some of the needs players have to keep egos healthy and motivated.

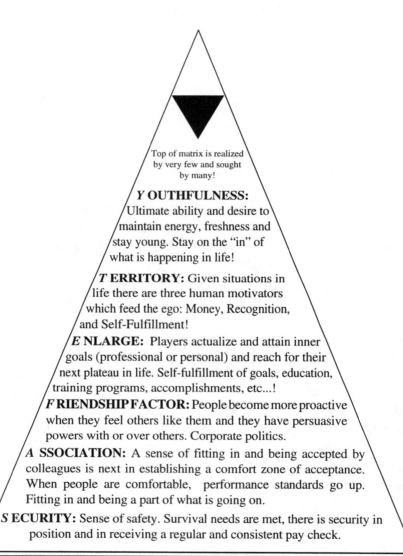

Top of matrix is realized
by very few and sought
by many!

Y OUTHFULNESS:
Ultimate ability and desire to
maintain energy, freshness and
stay young. Stay on the "in" of
what is happening in life!

T ERRITORY: Given situations in
life there are three human motivators
which feed the ego: Money, Recognition,
and Self-Fulfillment!

E NLARGE: Players actualize and attain inner
goals (professional or personal) and reach for their
next plateau in life. Self-fulfillment of goals, education,
training programs, accomplishments, etc...!

F RIENDSHIP FACTOR: People become more proactive
when they feel others like them and they have persuasive
powers with or over others. Corporate politics.

A SSOCIATION: A sense of fitting in and being accepted by
colleagues is next in establishing a comfort zone of acceptance.
When people are comfortable,   performance standards go up.
Fitting in and being a part of what is going on.

S ECURITY: Sense of safety. Survival needs are met, there is security in
position and in receiving a regular and consistent pay check.

EMPLOYEE "EGO GRATIFICATION" MATRIX

Players are very sensitive individuals and their egos need to be considered. With some players, the ego has to be continuously fed. By identifying the level in which a player is operating, management can help to make a player feel secure with that level and work to help move a player to the next level in the matrix. Remember, all players seek *SAFETY* in feeding their egos!

By observing a player or colleague you can begin to determine at which level of the *"Ego Gratification"* matrix they are operating; therefore, which level they will proceed toward once they have secured a hold on the level they are presently operating from. To establish better interacting relationships with people, help them help themselves via the six life levels - starting with Security and working ultimately toward Youthfulness!

Another way to look at the *"Ego Gratification"* matrix is to consider it a basic human motivator system - what is really the essence of a person and from which level in life is someone operating? Psychology through the decades has identified many different systems from which mankind can analyze what motivators there are in life, thus, what motivates people. The core basis of all of these charts, graphs, systems and theories is that motivators for individuals first play off some degree of inward personal ego gratification need. For some individuals the need level is very high and demanding, while with others the need level (while there) is not as demanding and doesn't override the majority of actions and thoughts.

With some individuals, the need levels also become more involved, complex and educated based upon one's conditioning factors and station in life - age, sex, race, educational perspectives/background, financial status/background, and professional perspectives/background. By understanding the individual person (Chapter Six), the ego gratification concepts will be more strategic and your analysis will become more focused!

Look at some of the players on your team and determine at which levels they are operating. On the following chart identify your team's Transformers and mentally or physically plot them on the matrix. Determine how you can assist those players to secure that level and what can be done with them to move toward the next level. Plot your team's Transmitters and Terrorists and determine the same developmental course of action for each individual player. This exercise will give management additional perspective on how to move a team closer to daily victories!

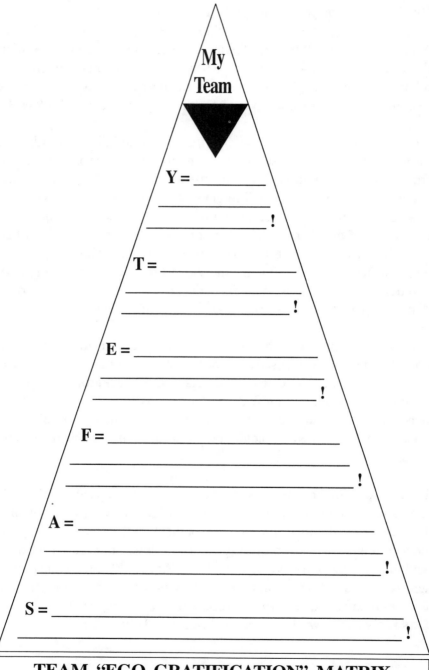

**My
Team**

Y = _____
_____
_____ !

T = _____
_____
_____ !

E = _____
_____
_____ !

F = _____
_____
_____ !

A = _____
_____
_____ !

S = _____
_____ !

TEAM "EGO GRATIFICATION" MATRIX

Jeff Magee International ® '94

Motivating The Player/Team Via Incentives

```
Team Route List
Return To: _____
           _____
           _____
           _____
           _____
```

Motivating the individual player on your team is the first step in motivating the team overall.

With a better understanding of the ego gratification need level of an individual player, you can begin to interact with players to develop each individually (MANAGER and COACH) and, at the same time, you can move a collective group of people (team) toward a greater good and organizational goal (growth). To design a winning team, all players must see a connection between their energy and involvement and where the organization is going. Each player has to see results and appreciation of those efforts. What may serve as a powerful motivator for one player on a team may be counterproductive for another. And what may motivate one time may not work another - you must always be assessing the environment, and players individually, to determine if your incentive plans and motivators are producing maximum yield!

Incentives are great as long as they work and don't have negative repercussions on management or among players. In order for incentives to work consider the following points:

- Is this incentive cost effective?
- If it works, can it be repeated?
- Does the incentive penalize any players or show favoritism?
- Does it meet a need level?
- Does it send the right message?
- How do I meet or beat this option in the future?

• Does it call attention to effort, work, accomplishments which have gone beyond the call of duty and expectation, or is this incentive paying a reward for merely doing one's job?
• Does the recipient of this incentive really appreciate it?
• Does the same person(s) receive the incentive reward more often than not?
• Does the presence of incentive plans create tension among players or within teams (departments, regions, divisions, etc...)?
• Have any of the players been involved in designing the incentive variables/plans?
• Are the incentives being used today the same as incentives used in the past? If so, how repetitive are the variables?

In order for incentives to work, they need to be thoroughly analyzed to make sure that these types of questions don't come to mind later (hindsight) and spell out disaster!

A very powerful means of identifying what really motivates a player and team is to have a team brain-storming meeting and solicit ideas for consideration from them as to what would motivate them and each other to greater levels of success! You may want to qualify this session with the players. Either have them offer ideas as a group, solicit three ideas to be written down and offered to management for consideration or even design a team of cross-sectional players to work on this objective and report back to the whole team at a later time and date. When soliciting ideas or when working on this task independently, break down incentives into three categories:

• Incentives that cost no money or revenue.
• Incentives which would cost $20.00 and less.
• Incentives which may be more involved, complex and would cost the team or organization some money.

Designing incentives can and should be fun. Consider the following chart for ideas or food for thought in designing your own player and team incentive program. These are examples of what motivates some players from professional organizations.

INCENTIVES

THAT COST YOU NO MONEY	THAT MAY COST YOU MONEY
Thank You! (genuine and sincere, is the number one human motivator in life!)	Balloons
	Flowers
	Concert Tickets
Letter of Recognition from Mgt.	T-Shirts
Increased Authority/Autonomy	Ball Caps
Increased Responsibility	Pay Raise
New Office	Increased Medical Benefits
New Projects	Increased Retirement Plan
Team Parties	Longer lunch
Flex Time Schedules	Comp. Time
Public Recognition	Cash Bonus
Job Security	3-Day Weekend
Merit Points	Training Opportunities
Letter of Accommodation	Take Individual or Family Out
Recognition In Newsletter	For Dinner
Recognition on Public Announcement Board	Gift Certificate
	Weekend Retreat
Temporary Title	Shorter Days
Permission to Dump One Project	New Office Decorations
Being Included In Brain Storms	Team Night Out / Party
Respect	Company Car
Extended Job Responsibilities	Company Parking Spot
Call From CEO	Merchandise ...
Employee Of The Month	Memberships ...
Unscheduled Evaluations	Holiday Greeting Type Cards
Time Off	Promotion
More Support/Back-Up/Flexibility	Paid Trip Vacations
Choice of Own Work	New Furniture
Team Leader Assignments	Updated Technology
Made 100% Accountable For ...	Expense Account
Suggestion Box/Wall	Awards/Diplomas
Reduced Delegated Tasks	Cash Bonus For Efficiency
Horizontal Job Movements	Ideas That Improve Org.

Whether or not you utilize any of the incentive motivator ideas presented on the preceding chart, are presently using similar ideas or designing your own, the use of incentive-based programs has to be done with extreme caution!

An incentive or incentive program once implemented has to accomplish its objectives for its intended purpose now, and it must not be counter-productive to the long-term development of an organization.

An incentive-based program can produce outstanding results from a player or team. However, think about the players who don't make the incentive program goal accomplishments and don't receive the incentive reward or award. How will those players or team feel? How will the future productivity levels be impacted based upon not receiving the previous incentive? What happens to their performance and attitude if they don't receive the incentive, but find out that other players that fell short of the goal but were closer to the target than they had received the incentive? Or, what happens to players' performance and commitment if everyone is receiving the same incentive, yet some players are not pulling their weight, forcing others to compensate for the slackers and dead weight?

Incentives have to be appreciated by the recipients. Incentives have to have impact and meaning. Incentives have to be timely. Iincentives should only be used as a way of saying a special thank you for effort and results far above those expected from a player. Player performance in the NORMS is recognized via a pay check already! Consider your team and list some incentives that you could utilize to stimulate additional growth and productivity.

PLAYER/TEAM INCENTIVES	
Free	$20.00 Or Less Range

Along with the following team and player incentives, immediate response via praise is another powerful motivator for human behavior! In management the act of genuine and sincere praise can ensure continued commitment from players in the tough times and stimulate players when they have fallen into a procrastination rut.

For praise to be most effective it needs to adhere to four basic ground rules:

- **First** - it needs to be *immediate*.
- **Second** - it needs to be *specific*.
- **Third** - it needs to be *given by a person who commands respect* from players and especially from the player receiving the praise.
- **Fourth** - it *must be appropriate and have meaning*.

Motivating and stimulating commitment from others through incentives and on-the-spot praise are major management tools for winning teams!

Motivating players and the team can be accomplished through both monetary (extrinsic) and nonmonetary (intrinsic) rewards, as you see from the previous chart. Examine each player individually, and your team overall, to determine what motivates and what doesn't.

Self-Assessed Motivators/Incentives: As an effective manager of resources and leader of people, have each player (employee) brainstorm and write down the ten extrinsic and ten intrinsic motivators that they would view as incentives, or merit bonuses, for work and energies that exceed expectation levels. Place each person's personalized list in their personnel file and draw upon their entries as needed (at the conclusion of projects, programs, work periods/cycles, appraisal periods, etc.). This list will provide valuable insight into what motivates your team overall and will motivate each player - individually!

Ultimate player and team motivation has to be focused on emphasizing what a player can do, not what a player can't do. Efforts have to be focused on building, strengthening and fostering a players' inner pride in what they do and what they are about. The greater the player's pride and self-confidence factor, the greater the player's commitment factor will become and the entire team benefits from greater energies.

Giving Praise (Recognition) and Incentives (Rewards): The fuel that maintains a winning team is effective and consistent recognition and rewards to its players. Individuals (and groups of people together that form your teams in life) need psychological reinforcement that what they are doing is correct and meaningful. When attention is given in a positive and constructive manner, more of that behavior will be gained. If people are left to guess as to whether or not their work is being appreciated and is meaningful, then typically the assumptions are proven wrong and work levels begin to even out and then decline.

First, differentiate between Praise (Recognition) and Incentives (Rewards). *Recognition* is that act of spotlighting or acknowledging a behavior (publicly or privately) that has lead to a success, accomplishment or substantial gain by an individual or team. This activity gets the person or team in question to recognize and "re-think" what it was that lead to that victory - by emphasizing this positive an individual or team can then repeat the activity as necessary!

Incentives (Rewards) are given for acts, service or delivery of something which exceeds expectations and norms. Incentives must have direct meaning to the recipient and have a level of value, meaning and even direct financial gain to the recipient.

---

6 Critical Factors To Successful Incentives & Praise

1. Emphasize the "can" and not the "can't"!
2. Allow all involved to celebrate a success or accomplishment when possible!
3. Must be given in a genuine manner!
4. Must be personalized to the recipient-meaning!
5. Should be appropriate to the act, the person and the timing to have lasting impact!
6. Must be connected in a clear communicated manner to the act being recognized and future goals!

Delegation Dynamics

```
Team Route List
Return To: _____
          _____
          _____
          _____
          _____
```

Effective delegation is both an art and a science. To effectively interact with other players and make requests from them, or assign tasks to them, and have them willingly and enthusiastically pursue those tasks, is ***the ultimate management goal***. Arriving at this point may, however, be another issue, and a stress filled issue at that!

Let's examine some of the reasons why delegation may go off track. Why some players seem to never get tasks assigned and delegated to them finished, while other players seem to always be in the line of getting dumped upon.

Delegation is a two-way interaction. For delegation to be effective and used as an educational development tool, management needs to be consistent about its approach and have a structure in place so all parties involved understand exactly what the mission is. When delegation goes off track, confusion, tension, defensive behavior, and player posturing takes place. The costs associated with misguided delegation to the organization are financially dangerous. To the players' attitudes and morale they are a killer and to the overall effectiveness of the team they are extreme!

Misguided delegation may result in non-productivity and a player on a team utilizing the following kind of response for work not completed. How many times have you heard: "Oh, I'm sorry, I didn't realize *what* you wanted;" "I didn't *know* I could do it that way;" "I didn't realize I could *use that*...;" "I didn't realize you needed it *right now*!!!"

To reduce these traditional responses from players who don't perform and produce the results necessary from delegated tasks, consider several of the following techniques with players (especially with Terrorists and Transmitters) in the future.

Delegation going off track may be attributed to several factors. If you can identify why this happens with a particular player, then future delegation should include an additional management step with that player to guard against repeated excuses and / or mistakes.

There are six basic elements which should be considered in delegation, with each step being presented at the time of delegation. To go back to a player after a task has been delegated/assigned, and then establish any one of the six core delegation steps, will be seen by the player as autocratic management and will imply to them that you don't trust them. When trust between a player and management is impaired, the level of commitment and enthusiasm by a player on a task goes down dramatically!

Consider the following *"Delegation Dynamics Matrix ©"*. Delegation is a systematic approach to entrusting something to another player. You need to approach the transfer of tasks from you to another player as a one-step-at-a-time activity.

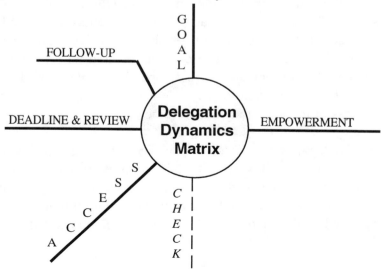

Utilizing this model requires that management slow down its interactions with players and take a systematic step-by-step approach to delegation. The *"Delegation Dynamics Matrix©"* requires the following:

Step One: GOAL - Explain in detail *WHAT* the goal or objective associated with the task which you are entrusting to this person is. Communicate what it is that you want to be done.

Step Two: EMPOWERMENT - Outline *HOW* you feel the player should proceed with the GOAL and *what* they can and can't do in the pursuit of getting it accomplished. Explain in essence, what authority they have directly associated with this GOAL, that the authority they have on this task is limited to this task only, and that this newfound authority is not universal (*Qualify the authority* and empowerment so as not to end up with a loose cannon on your team)!

Step Three: *CHECK* - At this point in the delegation sequence you must stop the delegation process and make sure via auditory or written questions that the other person understands, what is the GOAL and what is the scope of EMPOWERMENT. Until you receive some degree of response you feel confident about from the player, do not proceed with the delegation sequence. By getting an agreement from the player in question to the first two steps, you effectively eliminate the possibility of excuses like:

• "Oh, I'm sorry, I didn't realize that is what you wanted!"
• "Oh, I'm sorry, I didn't realize I could do it that way!"
• "Oh, I'm sorry, I didn't realize I could use that...!"

Step Four: ACCESS - Make sure that the player has ACCESS and can get ACCESS to any and all resources needed to facilitate achieving the GOAL or objective. Make sure that all other players know this player is working on this GOAL, and has authority (EMPOWERMENT) to ACCESS required resources, without a lot of additional or traditional authorizations.

Step Five: DEADLINE & REVIEW - Once you have gained confirmation via the communication interaction that steps one, two and four have been received and that there has been no miscommunication, you are ready to establish the due date and time frame associated with the task assigned to the player. Make sure the player has heard when it is due and allow for the player to communicate any concerns he may have concerning the DEADLINE. If there are no concerns and you have gained confirmation from him that the DEADLINE can be met, proceed to the REVIEW. After every delegation interaction (after the DEADLINE has come and gone), every player and MANAGER should invest a few minutes with one another to discuss and REVIEW what took place - pro and con. This REVIEW interaction is an educational growth opportunity and affords both management and player the opportunity to review successes and analyze any failures, so future actions will be more efficient and effective.

Step Six: FOLLOW-UP - At the time of delegation if you determine that the complexity of the task requires it or because of the player assigned to the task, you will need to have regular check-ups, then establish that FOLLOW-UP sequence. If you schedule the FOLLOW-UP before the player begins the task, the FOLLOW-UP will be seen as a positive. However, if you don't discuss the FOLLOW-UP and you merely keep checking in on him unannounced, the player will quickly begin to feel that you are baby-sitting him. This causes negative feelings and attitudes which will impact directly on the success of the task assigned (delegated) to him!

This is an auditory formula for delegation. If the situation or player warrants it, you should convert these steps into writing. With each of the six steps in the *"Delegation Dynamics Matrix©"* established and qualified and agreed upon by all parties, you can feel a greater level of confidence that the task assigned will be completed according to the predescribed plan of action!

As management interacts with individuals and groups of people, the interaction itself can be an opportunity for conflict and confrontations. A powerful way to structure management interactions with players, and with one another is to communicate and interact via the *"SMART"* formula!

The *"SMART"* formula for interaction and communication in delegation can lead to greater levels of player participation and increased positive player performance. Consider this as a map to effective human relations. As you follow the six steps in the *"Delegation Dynamics Matrix©"* , keep the *"SMART"* formula in mind as a behavioral map to improved relationships.

S	• Communication needs to be **specific** and not open to a difference of opinions - the *what* factors.
M	• Your interaction needs to be **measurable**. There needs to be an element to measure or gauge whether you are on track or off track - the *how* factors.
A	• Obtain **agreement** with the other player(s) on each point within this formula, prior to moving to the next.
R	• Inquire to make sure that the other player(s) believe what it is you are discussing (or tasking them with) is **realistic, reachable** and **reasonable**. If they don't, then don't proceed with the conversations, and especially don't proceed with delegation, until that sticking point is resolved - the *why* factors.
T	• Establish the working **time-frame** for the issue or task being assigned and be very specific - the *when* factors.

Delegation should be seen as a positive means to growing and developing players so a team can come together and accomplish greater levels of success. Delegation is also a point from which priorities can be assigned to appropriate levels of players so time being invested on issues and projects is efficient use of player time.

Management can only survive and grow toward market demands by letting go (delegation) of work, which would have traditionally been addressed by management personnel.

Some players will resist delegated tasks and attempt to divert attention and participation toward other projects to justify lack of or low levels of participation on issues and tasks which you had earlier assigned to them. If a player can go unchallenged for not participating on an assigned issue and management bails the player out, then management can expect similar behavior out of a player many times in the future. If, on the other hand, management doesn't allow a player off the hook when a delegated issue, task or project is not completed, then management can begin to change the educational process and hold players accountable for their actions!

Some players are also very good at appearing on management's door step at the most inopportune times. Think about how many times you have observed a player waiting until a MANAGER is on the telephone and then going to that MANAGER with questions and problems. If you watch what unfolds, the player has strategically waited for the MANAGER to become involved in an auditory conversation. When he appears in the MANAGER's office, neither party can engage in two auditory conversations. The MANAGER asks the player in the doorway to wait, the player waits a few minutes and then leaves a paper stack on the MANAGER's desk and the MANAGER then quietly says, "Let's get back together on this when I'm off the telephone." Recognizing that now the player's stack is on the MANAGER'S desk and the player is gone, when does the MANAGER typically see the player? When the MANAGER goes on a hunt to find the player!

In the environment of delegation, many times a player will wait until the assigning MANAGER is busy and then appear with dozens of questions or problems. The previous two management delegation techniques afford you alternative management actions with a player to ward off a large number of these typical problems.

Another management delegation technique that can be utilized to ward off the monkeys that land on your back is the *"Action Memo©"*! There are two basic steps to an *"Action Memo©"*. As management, the MANAGER can facilitate the technique in a number of ways.

- **One:** Management can initiate the first step and assign a player to step two.
- **Two:** Management can require that a player utilize an *"Action Memo©"* at any time he/she needs to interact with a member of the management team.

An *"Action Memo©"* allows the player needing management interaction to take a traditional auditory conversation or problem and convert it into a visual communication interaction. Management has to be careful not to alienate a player by refusing any of their inputs on *step two,* and work for interaction and linkage among a player's ideas and solutions, and those of management.

A typical memo can be drafted in writing and can be created on any piece of paper - scrap paper, sticky note pad, waste paper, note pad, back of a piece of used paper, etc... The following is an example of what an *"Action Memo©"* may look like:

ACTION MEMO ©

1)   **RE:** The issue, problem, subject, concern area need merely be written out for easy verbal and visual communication and understanding!

(the first objective is the identification of the *WHAT* factors)

2)   **Three Possible Solutions** or Alternatives to address above issue need to then be offered up as suggestions.

(the second objective here is to then identify viable *HOW* factors)

Jeff Magee International ® '94

Through the use of the *"Delegation Dynamics Matrix©"*, the *"SMART"* formula and the *"Action Memo©"*, management can develop healthy and educated perspectives of players and what can and cannot be delegated to each individual. Through player participation in these techniques and management tools, a MANAGER can begin to develop Transformers from Transmitters. A MANAGER can strategically utilize a Transformer to advance both himself and the team's performance!

Consider the application of these three techniques and the management tools as they specifically relate to a player on your team today!

ACTION INTERACTION DELEGATION PLAN

▼

Player Name: _____

Issue At Odds: _____

_____

Best Course Of Action Now: _____

_____

_____

_____

Date By Which I Can Interact With This Player And Attempt To Initiate These Techniques: _____

Now, make a notation on a calendar that as a MANAGER you will see this player on the date that you have identified above (mentally or physically) and on that date, you will now be reminded to see whether your actions have been successful or not!

The litany of techniques and differing management delegation tools which can be utilized to increase organizational production and decrease personal management work loads and stress is very diverse. Subjectively, consider some other powerful ideas for effective management delegation within your environment. Consider the following delegation inventory and determine if further management techniques can assist in team development.

MANAGEMENT TECHNIQUES/TACTICS -

• *Design Departmental Work Flow Charts* - Analyze each department independently to determine delegation patterns. Some management players fall victim to delegating similar tasks repeatedly to static players, without regard to whether that is the most efficient use of that player in the team perspective. Also, by flowing work through departments, you can determine unnecessary steps and then work to eliminate wasted time and misused resources.

• *Develop Player Experts* - Management should not have to play the role of expert on every task and job description element. Management should identify which player (see Chapter Six) desires to become an expert on specific tasks or issues and develop that player to be the team leader on given variables, thus reducing management work loads.

• *Technology Assistants* - Train colleagues and customers (internal/external), when appropriate, to utilize other means of communication, i.e., E-Mail, Fax, Voice Mail, to transmit work assignments, needs and help requests. This will free your schedule for other one-on-one interactions and actually increase your production level on all tasks and assignments.

• *Combine Delegation Task* - Low priority tasks should be ganged together for combination delegation of similar activities at the same time, saving player actions and reducing repetitive work assignments, trips, calls, etc...

• *Delegation Box* - If people delegate upward to you, horizontally to you or even vertically to you, consider placing a box to the side of your desk or on your door for those assignments. This reduces the face-to-face interactions, interruptions and socializing which may be associated with colleague interactions.

• *Write Ups* - Have players and superiors write requests which they throw your way in transit, walking or when you're not at your desk. By asking them to write it down and forward it to you, many times the requests will go away!

• *Player Logs* - Maintain a quick reference sheet on each player you delegate to regularly. When delegating tasks to a person, make a quick notation on this log as to the task name, date given and date expected and completed. Review your logs monthly to determine patterns in level of ease or complexity of tasks delegated. Evaluate to see if you are overloading some individuals and underdeveloping and thus underutilizing others.

Delegation is a powerful management tool, both for assisting management in addressing the top priorities for management and *in developing players* for a winning team!

While delegation is the single most powerful development tool in the manager/coach toolbox for organizational development today, it is also the most misunderstood and misused tool. View delegation as the fastest route to developing a player's level of self esteem, rebuilding a player with low self-esteem, and, for growing players both individually and as a group. Delegation is a tool that allows for the proper transfer of work and decision making from one individual to another. Think of delegation as the means to increased successes and proficiency internally - anything that can be pushed (meant as a positive management term) downward to another individual, should and must be!

---

del•e•ga•tion - *n*. 1. The act of delegating or state of being delegated. 2. A person or group of persons empowered to represent another or others. 3. A given task that grows and develops another person into a greater performer on a team.
del•e•gate - *n*. 1. A person empowered to act as representative for another.
dump•ing - *n*. 1. Needless tasking of an individual with mundane activities, that are seen to have no connection to what is suppose to be the main efforts of both an individual or the organization as a whole.

Designing Decision Making Teams

```
┌─────────────────────────────────┐
│ Team Route List                 │
│ Return To: _____│
│            _____│
│            _____│
│            _____│
│            _____│
└─────────────────────────────────┘
```

Designing a team of players and entrusting them with the accountability and responsibility for making certain key decisions in the absence of specific management personnel allows a team to competitively function and eliminates the traditional management structure and layers which typically impede growth!

Decision teams should be directed by Transformers and contain the appropriate cross-section of players to ensure educated discussions on challenges, so decisions can be arrived at and issues are not being placed to the side due to interaction requirements with a player who is not a member of the decision team and thus absent from dialogues.

Official "Decision Making Teams" should have the ability and authority (within reason) to make decisions on the run. Players need to be empowered to facilitate those decisions. Players on these teams should be educated and trained so that they can perform up to the standards expected, as management has identified each player to be capable of (as outlined in Chapter Six).

Each organizational level and individual department should have a designated decision team "on-line" in the event that a MANAGER is off-site and a key decision needs to be made for the organization to continue production and to meet market (customer) needs. There are problems with these teams. Management must ensure that the teams have a map or systematically structured formula to analyze situations and develop options prior to initiating a solution and committing organizational resources. It is this structure that many times is not given to decision teams and the team is first challenged with "how" to begin the process. Therefore, management must make sure that the teams have some decision making tools to start with.

When individuals are tasked with making decisions at any level within an organization, there are three variables which must be weighed in an attempt to arrive at a decision with the highest *value* level! The factors which must be considered are: *RISK, TIME,* and *QUALITY.*

The following chart will allow you to graph these three variables as they relate to you in any given situation within an organization (and within life as well). The point at which these three lines intersect is where you find the highest attainable level of *VALUE* and it is at that point in time that a decision must be made for the ultimate good of an organization and its players.

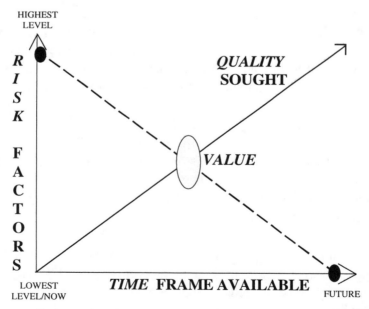

Teams must recognize there are factors which must be identified or associated with any decision. Each factor needs individual attention, but players must recognize when it is time to move on so as to not get pulled down by paralyses of analysis!

Three Factors To Consider: First, thoroughly analyze all associated *RISK* factors. Obviously the more time you can invest in analysis the more you can reduce the RISK factors (liabilities). However, if you invest too much time in the analysis of the RISK factors, it may be too late by the time the team makes a decision. **Second**, consider the reasonable amount *TIME* available for this analysis before a decision and action must take place. Again, the team and each player must realize in the beginning exactly how much time is allowable or available for the issue being analyzed. Too much time invested can spell disaster. **Third**, identify the *QUALITY* level sought or required. Obviously, the more time that can be invested in a cause (in theory) the better decision. This is not always the case. A realistic view of attainable *QUALITY* must also be identified.

When players, management and especially, official "Decision Making Teams" balance these three factors, sound and viable solutions can be designed. Weighing these three factors when they intersect is the point at which the ultimate *VALUE* will be obtained. To obtain the highest and most realistic level of *VALUE* from decisions, consider the next formula.

Psychology explains a great deal to individuals in terms of how the brain processes information and then how it acts upon that data. In making sound decisions, the brain processes that data in four systematic steps. When you interact with individuals on decision teams, these same four steps are at work within each player's mind. To thoroughly manage the dynamics of a team approach to decision making, each step needs to be identified at the beginning. Each player can then reference those four analysis points throughout the team's interaction. This will also reduce the level of tension, defensiveness, finger-pointing and increase effective interactions and ultimate decisions and solutions being acted upon!

How To Lead A Team: The Different Types Of Teams

Work Groups: A collection of people working together and toward a common goal. No true final decision making powers/abilities and most commonly used as a transition from traditional organizational structures to teams. **Temporary Team:** Designed to address a specific issue/concern and once addressed the team disbands. Short-term issues fit best here. **Permanent Teams:** Designed to address, monitor and handle consistent needs and on-going issues. **Management Teams:** A team made up of only management players to address strategic and directional issues. Only players with vested interest and management responsibilities should be involved. **Cross-Functional Teams:** Made up of all players necessary from across an organization (internally and externally) to address needs and make final recommendations and/or decisions. **Self-Directed Teams:** The ultimate team and decision body. These people have complete responsibility for planning, strategy and implementation. Final decision power is held with this group and therefore 100 percent accountability lies here as well.

The four psychological thought-processing steps are building blocks on one another. In order to smoothly progress from step one to step four, each subsequent step has to be thoroughly dealt with or players will mentally digress back to an already resolved step. The interactions will continuously go back and forth with no solutions being attained in reasonable amounts of time. Consider the following map for interactive analysis and decisions:

first	**S**	*stop* and *see* the issue
second	**T**	*target* (analyze) the -, +, risk factors
third	**O**	*organize* your *options* (solutions)
fourth	**P**	*pick* and *proceed* with an option

When you face an issue to which you dedicate analysis time, your brain has to become focused on one issue at a time. In essence, you need to dedicate both your conscious and subconscious brain power to the analysis. Then you have to rationalize why you have picked that issue or been tasked with it and explore all of the negatives and problems associated with it. Live and relive the traumas associated with what you have identified. From this analysis step, you then move to exploring solutions and options. The key factor with the third step is that options means more than one solution or idea must be available before considering an ultimate path upon which to proceed. When multiple ideas, solutions and options are raised, player and team synergy develops. This may ultimately result in a more viable option being arrived upon and will lead the decision process to the fourth step. From the brainstorming step (three) you can identify one viable solution (pick) and proceed to implement it (see Chapter Twelve for additional applications)!

The **"STOP" Formula** © leads an individual or team toward positive outcomes. Now there will be a map to follow when discussion gets bogged down. With this formula you can work to maintain and make decisions "issue" oriented and not "personality" oriented!

Focus energies toward positive outcomes and work to reduce the traditional *"Grief Cycle©"* (Chapter Five) of players with this technique.

Collecting and stimulating ideas from players in a decision situation or from within decision making teams is another challenge of management. Gaining ideas from players without criticism or judgments can be attained with proper management and ground rules. In order to stimulate input consider the three minimum factors associated with every decision within organizations: RISK, TIME, and QUALITY. Along with these three factors it is also necessary to ensure realistic standards and expectations within the decisions. A powerful and non-confrontational technique that can be utilized to accomplish this is the *"SMART©"* formula (as presented in the *Delegation Dynamics* section).

In arriving at an effective decision, one in which most, if not all, of the players have participated and will therefore be more inclined to participate in and support. Consider another application to this previous idea and what each letter represents in the acronym formula - *"SMART©"*.

S	• Communication needs to be **specific**. It should not be open to differences of opinions at a later date or at the time of initiation.
M	• Your interaction needs to be **measurable**. There should be elements of measure to gauge whether you are on track or off, ahead of or behind schedule. These steps need to be mapped out in black and white prior to initiation.
A	• Attain an **agreement** with each player on the above two and the remaining two factors, each independent of the other.
R	• Inquire through questions and dialogue with the other players to see and hear whether they feel that what is being discussed and decided upon is **realistic, reasonable** and **reachable**. If there is any negative feedback, those points need to be discussed, resolved or set to the side prior to progressing with any discussion and subsequent decisions.
T	• Establish the **time-frame** in which the decision will be acted upon. Any time-frame factors and deadlines need to mapped out here!

One effective way to stimulate thought and develop the options in making decisions within a team environment (or by oneself) is a technique called the ***Crawford Slip Method***. Professor C.C. Crawford, Ph.D., of the University of Southern California, structures decision sessions in such a way as to control interactions and idea fluency, while eliminating confrontations and criticisms through the ***Crawford Slip Method***.

Essentially, you assign and transcribe individual ideas or statements onto separate pieces of paper. One idea to a slip. When the ideas stop coming, then you go back and look at the ideas or suggestions. By having the ideas individually written down, you can now arrange the ideas in some order. By looking at each idea on paper and arranged in order, you have the ability to rearrange ideas. Also, by looking at what is written, you may also see patterns in your thinking and in what everyone is discussing. This slip method may stimulate additional ideas from participants or yourself - self-stimulated synergy!

When a team or player needs to make decisions where there may be some challenging personalities involved, you may also want to consider the three primary resources which will impact the final decision and from there, the action. Consider that typical decisions can have two of the following three factors in them, but never all three factors. Ask yourself, if you were to make a decision and could only have two of these three factors, how would that impact your decisions and what would they do to the actions one would expect from a decision. Which two factors would your supervisor prefer in making some of the pressing decisions within the daily schedules (if only two of the three could be had)?

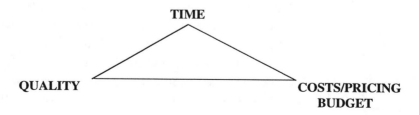

Reaching a consensus on decisions is not always easy. Consider some of these ideas and techniques for your next interaction involving decisions with others. Put some structure into your interactions for success!

Effective Meeting Management Skills

```
┌─────────────────────────────────┐
│ Team Route List                 │
│ Return To: _____        │
│            _____        │
│            _____        │
│            _____        │
│            _____        │
└─────────────────────────────────┘
```

Managing the amount of time management and players spend in meetings, and reducing the number of meetings that take place within organizations, is the aim of this section! So, how much time do you spend in meetings each year?

The Wharton School of Business studied that exact question. The findings are shocking! It is estimated that by the time a member of management retires, if that player held titles such as an executive, manager or supervisor, he would have spent roughly 33 percent of his/her working career sitting in meetings!

Can you afford to pay that much money to have your players sitting? Well, that is exactly what most organizations do. They pay staff to eat away every day by sitting in, blending in and in some cases sabotaging meetings!

Consider a typical meeting. They tend to be breeding grounds for Terrorists. One shows up and works throughout the course of the meeting to undermine management. If allowed to go on unchecked, that Terrorist can grow into a powerful subgroup and completely derail a meeting and organizational agenda.

In order to efficiently manage a team and to manage meetings, there has to be a structure that respects each player's position - yet keeps the meeting on course and guards against Terrorists. *Consider meeting management skills as a three-part approach:* **Before-During-After** *the meeting!*

BEFORE: Before any meeting there are several questions which management must ask. Then there are several steps which need to be addressed to ensure that a successful meeting takes place and for on time meeting management. Consider these questions and points prior to calling and arriving at your meetings:

SELF-IMPOSED QUESTIONS -

• Can the purpose of this meeting be communicated to the team and players by another means?

• Do I need the entire team for this meeting?

• Are there easier ways than a meeting to accomplish myobjectives?

• Am I calling a meeting for a limited scope of challenges which pertain to only a few specific players?

• Is this merely a regular meeting? Is there really no purpose for this regularly scheduled meeting?

• How much will this meeting cost financially?

- per minute participant wage/salary, times the length of the meeting = $ _____

- direct value/cost of lost productivity of each player in meeting times the length of the meeting = $ _____

- the add-on costs associated with lost production from other players on the team because they can't contact people they need, because those people are in your meeting. Cost of this = $ _____

- the cost of your time, times the length of the meeting = $ _____

- any other identified costs associated with this meeting (refreshments, speakers, materials, etc...) = $ _____

TOTAL FINANCIAL COST = $ _____ !

PREPARATION POINTS -

• *Agenda* - Design an agenda for the focus of this meeting. An agenda will give you the opportunity to mentally and physically plan, pull notes together, obtain the facts/data and documentation necessary to accomplish your agenda and objectives prior to a meeting.

• *Transformers* - Identify the Transformers on this team who would be in your meeting and interact with them prior to the meeting. Brief them on your objectives and agenda. Get their participation and "buy-in" to your position as this will assist you during the meeting in pulling Transmitters in your direction and in neutralizing the Terrorists.

• *Location* - Plan the logistics and location of the meeting site. If your traditional meeting environment is not conducive for success and allows for continuous interruptions, plan on a different location for your meeting.

• *Players* - Invite only those players that you need and who are directly impacted by this meeting agenda. If you don't need a player in a meeting, then don't require him to be there. Remember how much you are paying each player per hour. Take that figure and then multiply it for each player you will have in your meeting, times how many minutes or hours they will be in this meeting and you will quickly arrive at the rough dollar amount for your meeting.

• *Best Time Of Day For Highest Growth & Results* - Identify with your team what the most productive times of the day for meetings would be and schedule meetings for those time zones, regardless of what others, and especially the Terrorists, may say. Utilize time as a strategic success weapon in meetings instead of time being the enemy!

Ideally the best time of the day for any meeting is directly before something important; if there is nothing important or urgent on that specific day's schedule then always schedule meetings directly before ... *lunch or the end of the day*! These are the most important things to take place each day (going to lunch and going home at the end of the day) for most players. The positive of these two time frames is that everyone in the meeting understands what is to take place when the meeting is over, and the meeting's dominating talker gets peer pressure from colleagues to "shut up"!

With a meeting scheduled directly before something important, all players will typically be present for an on-time start;
unlike the first thing in the morning and right after lunch type
meeting, when there are always certain players arriving late and
blaming it on traffic. Now, though, the players are present and
can't blame the traffic for being late.

• *Facilitator* - Every meeting should have a designated facilitator
to serve as the navigator for that meeting and to ensure that the
agenda is being followed.

• *Perceived Outcome* - You should have mentally mapped out
your desired outcome for the presentation prior to
holding the session. You may even want to write a note as
reference to where the meeting needs to move and to
serve as a reminder of what your worst-case scenario may be
for this interaction!

• *Three Types Of Meetings* - There are only three different styles
or types of meeting which management can call to order. The
are: *Information-Sharing, Information-Gathering,* and
Information-Creation.

• *48-Hour Notice* - A written meeting announcement or reminder
should go to all players expected at the meeting. It should
mention by name all of the players you will need or who you
expect to present any type of report or update. This warning
gives all players a chance to prepare and will save time in player
reports. This announcement carrying the very specific names
of those players who will be reporting will also serve as a
powerful way to tell the typical meeting Terrorists to keep their
mouths shut during the participants' reports!

(❑This step ties into the two additional steps. The three utilized together
serve as a powerful three-punch for improved meeting management skills.
See DURING for the next two steps.)

These *BEFORE* points serve as a preparation checklist to greater meeting participation, interactions and overall meeting management success for *DURING* stage.

DURING: Once the meeting has started, it is critical to maintain balance within the meeting and to enforce the structure which you have put into place. Players in meetings are like children and they all start by seeing what they can get away with and what you are all about! If you let players have an inch, they will take a mile, and it will seem like you are running the distance to regain control of your meetings.

To ensure the highest level of productivity, greatest level of player participation, decrease Terroristic attacks and reduce the amount of time everyone has to invest in meetings, consider strategic questions prior to the meeting's commencement and throughout the session:

SELF-IMPOSED QUESTIONS -
• Have I established the proper structure for this meeting to be successful?
• Are we on or off track in the meeting in regard to the agenda?
• Are we on the right issue or are we jumping around on the agenda. If so, how do I get back on track?

MANAGEMENT TECHNIQUES/TACTICS -
• *Start and Stop* - Start your meeting exactly when you say you will and don't wait for anyone. If you wait, that person will never be on time. Then everyone who is there on time becomes alienated and you convert them into pseudo Terrorists!

Stop your meeting when you say you are going to. Even if you are not done you must stop, shut up! If a meeting is to be done at 10 AM and you still have items to discuss at 10 AM, pause and make sure the players in the room are both mentally and physically with you. Most players will have things planned at 10:01 AM and sitting in another of management's meetings is not on their list! Ask a question to determine if the team needs a brief break, needs to reschedule or should continue on with an agreed upon amount of additional time. If you stop the meeting flow and get the players back with you, the remaining minutes of this meeting will be significantly more productive!

• *Player Assignments* - Every meeting has several players who attend and believe that they have an "unofficial" official role in the meeting. Management can facilitate effective meetings with these players by putting them in a position where they are not challenging the meeting coordinator. Officially, at the beginning of the meeting, in front of all the other players, ask these players if they would "officially" assist in the management of that specific meeting by serving as the: *Official Time Keeper* (signified by that colleague who typically attends meetings and maintains eye contact with the wall clock, or if there is no wall clock, takes their wrist watch off and places it before them on the table for all to see); *Official Secretary* (signified by that colleague who takes notes during the meeting on everything that is said and by whom).

The time keeper will keep the meeting flowing and they (not you) will now non-confrontationally redirect any player who is off track. The official secretary and his notes will become the official meeting minutes so you can follow-up your meetings with visual confirmation of what was discussed and resolved. Each player is informed and you can now control post-meeting miscommunication!

• *Agenda* - Everyone attending the meeting should have a copy of an agenda so they can understand what to focus on and accomplish! The agenda serves as a map and should be visible to you as a tracking tool of where you are, how much time you have invested on any specific item, therefore assisting the coordinator or leader in managing that meeting.

If anyone goes off the agenda, you can now non-confrontationally move the conversation and other players back to the purpose of the meeting by comfortably pointing at the last agenda item discussed and redirecting the group's momentum to that point.

• *Two-Minute Warning* - Every player, mentioned in the "48-Hour Notice" who is to actually give a report or make a presentation will be informed that each will have two minutes only at the beginning of the meeting to either give their entire report or to give an overview of their report. No Q & A will take place during or immediately after the two-minute reports. Once all identified players have given their two-minute reports, then the first person will be called upon to complete their overview and then the Q & A will take place. This cuts down significantly on senseless dialogue and questions, speeds up reports of fact and data and cuts down on the volume of fluff typically presented in reports!

• *45-Minute Limit* - No meeting should require participants to absorb more than 45 minutes of the same topic. If a meeting needs to go more than 45 minutes due to content issues (as very often is the issue), then the facilitator should make plans for breaks, activities or interactions to stimulate energy and counter agitation and day-dreaming!

• *Three Types Of Meeting Management Styles* - Depending on the meeting type you are calling and participating in, there are three different management styles which you must assume to maximize that type of meeting. If you are having an Information-Sharing meeting, then you should serve as an *Autocrat*. If the meeting is Information-Gathering, act as a *Democrat*. And if the meeting is an Information-Creation session, then you serve via *Laissez-Faire*.

• *Six Power Questions Stimulate Involvement* - If you find yourself in a meeting and are unclear of what is being said, proposed or challenged, don't become defensive or engage in a war of words. Initiate a strategic series of questions which stimulate the other player into conversation and away from confrontation. This conversation will afford you additional knowledge and assist in designing your management response. The questions are W, W, W, W, W, and H!

If these letters don't mean anything to you, then go back to your high school English course. The person who asks the questions typically wins the interaction and the person who dominates the interaction and conversations ultimately loses! Still confused? Reflect on any interaction you have had with a four-year old. The letters represent: Who? What? When? Where? Why? and How?

• *Punch List* - During the meeting make a listing or chart of each issue addressed with the status of each. The status should include: actions to be taken, date initiated, who initiated it, date to be completed, who is accountable, and comments. A copy of this should be maintained in an official meeting log and copies given to appropriate players!

• *Time* - At the beginning of any meeting with an individual or a team, state how much time is allotted to this meeting.

• *Know Player Work Load Liabilities* - Realistically understand your present work load and that of the other players in a meeting. Be cautious not to overload a Transformer or Transmitter to the point that the productivity level turns negative.

• *Multiple Layered Player Participation* - If you're going to have more than one management layer/level present at a meeting, meet BEFORE the meeting or presentation with those players and assign roles and responsibilities so that DURING the meeting management isn't fighting for power in front of the team. Lines of authority in this meeting need to be clear (who is the actual facilitator) and whose meeting is it!

• *Mind Mapping or Growth Wheels* © - Utilize alternative note taking techniques in the meeting. Allow yourself to stay connected with everyone else so you don't get caught up in taking notes and then miss some of the communication.

• *SMART Formula* - Utilize the SMART formula (see "Delegation Dynamics" techniques) to ensure player understanding and buy-in to meeting issues.

• *Questions* - Make sure that all meetings have extra time budgeted for expected and unexpected questions from players. Solicit input and feedback on issues throughout the meeting from colleagues (both Transmitters and Transformers).

• *Negative Participants* - When a negative participant appears in a meeting or challenges a position presented by management or another player, don't <u>react</u>. Instead, take immediate logical control and <u>act</u>. Consider the following techniques designed for tactical interaction with the negative meeting participant player (i.e., Terrorist):

1.   *Empathy.* Immediately acknowledge his position o statement. You are not agreeing or disagreeing with him, merely acknowledging him. A negative person expects you to challenge them, defend your position or react. He doesn't expect you to be rational about his attack!

2.   *Stimulate A Conversation.* Immediately upon acknowledging them, utilize one of the six questions (W,W,W,W,W,H) to get the other person talking to educate you, or for you to gain a better perspective of where he is coming from. This will give you a better response position.

3.   *Demand An Alternative.* No one has ever made him accountable for his challenge. Don't let him off the hook. If a player challenges your position in a meeting you must stop the meeting process right then, keep the conversation (not confrontation) "issue-oriented" and not personality oriented (which is what the negative player has come to expect and may even want) and demand an alternative from him. If you solicit an option or alternative from him once and he has no offer,

repeat, up to three times, "What do you feel we should do?" And then move on if he has no options. If he does, objectively analyze and consider them.

4.   *Assign 100 Percent Accountability.* Place the project, task or issue directly in his hands and make him 100 percent accountable for it. Directly move onto the next agenda item!

5.   *Request Write Up.* Ask the player to write up the point he wants to discuss, and several alternatives for resolving it, and get with you one-on-one later in the day or week. Then directly move onto the next agenda issue!

6.   *Avoid Argument.* At all costs avoid getting drawn into a debate with a negative person in front of an audience. They seek these situations. Reschedule the negativist's issue for a one-on-one, in private, after the meeting!

7.   *Set Up.* If you know going into a meeting that there may be a vocal objector, then go for him in your opening statement. Don't let the negativists attack you or attempt to steal the show. Professionally (and issue-oriented) go for the negativists before they get a chance to come after you.

For example. "In considering the proposition of purchasing blue pens for the entire department, I would like to spend a few minutes to solicit feedback as to whether this is a good idea or if there may be other options. If so, I would like to analyze each alternative pro and con as it is raised. Let's get this meeting going with a few ideas. John (perceived negativist, challenging person, Terrorist), what are your feelings on the blue pen order?"

Management must maintain control over meetings or they will destruct right before your eyes and those players who were Transformers and/or Transmitters may revert to pseudo Terrorists. This will be due to management allowing the meeting to go off track and wasting their limited time!

AFTER: Once the meeting is over, there are several key requirements of that meeting's facilitator (MANAGER) in order to ensure that the outcomes of the meeting are actualized! Consider the following questions and points as a map for post-meeting success:

SELF-IMPOSED QUESTIONS -
• Did we accomplish what we set out to in the meeting?
• Did the Terrorists or the Transformers win this meeting?
• Do I have a clear understanding of what the next course of action is? If I do, do the other members of the team have a clear understanding of what the next step is?
• Did we follow the meeting outline as designed BEFORE the meeting? If so, how? If not, why?

MANAGEMENT POINTS -
• *Self Meeting* - Make sure that you schedule some private time to focus after a meeting on what happened and what the next steps are.

• *Notes* - After every meeting review your notes/minutes briefly to ensure that the play-by-play notes which you took while the meeting was in progress are accurate and if additional notes (perspective) are necessary to get those thoughts down while they are fresh in your mind! Then store all of your notes and any other documentation from the meeting for historical purposes. Never throw away meeting notes!

• *Follow-Up Times* - Immediately transpose dates onto your working calendar for any follow-ups and with whom.

• *Mini Meeting* - If appropriate, after the meeting and on reflection of what transpired DURING the meeting, you may feel it necessary to get face-to-face (once again) with a certain few players to ensure that the issues addressed in the meeting are being initiated and that assumptions are not setting a stage from which problems will surface later.

To maximize both your time and the time of each player on your team, consider the follow checklist for managing meetings.

Effective Meeting Management Index
(Prior to any meeting reflect upon the following points to determine if all options have been considered and whether there are any points that have been overlooked.)

BEFORE	DURING	AFTER
❏ Costs	❏ Structure Set	❏ Did We
❏ Agenda	❏ Start/Stop Times	Accomplish ?
❏ Transformers	❏ Player Assignments	❏ Notes
❏ Location	❏ Agenda Usage	❏ Follow-up
❏ Players	❏ Two-Minute	❏ Mini-
❏ Best Times	Warnings	Meetings
❏ Facilitator	❏ 45-Minute Limits	❏ **Other:**
❏ Perceived Outcome	❏ Three Types of	
❏ Type of Meeting	Meeting Styles	
❏ 48-Hr. Notice	❏ Six Power Questions	
❏ **Other:**	❏ Punch List	
	❏ Time	
	❏ Player Liabilities	
	❏ Self-Meeting Need	
	❏ Mind Mapping	
	❏ SMART Formula	
	❏ Questions	
	❏ Managing The	
	Negative Player	
	❏ **Other:**	

Managing The Difficult
And Challenging Person

```
┌─────────────────────────────┐
│ Team Route List             │
│ Return To: _____  │
│            _____  │
│            _____  │
│            _____  │
│            _____  │
│            _____  │
└─────────────────────────────┘
```

For the past thirty years, Peter Drucker (organizational management writer, consultant and sociologist) has studied organizations and strongly feels that problems and challenges facing any group of people (team) today, within any organization, can be traced to two differing variables: *Systems* and *People*!

It is the second variable which typically dominates the management scene and which typically creates the most stress and tension among players on a team. Yet, Drucker finds that of the two variables (*Systems* and *People*) the percentage value attributed to the two variables is disproportionately weighted toward the *Systems* - nearly 85 percent of organizational problems can be traced back to the *Systems*; while only 15 percent of the problems are traceable to the *People*!

These two variables are very interesting, especially given the fact that it tends to be the *people* within those organizations that cause the problems (on the surface) and not the *systems*; which cause the tension and stress within a team! Therefore, techniques for "managing the difficult and challenging person," whom management comes in contact with on a daily basis, will assist in facilitating the management styles (hats one wears outlined in Chapter Four) of: MANAGER, MENTOR, COUNSELOR, COACH!

Challenging people may be either external or internal. Management deals with people from the positive end of the spectrum to those players on the negative end of the spectrum. They may be customers, colleagues, clients, subordinates or supervisors. They may be friends, family or kids and they may be powerful or wealthy people. It doesn't matter who they are, only that they are difficult and challenging. So, how can you interact with these people?

The fastest way to interact with these people for a positive outcome is to change your typical approach with these people. In this subsection a three-step process is proposed. Step one sets the foundation from which the second and final steps will develop. *The three steps for managing difficult and challenging people for positive outcomes are*:

> • **First:** *Neutralize* or condition the person or player.
> • **Second**: *Interact* with the person or player.
> • **Third:** Stimulate a *change* within the person or player.

As you analyze these three steps, notice which step management typically jumps directly into when faced with a difficult or challenging person. Perhaps phrases like crisis management, conflict resolution, putting out fires seem familiar! If they do, then recognize this is a BLEND because management and players are always jumping directly into the *Interact* step or stage without ever *Neutralizing* the other player!

To begin to change the paradigm of traditional interactions with difficult and challenging people, which turn confrontational and lead to heightened stress and team tension levels, consider conditioning the environment differently than what you might traditionally do and that the other player would expect you to do. By *neutralizing* the other player (reverse psychology), you condition them for a greater level of *interaction* and that can lead to a more productive outcome - *Change*!

NEUTRALIZE: First, establish nonthreatening ways to create a more relaxing atmosphere in which your interaction has a chance of being heard and thus accepted and acted (not reacted) upon. There are several ways to *neutralize* the other player in conversations, one-on-one situations and when challenged in a more public environment where there are witnesses to this interaction. Consider a profession that is trained in the importance of neutralizing first in order to attain desired interaction levels and safe productive outcomes - law enforcement. Consider the management parallel to your environment and personal/professional interactions:

Trooper Jeff Kistle of the New Jersey State Police and member of a special task force unit, trains weekly on special drills (MANAGER role) so that when in a situation for which he and his team have trained, their actions and response will be systematic as trained for and structured for. By following your logic track and not your emotions, you can neutralize practically any situation!

Consider how law enforcement officers (Troopers) on the highway position their patrol cars when making a traffic stop on the highway. They have learned through analysis and observation to position their car on an angle to serve as a shield if necessary, thus giving them an element of neutralization!

If there is more than one person in the vehicle the law enforcement officer (Trooper) has stopped, he requests one person at a time to step out of the car. He requests hands be maintained at a level where they can be seen at all times. The person is instructed to move at a slow pace in one situation and a faster pace in another - given the situation. If the officer (Trooper) finds himself outnumbered and determines a need for greater levels of neutralization (control) for increased interaction success, the officer (Trooper) will have the players assume a standard position against the vehicle and, one at a time, place the players into handcuffs.

But if the officer (Trooper) was immediately interacting with the players beside the car, and while the interaction was in progress determined to handcuff the players as they all stood within close proximity to him, can you imagine how difficult maintaining a neutral zone would be? Imagine how easy it would be for one of the players to incite a problem, challenge, fight, or run from the scene?

The first step to people interaction has to be *Neutralization*!

MANAGEMENT TECHNIQUES/TACTICS

STEP ONE: *NEUTRALIZE* the challenging or difficult person before ever attempting to *Interact* with them. Consider:

• *Empathy* - Immediate acknowledgment will many times defuse a negative, challenging or difficult person. Acknowledgment means you recognize him and his position. It doesn't mean you agree or disagree with him. Many times these challenging people feel they have to be difficult to get attention. Your immediate acknowledgment throws them mentally off balance and gives you management control.

• *Avoid Challenging Vocabulary* - When interacting with these people, and in your initial attempt to neutralize the environment, avoid words that mentally poke a finger at them and solicit defensiveness. Words like: You; However; But; And; Think; Opinion. These are all words that the listener feels compelled to defend his position against as he feels you have just attacked him.

• *Utilize Ownership Words* - These are words that send the message of "we are in this together" and "no one is trying to control any one here." Words like: I; We; Us; Feel.

• *Venting* - Let the other player vent 100 percent of what is on his mind. As he vents, you take notes so that he can see that you are writing as he talks (or yells). Taking notes helps you to pay attention, track what he is presenting from a logical perspective, and it helps the listener to keep his mouth closed (which typically opens and pulls the listener directly into the negativity).

• *Apologize* - If the threat is an organizational problem, don't join in to point fingers or defend a known problem. Admit the negative point, offer a broad apology for the event and then immediately direct the conversation (not confrontation) back to the person in question and ask him for this input on solutions!

• *Go It Alone* - Increase the number of activities that you do by yourself which would traditionally involve interacting with a challenging and difficult person. This degree of exclusion will bring about change in the other person's behavior. You are being realistic with this approach. Think about how many times you end up doing the task yourself anyway - only with increased personal stress and tension.

STEP TWO: *INTERACTION* is the objective of dealing with challenging and difficult people. You don't want a personality grudge match, merely an issue-oriented interaction. By first *NEUTRALIZING* the other party, you increase the prospect of the following techniques being successful! Consider:

• *Avoidance* - This is the most powerful technique for dealing with these people. You are cutting down your exposure to them and the ramifications of that exposure. It is easier to walk away from a negative interaction than to remain engaged in that interaction - easier said than done for most people.

• *Isolation* - Separate the challenging and negative players from the team and keep them focused and busy at what they are good at doing. If there are times when you have a person on your team who is difficult for the team overall, but his skill or knowledge is such that you need him, then refocus your utilization of that player and how you and others are exposed to him. Isolation can mean to isolate him away from the team or it could mean to isolate yourself away from him!

This is a lot like having two children fighting over which toy is theirs. You give a toy to each, separate them and tell them to remain by themselves and play with their own toys! You then observe one of the players (who had been isolated from the other) make a behavior change to get back with the other!

• *Demand An Alternative* - When a player is causing difficulty and contradicting what others (or you) are saying, neutralize the situation via empathy and then demand that they offer an alternative (up to three times). Don't turn this step into a personality interaction. Keep energies focused upon the issues and don't let the player off the hook. Typically, people challenge this situation and the interaction becomes an instant debate.   No one ever thinks to professionally require that the player who started this debate offer alternatives or options.

• *Don't Rush In* - With a response when a player becomes difficult. Allow the use of silence to help you gain or regain logical control over the interaction to increase the success quotient.

• *Visual Notes* - When you are challenged by a player, start taking notes while he is talking, venting, threatening. By taking notes you will assist yourself in remaining quiet, assist yourself in determining what the root problem is under all of their negative energy; and he will see how out of control he is by watching what you are writing down - no one wants documented, via notes, his bad language or out-of-control emotions. These people slow down and calm down and you will not have said one word!

• *Education* - Many times the reason for difficulty is differing levels of education and awareness on an issue. Determine if you need more education - solicit it, or if the other party needs additional information - then provide it!

• *Seek Linkage* - Determine points of commonality between your position and the other person's and merge those elements. It will be easier to interact when both parties see the commonality (linkage) and, thus, the challenge; and defensive posturing will decrease and productive interaction will begin to increase.

• *Use Double Standards* - Between what the player has raised and another issue within your environment so they can see direct association.

• *Ask Questions* - When faced with an uncertain situation or player, don't initiate a conversation from the perspective of solving the presented problem. Instead, stimulate a conversation by using one of the six power words learned in school - W, W, W, W, W, H - WHO, WHAT, WHEN, WHERE, WHY,   and HOW! If one of these words turned question doesn't stimulate a conversation, don't rush in. Merely move on to the next letter, word, question!

• *One-On-One In Private* - If a player remains difficult and challenging to you and the management structure, you must go one-on-one with them and do so in private (put on the COUNSELOR HAT outlined in Chapter Four). Consider what your objective is for this meeting prior to meeting with the player. Consider trying to identify why he is negative, as he may have a realistic position and once you determine what it is, then you will be able to start to work to *NEUTRALIZE*   him for better *INTERACTIONS*.

• *Seek Consensus* - Before moving on to additional points of discussion, make sure that the people involved in the challenging interaction have attained an agreement point on the issue at hand prior to moving on to new points.

• *Pain Factor/Pleasure Factor* - Ultimately, another person will not change his behavior unless there is a reason to: either PAIN, more pain to do it his way than an alternate way; or PLEASURE, meaning more gain doing it another way rather than his way.

• *Subgroup Dynamics* - Interact with your positive players before dealing with the challenging and difficult players. By interacting with your Transformers and getting their buy-in on an issue and their ability to persuade the Transmitters to move in your direction, your interaction with the Terrorists can be

NEUTRALIZED and a greater INTERACTION level can be attained via peer pressure!

• *Note Pad Management* - When you are interacting with more than one difficult or challenging person, you have to manage those interactions and conversations more wisely. Move from auditory conversations to visual communication. If, for example, you have multiple bosses tasking you with issues and projects, take a piece of paper and, when one approaches you with a request, write out next to a number one his request and place his name below your entry. Now when the next boss approaches, get the same piece of paper and next to the number two, write out his request placing his name next to or below that request. Now that the second boss has seen the order of work and who his colleague is who has also tasked you, he may not accept the placement that you have assigned to him; yet notice thus far in the exercise that you haven't said anything. He will inquire as to what you are working on and you will notice that you are engaged in a conversation, whereas traditionally you would be engaged in a confrontation.

• *Involvement* - Most importantly of all when interacting with challenging and difficult people, you have to get them involved in the process and decisions. The more involved the player is the less likely he will be to attack others and cause problems.

STEP THREE: *CHANGE* will develop when you *NEUTRALIZE* the other party and then *INTERACT* with him from an issue-oriented and not from a personality-oriented perspective!

By focusing your energies on conditioning the environment for efficient interactions, you can go about stimulating change without people really getting upset over it. First *NEUTRALIZE* and second *INTERACT* for a proactive response perspective (not reactive mode) and the *CHANGES* will come about. If, however, you approach someone and immediately work to stimulate a change that becomes manipulation and everyone can sense when someone is trying to manipulate him!

Difficult & Challenging Player Index
(3-Step Approach)

NEUTRALIZE	INTERACT	CHANGE
❒ Empathy	❒ Avoidance	❒ By-Product
❒ Avoid Challenge Words	❒ Isolation	Of Effective
❒ Use Ownership Words	❒ Demand Alternatives	Interaction!
❒ Venting	❒ Don't Rush In	
❒ Apologize	❒ Visual Notes	
❒ Go It Alone	❒ Education	
❒ Other:	❒ Seek Linkage	
	❒ Use Double Standards	
	❒ Ask Questions	
	❒ 1-on-1 In Private	
	❒ Seek Consensus	
	❒ Pain/Pleasure Factors	
	❒ Subgroup Dynamics	
	❒ Take Notes/Note Pad Management	
	❒ Involvement	
	❒ Other:	

Counseling The Difficult Player

```
┌─────────────────────────────┐
│ Team Route List             │
│ Return To: _____  │
│            _____  │
│            _____  │
│            _____  │
│            _____  │
└─────────────────────────────┘
```

Interacting with the difficult, challenging and negative player on your team for a positive growth outcome is the ultimate goal of every leader and MANAGER in an organization. When that player becomes so difficult that his behavior, actions, comments and position become counter-productive for you and members of a team, management has to assume the management style of COUNSELOR and go one-on-one with that player.

The management cliche of "out of sight, out of mind" won't work in any successful growth organization of the future. The problem player may be out of the mind and sight of management, but all of the other players on the team know exactly what is and is not happening. One negative player (Terrorist) unchecked can cultivate additional negative players (Terrorists) in your organization.

There are several ways management can approach this interaction, whether the aim is to educate and train a player to peak performance, take corrective actions with this player, discipline the player, or work to eliminate the player from the team.

Worse case scenario first! Ultimately, management has to be willing to live without a negative player if he becomes disruptive enough to hold other players back from attaining results. If a player can be specifically seen as the negative spark plug in an environment, then let him know up front that interactions are designed for a positive outcome or he will be removed from the team - until the ultimate PAIN factor realization is levied, some players will keep pushing management to see what they can get away with!

Based on the analysis techniques presented in Chapter Six, your perspective of a player may or may not change. The analysis of a player is critical prior to going into a counseling session, as it may assist you in whether to have a counseling session. If you are to have a counseling session with a difficult player, consider this subsection as a map of what to consider **BEFORE-DURING-AFTER** the encounter.

BEFORE: *BEFORE the COUNSELING Session*   consider the following guideposts for increased success and decreased liability.

> • *Agenda* - Develop what you believe to be the key issues which need to be addressed. Having them down on paper will afford you the opportunity to secure all documentation necessary for this interaction. It will give you time to get your thoughts and notes together and a chance to investigate your assumptions and positions to gather additional data, facts and documentation necessary to keep this interaction issue-oriented and not a personality issue.

> • *Location* - Consider the most nonthreatening and most conducive place for the interaction where the other person is most inclined to open up and verbalize his positions without feeling threatened.

> • *Time* - Consider the best time for you (not him) to hold the session to further impact your missions. Is it at the beginning of the day or week, toward the end of the day or week, or directly before something important?

> • *Observer* - Consider having a neutral third party (your equal or superior, not the other player's equal) sit in on the session to take notes and observe. He is not there to lend his perspectives, comments or take sides. Pre-establish with this party his role before the session. Remember, in some work environments the observers are posturing points and merely used to

psych the other party out!

• *Alternatives* - Are there other options available to management for interacting with the difficult player to stimulate a change in actions or behavior besides a formal or informal counseling session?

• *Third Party Information/Leads* - Many times problems concerning players on your team are not actually experienced by management. The concerns about a player are brought to management by another player (tattle-tellers). For this reason management must protect its position against "would-be" Terrorists on a team. For those rare occasions when a player on a team may be instigating trouble and even trying to set up a particular management player, it's good to be cautious.

If a player brings a concern to you about another person, ask the player talking to you to write those concerns down citing specific issues. If he won't, be aware that he may be the problem player not the person he is pointing fingers at. If he does write the concerns down, you have a map for future observations. Once the informer writes down the concerns ask that player to sign the paper. Once signed you have an official document. If he won't sign the paper, let this be a second opportunity to analyze where the real problem is.

• *Solutions* - Establish several options or strategies for working through the difficulty in case the player you're going to meet with becomes unresponsive. Then you can maintain control of the session and stimulate conversation between the two of you by posing your alternatives or options.

• *Pain Factors* - Identify the penalties for nonconformance and nonchange. Determine the level of severity to take place in this session. If you have exhausted all pleasure factors to this point and the difficult and challenging player is still refusing your position and authority, it is now time to get serious!

DURING: *DURING the COUNSELING Session* you are primarily there for your own benefit (as you represent the organization) and not the difficult or challenging player's! The interaction needs to be highly professional, structured and focused. Consider the following techniques for maintaining a productive, controlled session:

> • *Agenda* - Start off by presenting the other people in the session with a copy of your agenda so that everyone can visually see what this meeting is about. With an agenda, everyone will know what is to be discussed, and, therefore, what is not to be addressed. If someone goes off the agenda, you can point at it (and not the other person) and make a directed comment focusing energies and the conversation back to the next item on the agenda.

> • *Expectation Statement* - Your opening statement should contain a reference to what your expectations are for this session. By doing this, the other player(s) will understand your level of seriousness, commitment and what this session's goal is!

> • *Time* - Make an immediate reference to the amount of time allocated to this session. By doing so, all players will know how much time has been budgeted for this agenda, and if anyone goes off track, you can reference time as another factor for getting back on schedule.

> • *Neutral Third Parties* - If you have an observer, introduce the person and what his participation will be and move directly on to the agenda!

> • *Follow-up* - Establish what the follow-up plan and schedule will be for the agenda items about to be discussed. If the player in question knows up front that there will be a follow-up plan and that he will be getting back with you face-to-face in a limited number of days to measure the progress made based upon this meeting and what is discussed and agreed upon, the follow-up date will also serve as a motivator for the player(s) in question to stimulate some change.

• *Mini-Agreements* - During the session work through the agenda items one at a time and work to obtain an agreement on each individual issue as to what it is and what will be done jointly to resolve it and obtain an agreement on the battle plan before moving onto the next item. By establishing these mini-agreements you will be able to manage the overall session more wisely. Also, if the session breaks down, you can go back to the last point where the parties had an agreement and begin again from there.

• *Take Notes* - Everything the other party says, suggests, or claims needs be documented and attached to the agenda at the end of the session. Whenever a player in a session talks, as long as he is on the agenda, don't interrupt him, merely take notes. This note taking will help you understand his perspectives and help you document what took place within the session.

• *Solutions* - Several solutions to issues raised should be discussed before making a decision on the course of action. Stimulate a conversation with the other player to solicit solutions. If none are presented, then suggest some of the solutions you designed BEFORE the session and get the other player's feedback.

• *Confidentiality* - Discuss and agree upon what will be expressed to other members of the team after the session, if they inquire.

• *Silence* - Use silence as a tool to reinforce your seriousness on issues and to stimulate responses from the other person. Don't let the other person be unresponsive in this session!

• *Agenda Manager* © -Consider the following agenda format for presenting your concerns to players and have all parties sign the agenda in the appropriate places. After the session, each participant should leave with a copy of the agreed-upon agenda items and solutions. This documentation is another powerful means for stimulating change.

AGENDA MANAGER ©

_____
(Issue to be dealt with)

Date: _____   TIME: _____

ITEMS/ISSUES:

Agreement Initials:

People Present: _____
_____ !

•*Agenda Manager* © (continued) - Using this system is very easy and serves to facilitate a session from a very structured and professional perspective. The steps for using an *"Agenda Manager©"* are:

1. Identify across the top of the page the core issue or subject matter to be addressed at this COUNSEL-ING SESSION!
2. List the actual date and time of the session.
3. Write or type out the individual item(s) or issue(s) to be addressed under the ITEM/ISSUE section. Note each additional item with numbers, so all parties can focus on one numbered variable at a time.
4. Identify all the names of the people in the session at the bottom of the form. This will serve both as historical documentation and as a reminder of all of the players in the session if your mind blanks out.
5. In the shaded vertical grid section on the far right side of the form noted as "Agreement Initials," place your initials. The player in question should place his initials in this section and adjacent to each line item discussed when it has been finalized and a course of corrective action has been mapped out. If the player refuses to sign it, then be aware that he more than likely has not resolved that issue and further conversation is required. If he still refuses to sign each item, then make a vivid note to that fact in the shaded section. Then move on to the next line item to be addressed.

This system is designed to allow all parties involved to maintain professional controls and for all parties to address issues one step at a time for positive outcomes. Should the player in question (or in some environments, the player's representatives) refuse to participate in the "AGENDA MANAGER©", then there is a serious issue of lack of trust among the entire group that should serve as a topic of conversation in another session!

AFTER: *AFTER The COUNSELING Session* you must invest a few minutes away from the team, your colleagues and the players just in the session with you and away from interruptions to finish the third and most critical step in the successful facilitation of a COUNSELING session. To ensure greater levels of transformation with the difficult player you just left and to ensure no liabilities later, consider:

> • *Agenda* - Review your agenda to ensure that all items listed were addressed and that nothing was overlooked or short-changed. Look at the "Agenda Manager©" and make sure all points were addressed and initialed.

> • *Notes* - make sure that the play-by-play notes you took DURING the session make sense to you in retrospect. If you need to add additional perspective or edited notes so they will make sense to you six months or a year later, then do so!

> • *Observer's Notes* - Take the observer's notes and review them. In a second color ink (noted as your additions), add any perspective to these notes, if necessary, for future understanding!

> • *Follow-Up* - Make sure that the agreed upon follow-up sequence will be maintained. If necessary, put notes in your professional daily calendar of those future dates and what you are to be doing. If you want the session's observer to participate in the follow-up activities, then coordinate that now and not later.

> • *Player Formal/Informal Follow-Up* - Immediately after the session, make a photo copy of the "Agenda Manager©" page. Write a follow-up P.S. to reinforce the session's issues and remind the player(s) that this is what we discussed and agreed to and this is when we get together to measure our progress. Handwriting the note still conveys the message, yet it is less threatening than a typed follow-up note!

Consider the following chart prior to your next COUNSELING session!

Counseling Session Check Sheet

BEFORE	DURING	AFTER
❐ Agenda	❐ Agenda	❐ Agenda
❐ Location	❐ Start With Opening	❐ Notes
❐ Time	Statement Expec-	❐ Observer's
❐ Validation Of	tation Statement	Notes
Concerns &	❐ Time	❐ Follow-Up
Key Issues	❐ Neutral 3rd Party	❐ Player
❐ Alternatives	❐ Follow-Up Plan	Follow-up
❐ 3rd Party	❐ Mini-Agreements	❐ Other:
Observer	❐ Many Agreements	
❐ Predesign	❐ Many Agreements	
Solutions	❐ Take Notes	
❐ Pain Factor:	❐ Collaborative	
Leverage Point	Solution Develop-	
To Change	ment	
Behavior	❐ Confidentiality	
❐ Other:	❐ Utilize Silence	
	❐ Agenda Manager ©	
	❐ Other:	

Editor's Note: Treat problem/challenging players like the Terrorist (Chapter Two). They are a cancer to an organization. Treat the cancer with the tools presented herein. If the treatment doesn't take and they refuse to join the team, document your actions for corrective behavior, document your multiple attempts and their repeated cancerous actions and then remove them from the team - FIRE THEM!

They may yell a lot, but <u>with the proper documentation and management fortitude to do one's job</u>, the Terrorist now removed allows the team to develop and flourish once again. Their chances in court will most likely be zero; documentation always holds up. Most Terrorists have learned how to play systems and no one has ever really called their bluff - HOLD THEM ACCOUNTABLE!

Dealing With Procrastination And Burn-Out

```
┌─────────────────────────────┐
│ Team Route List             │
│ Return To: _____  │
│            _____  │
│            _____  │
│            _____  │
│            _____  │
│            _____  │
└─────────────────────────────┘
```

Infusing energy and experiencing the rebirth of a player on a team who has digressed from participation and contribution to the organization to liability and procrastination is possible. Most players (including yourself) fall victim to procrastination for simple reasons. Left unchecked, this state of procrastination can digress further to a state of burn-out!

When procrastination occurs within an organization, it causes low levels of productivity, which can lead to player tensions and difficulty. When burn-out occurs within an organization, it causes work shortages, accidents, errors, apathy and player turnover.

So what causes procrastination? Consider procrastination in a player on your team and determine whether or not any of the following factors apply. Procrastination occurs due to:

- Dislike for task being delegated routinely to a player.
- Dislike for the players around them.
- Dislike for the specific task assigned to them.
- Degree of confusion as to what the first step might be.
- Degree of confusion over how to begin.
- Unsure whether enough data are available from which to make an accurate decision.
- Afraid of making the wrong decision on their own and a fear of interaction with management necessary prior to final action.
- FEAR, representing degrees of *False Education* (or evidence) *Appearing Real* and psyching oneself out of action.

There are ways management can work to deter, and even avoid, situations which lead to the state of procrastination. By avoiding procrastination, management can avoid significant numbers of burn-out situations with players. Consider:

MANAGEMENT TECHNIQUES/TACTICS FOR PROCRASTINATION

• *FEAR* - Most procrastinators will hesitate to act because something is making them feel uncomfortable. Management needs to interact to identify what that factor is, deal with it and then move on. Most players' *fear factor* is based upon *False Education* (or evidence) allowed to *Appear Realistic*. And this factor is what is psyching them from moving forward.

• *Deadline* - Establish a very specific deadline associated with the task which the player has been assigned. Many times a specific deadline will serve as the motivator or stimulant to get a person who may otherwise procrastinate to either come forward with questions or to become productive. Unfortunately, management will at times be dealing with a procrastinator and request something by the end of today. Is that deadline specific or general? Does end of today mean, 3 PM, 4 PM or 5 PM? And then when management returns at the end of the day and it is not done, tension and conflict are the outcome!

• *Schedule Enough Time The First Time* - Many times, management will task a procrastinator with something and request it back in a certain amount of time. Next time, in light of the player you're interacting with and the issue you are interacting on, schedule enough time the first time. If a procrastinator will take one hour for something, and in your estimation it should take 45 minutes, then schedule one hour. If the player gets it done in one hour or less, he will be in a positive mood which means greater quality results. However, if you schedule 45 minutes and he takes one hour, then the player will be in a bad mood for he is behind schedule and it is because of another --- project!

• *Schedule It To Later In That Day* - Take the issue which has you stuck or which has another player stuck and set it to the side for a few minutes or hours. Place a note strategically where you will keep seeing it as a reminder to go back to this certain project later on. A procrastinator would push it to the side also and say, "I will get back to this later." Only problem is he doesn't define when later is. Here you are defining the later! If, for example, it is 10 AM and you find yourself stuck (wasting time, day dreaming, getting upset, talking to yourself, etc...), take that project and set it to the side somewhere and write a note reminding yourself to go back to this project at 2 PM, then attach that note on your telephone. Consciously move on to another project with a different mental perspective. Every time your eyes scan past the telephone and you consciously see the note you are telling your subconscious mind to work on that issue. When 2 PM comes around, what had you stuck earlier in the day is easily dealt with in the PM!

• *Ask Questions* - When you find yourself or someone else in a procrastination state, you must identify how the situation came about and what has caused productivity to come to a stop. Once those answers can be identified, then management can work to avoid similar situations.

• *See-Say-Do* - Instead of showing (see) a player what needs to be done or telling (say) a player what needs to be taken care of, have him do it! Next time when you find a player procrastinating have that player show you and himself that he can do what he was stuck on. The next time he is tasked with something, his last mental point of reference will be that he had done it before and therefore he can do again!

If management does not interact with a player on a team that seems to be a procrastinator, even if he is just a casual procrastinator, that player, over time gone unchecked, can revert to a person who feels burned out. When a player hits this stage, there are a limited number of options available to management.

MANAGEMENT TECHNIQUES/TACTICS FOR BURN-OUT

• *Do Something Different* - Have the player do something completely different from his norms. Don't have the player continue to do more of what he is presently doing, as there is a good chance he doesn't like any of it. This could mean something different professionally (assignments, tasks, duties, trips, interactions, volunteerism, etc...) or personally (community activities, social involvements, sports, etc...).

• *Delegate Something Different* - Consider what the burned-out player typically receives from management with respect to tasks. To stimulate life and energy in this player, delegate something completely different to push him out of his norms.

• *Volunteer For Something Different* - Assist this player in getting involved with something different, either through volunteering or not allowing him to volunteer for the things which he typically does. The point here is to get the player into a new habit and spend his time in different activities.

• *Movement* - Have the player make a lateral or vertical move to stimulate a new psychology. Get the player professionally out of his routines and into something new, challenging and different.

• *Mentor* - Have the player serve as a mentor to new players and have him gain energy from new life. This will at the same time giving the older or burned-out player a new mission and feeling of worth.

Dealing with procrastinators or burned-out people takes energy from management and from other players. You have to consider a few universals with both players to maintain your level of organizational success and to guard against falling into one of the same traps. Consider a few ways to ensure productivity and work to stimulate subtle changes in these two players at the same time.

MANAGEMENT TECHNIQUES/TACTICS FOR PROCRASTINATORS & BURN-OUTS

• *Avoidance* - Work to avoid direct interaction with these players if you know of alternative ways and means to accomplish your objectives. This reduces both (yours and their) stress or tension levels. Also, by avoiding these two difficult situations, you are reducing the volume of negative strain on their psyche. Everyone wins and now the other players can focus their energies on being productive.

• *Education* - Increased education and training on your behalf or the other players in question will reduce the volume of unknowns which leads to nonproductivity.

• *Pairing Up* - Strategically place the team expert on an issue with a player who is typically slow or nonproductive to see if the mini-teaming stimulates positive interaction and productivity. Observe to see if the procrastinator or burn-out learns from your team expert and whether or not that player increases his levels of efficiency.

• *Re-Assignment Of Tasks* - If procrastination continues, then reassign the typical work flow so that the procrastinating player you want to keep on the team is no longer in the receiving line for those negatives.

Dealing With Time Wasters

```
Team Route List
Return To: _____
         _____
         _____
         _____
         _____
```

Gaining control of time in the work place seems to be a never-ending pursuit. Imagine being able to save time and place it in a time savings account; so when you need additional time you can make a withdrawal. Unfortunately, it doesn't work that way!

Saving time now, for utilization in the future, is the reason management needs to work to eliminate as many time-wasting activities as possible. The *"Law of the Competitive Edge"* © states that if you could save just one hour a day, or regain one hour a day of misspent time, over the course of the year that one hour daily would add up to more than 45 eight-hour days of time!

Gaining that one hour a day is the objective of this short management course on organizational time management, project time management, personal time management and people time management!

In order to manage that time you must first recognize that there are three different types of time environments which encompass your daily professional schedule. Only when you are in one of those three environments do you have 100 percent control. When you are within the other two environments, you don't have control capabilities. At best, you can manage these two environments. On the following chart the three different professional time types are detailed. Identify percentage-wise how much time you spend daily in each!

TIME ENVIRONMENT ANALYZER CHART

Boss-Imposed Time = _____

System-Imposed Time = _____

Self-Imposed Time = _____

There are three time types each professional day. Consider what these three environments are all about: *Boss-Imposed Time* is those situations where your boss has placed demands on you and there is no recourse and you cannot change the situation. *System-Imposed Time* is the time constraints and demands placed upon you by the procedures, regulations, policies, laws, customers, vendors, culture within your professional environment (system) which you have no control over and more-or-less have inherited. Whereas, the *Self-Imposed Time* environment is where you have direct control and power of choice and actions over what you are doing. This is where you typically find peak performance (and for many is thus defined as before work, during lunch, after work and on the weekends).

Based upon how you feel your time is spent or invested each day, you can maximize the time falling within the three environments and especially the *Self-Imposed Time*!

One very powerful way to determine objectively what the time wasters in your environment are, would be to utilize a *daily time log* (sort of a time and motion study of yourself) for an entire day. At the end of the day or the following day, invest some time in analyzing where you spent your time and, thus, where wasted time may be lurking. In order to successfully decide which time management techniques to utilize from this section (and from throughout this text), you must first have a clear perspective of where you spent time and the *daily time log* will show you exactly that!

If you utilize this time log, remember it is for your edification only. No one else needs to see what you're doing throughout the course of the day as you log on the chart, nor does anyone need to see the finished daily log. Consider the following *daily time log* for your immediate use:

DAILY TIME EFFICIENCY LOG

Name: _____   Date: _____

Time:	8-8:30	8:30-9	9-9:30	9:30-10	10-10:30	10:30-11	11-11:30	11:30-12	1-1:30	1:30-2	2-2:30	2:30-3	3-3:30	3:30-4	4-4:30	4:30-5	5-5:30
Category:																	
meetings																	
socializing																	
telephone																	
voicemail																	
delegation																	
crises																	
conflict																	
discussion																	
debate																	
filing																	
paperwork																	
project mgt.																	
comm.																	
directing																	
call backs																	
drive time																	
waiting																	
day dreaming																	
procrastination																	
worrying																	
other:																	

Jeff Magee International ® '94

DAILY TIME EFFICIENCY LOG

Name: _____   Date: _____

Time: Category:	8-8:30	8:30-9	9-9:30	9:30-10	10-10:30	10:30-11	11-11:30	11:30-12	12-1	1-1:30	1:30-2	2-2:30	2:30-3	3-3:30	3:30-4	4-4:30	4:30-5	5-5:30
meetings																		
socializing																		
telephone																		
voicemail																		
delegation																		
crises																		
conflict																		
discussion																		
debate																		
filing																		
paperwork																		
project mgt.																		
comm.																		
directing																		
call backs																		
drive time																		
waiting																		
day dreaming																		
procrastination																		
worrying																		
other:																		

Jeff Magee International ® '94

DAILY TIME EFFICIENCY LOG

Name: _____ Date: _____

Time: / Category:	8-8:30	8:30-9	9-9:30	9:30-10	10-10:30	10:30-11	11-11:30	11:30-12	1-1:30	1:30-2	2-2:30	2:30-3	3-3:30	3:30-4	4-4:30	4:30-5	5-5:30
meetings																	
socializing																	
telephone																	
voicemail																	
delegation																	
crises																	
conflict																	
discussion																	
debate																	
filing																	
paperwork																	
project mgt.																	
comm.																	
directing																	
call backs																	
drive time																	
waiting																	
day dreaming																	
procrastination																	
worrying																	
other:																	

Through the utilization of a time tracking chart like the previous page, you will be able to determine where your time was spent negatively and where specific time wasters may be within your environment. Once you can identify the time wasters in your three time environments, then you will be able to strategize ways to regain productive usage of that time!

The purpose of the *"Daily Time Efficiency Log"* is to aid you in determining what you have and have not been doing, every 30 minutes. By logging on your personal chart every 30 minutes (or so), at the end of the day you can reflect on what the day contained for you. By identifying any patterns in your behavior (or others') which lead to either a productive day or major down times, then you can plan accordingly.

Ultimately, from physically using a chart like this one, you will be able to objectively answer the two major questions which management reflects upon for hiring, keeping or dismissing a player from a team. The two questions which every position must answer are:

    1. How can this position and player make the
    organization money?
    2. How can this position or player help the
    organization save money?

From the utilization of a *"Daily Time Efficiency Log"* you will then be able to determine two answers:

    1. How did I spend my time?
    2. Who else spent my time and how did they do it?

The answers to these four questions are the powerful answers which Peter Drucker outlines to be management's requirement to be able to maximize people as valuable resources in an organization. These responses and answers will also prove valuable in managing time and dealing effectively with time wasters. The remaining pages of this subsection will assist you in maximizing your time within some of the major time-wasting environments. Consider:

Telephone: Telephones seem to never ring when you have free time or when you are between projects. The telephone always rings when you have no free time, you're late on a project, you're dealing with a crisis or when you are alone in the office and trying to handle several things at one time. Some general rules to live by to turn the telephone into your power time-saver tool are:

MANAGEMENT TECHNIQUES/TACTICS -

• *Voice Mail* - Activate voice mail or your answering machine once each AM and once each PM for 30 minutes of uninterrupted telephone time and focus your energies on critical work tasks. Leave a personal message for the caller so he knows what is happening (*"Thank you for calling, this is Jeff and I am working on a critical project for the next 30 minutes. At the tone please leave your name, a short message and the best time to return the call. I will be checking these messages at _____. If it is an emergency, dial _____ and ask for _____. Thank you*).

• *Hold Button* - Don't utilize this function until you have asked and received an answer from one of two powerful questions. (1) "Can I put you on hold/can you hold please?" or, (2) "Can I take your number and name and call you right back, as it will take me a few minutes to obtain this information?"

Otherwise, the caller is restricted at his end as to what he can and cannot do. If that caller is upset or hostile, the entire time he is on hold he is being reminded of his level of negativity and when you return he is even more upset.

• *Chunking* - Gang up all the phone message slips of people you need to return calls to and return phone messages at one time. For example, if you know that during the last few minutes in the AM before lunch certain people will be less likely to socialize, then call those people right before lunch time (or use the same philosophy and call them at the end of the day).

• *Outbound* - Determine which contacts have voice mail or answering service/machines that you have to contact. If they have an alternative phone message system, ask yourself whether or not you need to relay information or you need to talk with this person live. If message relay is the objective, never talk with him live. This will reduce substantially the volume of time you spend on the telephone, while at the same time increasing productivity.

Paper Stacks: The volume of paper in the professional organization today is unbelievable. No matter how electronic your environment is or becomes there is and will always be paper work, paper flow, paper stacks and paper collecting in file cabinets and drawers. To manage paper more efficiently consider the following ideas:

• *RAFT* - Invest the first few minutes upon arriving at your work environment and immediately *RAFT* your stacks each morning. When you return from breaks, lunch, from meetings or look in your in box, etc... in essence all about you is paper looking for a stack to call home.

Any paper pile or stack can be rafted in a matter of seconds with this technique. You pick up the main stack and ask yourself one of four key questions as you touch each item. The answer to these questions as you are touching each item will direct you to which subpile the item belongs. Once you have converted your primary paper stack or pile into four substacks, then you can manage the paper and work to eliminate paper stacks from collecting about you.

The *four power questions for managing and eliminating paper stacks* from your life are:

1) **R = Refer**, can I refer this item to someone else?
2) **A = Action**, does this need my action?
3) **F = File**, does this need to be filed?
4) **T = Toss**, can this be recycled or tossed away?

From the primary stack you have now broken the pile down into four substacks. From these four substacks, set to the side those two stacks which can be dealt with at any time (the "R" and "F") and focus upon the immediate items for action ("A"). With the two substacks to the side, you can deal with them at your discretion and you can also utilize them as props should someone corner you during the day and begin to waste your time. Grab an "F" or "R" and proceed non-confrontationally with that pile or stack. As for the other person, invite them to assist with your endeavor! Consider the flow to work like the following diagram:

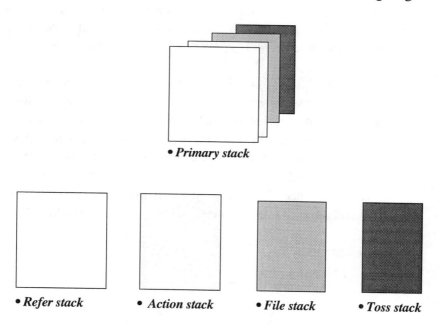

• *Primary stack*

• *Refer stack*   • *Action stack*   • *File stack*   • *Toss stack*

Correspondence: How many times have you read a letter, fax, memo, or contract and had no idea of its contents on second reading? Now you invest time again to glance over or read it again!

Even if you utilize a system like the *RAFT* formula, the material you sort through and place in the appropriate stacks is only half the issue. Establishing your own note-taking system on the paper and documents for easier future access is necessary. Several powerful techniques you can utilize to increase your comprehension of written materials and help yourself with the filed paper work activity is through the use of:

> • *Growth Wheel* s © - A type of mind mapping note-taking that assists you in becoming a whole brain communicator. As you read a letter for example, underline or circle all power points within the text. Upon finishing the text go to the upper right-hand corner of the paper and draw a circle. In that circle, in your own words, write down what the major point of text was about (like-RE:). Off that circle you can place lines and transfer the names, figures, dates, etc... from the text of the letter to these new lines at the top right corner. In essence you are creating your own condensed note section on every letter or document you read.

Placing these notes in this area of the paper and in this new manner will assist you in finding information contained within letters. As you reference a paper stack or file folder within a cabinet, all you need do is look at the upper right-hand corner of each page until you reach the desired page. Then you can open the entire folder and pull that individual paper out for further reference. You can eliminate the time spent looking over and through every piece of paper to find one specific item.

For example:

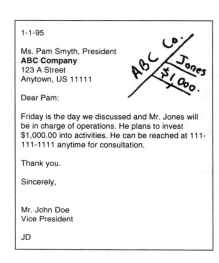

• *Immediate Action Correspondence Turn-Around (I-ACT)* -
Immediately upon receiving a letter, memo, fax, document or
any visual piece of communication from another person that
requires your reply, consider the level of formality which must
be maintained. If the level is low or the relationship you have
with the sender of the communication allows, then save consid-
erable time and resources by merely writing the answer
directly on the document sent to you. Return the document or
a copy of it immediately.

Consider whether you can merely hand-write
the information or response to the sender's letter directly on
the letter sent to you. Write your reply on the bottom portion
of the letter where space is available or on the reverse side
of the letter immediately after reading it. This saves valuable
formal writing time by merely replying on the sender's
paper. If you need a copy for your files, make a copy of the
original letter with your reply written on it.

• *Reading File* - Place low priority letters and correspondence
in a reading file and review this file at regular time periods. If
you travel, this reading file can be saved and read during
trips to maximize that down time.

General Time Management: Consider alternative management techniques for dealing effectively with other time zappers as well. No matter
how effective you are, there is no getting away from paper stacks, paper
work, people who like to socialize, getting yourself and others organized
to get the top priorities accomplished and endless file folders carrying
projects. Consider the following techniques for increased effectiveness:

• *Delegation Dynamics Matrix* © - Consider the five-step delegation formula presented in the "Delegation Dynamics" section.

• *Action Memo* © - This is a powerful technique for getting the
monkeys strategically placed on your shoulders by others
off. Review the "Delegation Dynamics" section for a step-by-
step approach to this technique and management tool.

• *Quadrant Manager* © - This powerful prioritizing system can be utilized in concert with any other day-planner system or as a stand-alone tool. Break daily work into one of the four appropriate work categories and focus energies accordingly. Refer to Chapter Seven for a detailed approach to this technique!

• *Tickler Systems* - Save your memory for important items. Utilize your calendar or a file system and write down the people to call and things to do on the appropriate dates. Once logged in, concentrate on other issues and don't worry about remembering lower priority items.

• *File Folders and File Folder Management* - These are the most obvious tool for managing projects. Each project needs and deserves its own folder. Don't try to manage work by zig-zag stacks on your desk. Place each project in a separate file and then use the next three steps for file folder management:

1) "Next Step Is" - Whenever you leave a project for another task, always grab a piece of paper or sticky note and leave a brief note to yourself as to *what your next step is*. This saves you valuable time later when you return to a project and attempt to determine what you're supposed to be doing. This also allows you to refocus your mental energies to where you were when you left - instant creativity!

2) File Folder/Project Management Quadrant Manager - Utilize the upper half of the inside cover of every file folder to design a Quadrant Manager © as it relates to that specific project or task. By designing the specific "Do/See/Call/Write" tasks you can monitor each project individually to determine whether you are on track. This system also affords you the ability to delegate a project and allows the other player to have a starting point or map of that project - right there on the inside of that file folder are your notes as to the minimum course of action required to facilitate that project.

3) File Folder/Project Growth Wheel © - Utilize the bottom half of every file folder to design a specific Growth Wheel ® with your notes that will assist in accomplishing this task or project. As each item on this map of notes is accomplished, put a check mark next to it designating that it is no longer relevant. This also serves as a fast track glance as to what is next.

These last three ideas may look like the following diagrams:

Ex. Step 1)

Ex.
Steps 2 & 3)

Use these specific time management savers along with the ideas presented throughout Chapter Nine in each subsection as additional ways for dealing with time wasters!

Chapter 10

Improving
Interactive
Communication

**"Communication and access to knowledge
(information) will be the key to power and influence
for the future ... Communications impact - It is not as
much what you say, as it is how you say *it* that directly
impacts the response others have to your message!"**
• Nido Qubein

Improving
Interactive Communication

Communication is the vehicle for motivation and management. Through communication, action and reaction take place. Through communication, people can express and share ideas, feelings and thoughts. Through communication the interactions can be understood, whereas through assumption, communication problems can develop. Communication, the ability to communicate clearly and nonconfrontationally, is the hallmark of an effective management player.

Nearly 30 years ago Peter Drucker profiled (and it still holds true today) that problems within an organization can typically be traced back to two sources. One source is problems with *systems*, and the second is problems with *people*. Of these two sources, *systems* account for nearly 85 percent of all organizational problems and *people* account for roughly 15 percent of the problems. Of the two sources it is typically the *people* source which leads to the dominant trauma and tension with players - not *system* problems!

It is estimated that nearly two-thirds of all inner-office problems are communication related - poor communication, over-communication, under-communication, negative communication, miscommunication, etc... It is no wonder that communication is a major factor in management success!

For communication to become more interactive and successful, the sender of the communication has to make major changes in behavior accountability. One can no longer merely send a signal and view his responsibility as completed and that it is the responsibility of the receiver (the listener) to receive, understand and act upon that signal. If the receiver doesn't act accordingly, then it is the receiver's (the listener's) fault and problem!

Interactive communication implies that the parties involved in the communication exchange are interacting with positive signal exchange and that all parties involved are each equally assuming 100 percent accountability for the signal exchange. Each party has to be maintaining control over the entire communication interaction and neither party (especially management) allows assumptions to play out, either internally in one's own head or out loud with another player!

Interactive communication depends upon the sender of the signal and the receiver of the signal (whether you serve in either position) taking communication as a step-by-step process. There are three phases to interactive communication which the sender has to ensure have been accomplished - each step completely accomplished prior to moving on to the next communication phase. For example:

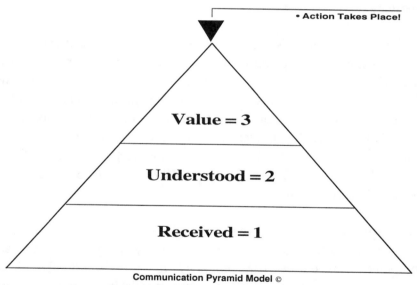

Communication Pyramid Model ©

Interactive communication rests upon the above foundational model that there are three phases which communication must pass through in order for the signal to be acted upon. As you nonconfrontationally move from one level upward to the next, you have to become interactive in order to facilitate the communication process for the success of all parties involved!

The first responsibility of the communication sender is to ensure that the other party actually gets the message - *RECEIVED*. Once this first phase is attained, then the communication signal must be comprehended by the receiver - **UNDERSTOOD**. Only when the signal is *RECEIVED* and *UNDERSTOOD* will there be an opportunity for the receiver to mentally digest the signal and for there to be any sort of action. Therefore, for the receiver to be motivated by the signal and for there to be any action, there must be **VALUE.**

As the signal is *RECEIVED* by the receiver (listen), that signal can be intentional or unintentional, linear or interactive. The receiver's perception of the signal is all that matters, not intentions. Communication signals that are intentional are logic driven and have been calculated. Communication signals that are unintentional are emotion and feeling based and driven and are transmitted outbound without the sender realizing it. Traditional management communication in most cases is very linear (one-way).

Linear communication is one-way based. The sender sends the message and does not feel obligated to follow-up to ensure the message was *RECEIVED, UNDERSTOOD* or *VALUED*. When this takes place, the communication exchange is one-way and thus linear. Linear communication typically leads to miscommunication and further organizational stress. On the other hand, interactive communication suggests that the sender and receiver assume 100 percent communication accountability to ensure that a message sent is *RECEIVED, UNDERSTOOD* and *VALUED* - zero assumptions!

To reach the level of interactive intentional communication, the mechanics of communication need to be analyzed. Every time you communicate outbound to someone else (the technical term for this is ENCODING) or receive the signal inbound from someone else (listening technical word is DECODING), there are three basic psychological steps to effective interactive communication.

Improve your communication ability with others and reduce negative communication with others by mentally reflecting upon what these three phases (or steps) have to do with the communication exchange with others. Consider the following diagram:

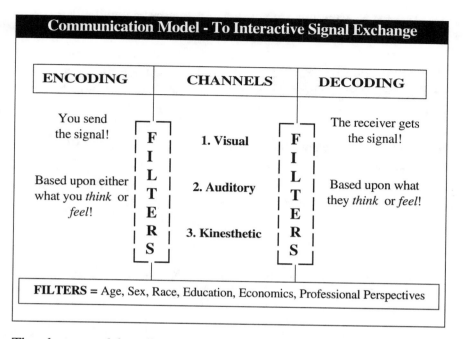

Communication Model - To Interactive Signal Exchange

ENCODING	CHANNELS	DECODING

You send the signal!

F I L T E R S

1. Visual

F I L T E R S

The receiver gets the signal!

Based upon either what you *think* or *feel*!

2. Auditory

Based upon what they *think* or *feel*!

3. Kinesthetic

FILTERS = Age, Sex, Race, Education, Economics, Professional Perspectives

The above model outlines the process through which communication outbound and inbound works. **Step One: Encoding**. As ideas and signals surface with the sender, they are then shaped by what the sender thinks (logic) or feels (emotions), given one's six core Filters, which condition and shape individuals to think and feel the way they do. Based on the initial thought, you then move toward **Step Two: Decoding**. Pause and mentally reflect on what you know about the other person and what you know about their Filters before you send the signal. This may serve as an insurance policy to protect you from a communication error!

After reflecting on what shapes the formation of the signal, the sending of the signal and how the signal is received and digested, you are then ready to send the signal to the other person(s) via **Step Three: Channels**. There are three channels which you can utilize to send the signal from your brain to the receiver's brain - *Visual, Auditory* and *Kinesthetic* (VAK). Peak performers utilize all three channels whenever possible when transmitting signals. Start by sending the signal via the channel you are best at. Then follow-up with the other two complementary channels. The more effectively you send the signal via channels, the greater the interactive communication impact will be.

The process of sending signals via the three channels and ways to interactively communicate in any one channel will be explored in greater detail later in the chapter. In order to successfully communicate to another person within an organization (or outside the organization), consider very strategic ways to ensure success in each of the three phases or levels of communication (via the *Communication Pyramid Model*).

Making sure that the communication signal has been RECEIVED is the first and most critical step or phase in interactive communication exchanges. Think of the volume of experiences in your organization where it has been assumed that someone else received a message, note, letter, document and, only when it is too late, did the players involved realize that the assumption of receipt led to the crisis then being experienced!

Consider some of the following ideas as means to ensuring the signal is being ***RECEIVED***:

> • *Checking Questions* - Immediately after communicating to another person or forwarding a message to them via some vehicle, you need to develop the habit of asking to make sure they received the signal. This only takes a few seconds and may result in the saving of valuable minutes being misused!

> • *RSVP* - This is some sort of return mechanism or request that the receiver acknowledge receipt of the message/signal.

> • *BRC* - Use some sort of business response card, return response letter with an enclosed stamped, self-addressed envelope. Some visual means of receiving something back from the receiver of your signal that would indicate they received your signal is invaluable.

> • *1/2 Day Rule* - This directs you to follow-up any signal you have sent outbound to another person and make auditory contact with him to ensure he received the signal. If the answer is yes, then you have accomplished the first phase. While you are talking with him, you could inquire about any questions concerning the signal and nail down the second phase of the

communication exchange. You can make this follow-up technique the 1/2-hour rule or ten-minute rule. It doesn't matter what the time delay is. What is critical with this technique is that you assume the responsibility to follow-up quickly to ensure receipt of the signal!

• *Phone Call* - Make a quick phone call to the receiver of your signal. This time, if you are short on time and have sent a visual signal, you merely access his voice mail or answering machine and leave a message to follow-up. If the receiver has neither, then leave a follow-up auditory message with one of his colleagues and direct him to find the signal you sent earlier.

• *Repeat* - Have the receiver occasionally repeat what you have said. This will afford you the opportunity to hear his perspective on what you are saying and whether he has received and understood you correctly.

Once the signal has been *RECEIVED,* then, and only then, should you concern yourself with assuring that the signal has been *UNDERSTOOD* by the player(s) involved in this communication interaction. Before you even send the communication signal there are elements which should be considered. Plan and organize your thoughts so that when you present them they are systematic and each idea flows into the next. This always makes it easier for the receiver of your signals to *UNDERSTAND* you.

To ensure the signal is being ***UNDERSTOOD***, consider some of these techniques and ideas:

• *Clarify* - Occasionally in the communication exchange, you need to stop and clarify any points that are obvious to you, but which may not be so obvious to the other person.

• *Feedback* - Gain some sort of verbal or nonverbal response from the intended receiver of a signal and ensure that what you have intended the communication signal to be equals what their perception is!

• *Ask Questions* - More specific questions are used in this second phase to ensure that the elements of your signal are being *UNDERSTOOD* by the receiver. The more information and individual details attached to your signal, the more important it is to ask strategic questions to accomplish your objectives. There are four specific types of questions which you may consider:

1) probing questions to solicit additional information to further assist you in your delivery and in mentally deciding what needs to be expanded upon for the receiver.

2) evaluation questions to make sure that what you have sent is what has been interpreted as well as evaluation questions to measure the responses to make sure that you *UNDERSTAND* them!

3) advice questions allow you to ask questions while giving additional direction.

4) interpret questions allow you to digest responses to your signal to ensure that your understanding is equal to the receiver's.

• *Obtain Signatures* - While you are interacting with the other person(s), devise a way to have him sign off on what the two of you have discussed. If he didn't *UNDERSTAND* you he will hesitate signing something. You gain the feedback necessary to accomplish level two.

• *Nonverbal Signals* - Look at the nonverbal signals the receiver is sending as you interact with him through his face, body language, head nodding and breathing patterns to help in determining whether he is following you, *UNDERSTANDING* you or is lost or irritated. All of these factors impact the effectiveness of level two.

• *Create Mental Imagery* - As you communicate, utilize words which paint a mental picture of what you are communicating. The more vivid your words, the greater the mental impact on the receiver and thus the greater the interaction will become.

This helps you gain *UNDERSTANDING.*

• *Utilize Visual Aids* - As you communicate, consider the opportunities to increase interactive communication effectiveness by incorporating visual aids into your signal exchange. These aids could be charts, folders, diagrams, brochures, maps, business cards with additional notes written on them, pictures, etc...

There are only two rules to visual aids. First, use a visual aid only if it is appropriate. That means the visual is timely, in good shape, will assist and reinforce the signal, and presents a quality message. Second, don't use a visual if it doesn't aid the signal. Don't use a visual aid if it is in bad shape, poor taste, outdated, or detracts from your message.

The Wharton School of Business (PA) studied the issue of communication exchange and communication information retention on signal receivers (listeners) and determined that a message heard once is 68 percent forgotten in 48 hours. Within 30 days less than 10 percent is retained. However, if that same signal is communicated with the complementing use of visuals, you can increase retention (*UNDERSTANDING*) of the signal by as much as 73 percent!

• *Reinforce The Signal* - There are a lot of ways to reinforce what you have sent. The use of visual aids is one. You may also want to send a follow-up fax or electronic message. The use of examples, statistics, analogies and stories can lend further impact and actually help the receiver to *UNDERSTAND* what is being sent.

With the communication signal *RECEIVED* and *UNDERSTOOD* by the other person(s), the interactive communication exchange now proceeds to the most important phase of all - *VALUED*. Only when the receiver senses some degree of *VALUE* in a signal will there be any degree of action on your signals. There are many ways to ensure *VALUE* is received from your signals. Consider:

• *WIIFM & WIIFU* - When sending signals to other people keep focused on the fact that the underlying psychological motivator in human behavior is that all people are tuned to a constant psychological radio frequency (**WIIFM**), which tells him, "*What's In It For Me!*" In group situations, leaders of groups are tuned into a larger frequency (**WIIFU**), which tells them to focus on, "*What's In It For Us!*"

Keep in mind that people read signals with WIIFM in mind. Some people are focused on this position loudly and others have it on as quiet music in the background and occasionally refer to it.

• *Timing* - Consider your timing when sending that signal. The wrong time of day or week may impact its reception. Whether or not there are distracting activities taking place in that recipient's personal or professional environment may also impact the signal reception.

• *Benefit* - The payoff and benefits attached to your signal and how they impact the recipient's work schedule and mental agenda also impact how the message will be acted on.

• *Territorial Issues* - Your sensitivity to the other person's traditional territorial concerns will also impact the value of the signal you send. Territorial issues, for example, are those areas (territories) that if violated will prevent the other person from listening. He may be looking at you while you continue talking, but he won't be listening.

Territory is like education. You may need to interact with another person on an issue dealing with a subject which that person feels he is versed in. However, you need to interact with him on that subject from an instructional standpoint. Approach the subject matter with guarded caution so you don't violate his education and cause confrontation.

• *Messenger* - Sometimes you can increase the value of the signal by adjusting the person who delivers the signal. Utilize other people to deliver your signals as necessary to accomplish your objectives.

• *Enthusiasm* - You have to believe in the signal you're sending and have genuine energy and motivation if you expect the recipient of your signal to become motivated. Remember, the *'iasm'* in enthusiasm stands for, "*I Am Sold Myself!*" Ask yourself if you're buying into this signal prior to delivering it. If you're not, it will be written all over you face when you deliver the signal. Your enthusiasm for a signal sets the stage for how the recipient will *RECEIVE* the signal.

• *Tie-In* - Establish the linkage between your signal and how the recipient will benefit from this signal. Establish how it will help develop him as he progresses toward his professional goals. Many times, if the receiver of the signal can see the tie-in between what you're communicating and the bigger picture, he will be motivated to action, as now he sees the *VALUE*.

• *Ownership Words* - Utilize more words that focus on the "we" and not the "you" in conversations. Ownership words are words that as used imply all parties are in this together and no one is pointing fingers at the other person. Ownership words are words like: we, us, team, I.

The importance of maintaining a step-by-step approach to communication is that you can control the flow of communication and measure whether the signals you are sending are being *RECEIVED, UNDERSTOOD* and *VALUED*.

Another aspect of interactive communication and attaining peak performance states within management is reflected in the percentage of your signals which the recipient internalizes.

Some communication study's explore the three levels of communication and the communication model of how the signal flows from the sender to the receiver. 100 percent of what the recipient *RECEIVES* and internalizes (*UNDERSTANDS*) for interpretation (*VALUE*) breaks down into three different elements of the signal.

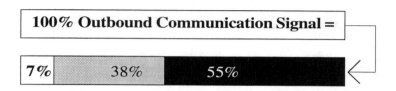

100% Outbound Communication Signal =

7%	38%	55%

- 7 percent of your signal's impact is from the <u>words</u> you use! This means **WHAT** was said.
- 38 percent of your signal's impact is based upon <u>para language</u>: the tone, pitch, pace, rate, volume, etc... This means **HOW** the what was said.
- 55 percent of your signal's impact is the <u>nonverbal</u> signals. This means **WHY** the what was said, the support components of the signal.

Interactive communication also rests upon how effectively you merge these percentage values as you send the signal. The three factors combined make for the total 100 percent signal which you send outbound, and directly impacts the *VALUE* seen in your message.

You can obtain greater impact with your communication signals by flexing the three channels and by using variations of the three channels at different times. Consider the following examples of communicating via the three channels to gain immediate *RECEPTION*, faster *UNDER-STANDING* and precise *VALUE* with your interactive communication.

When communicating outbound consider which channel the brain needs to receive the signal through to effectively *RECEIVE, UNDERSTAND,* and *VALUE* the signal. If you are communicating outbound via the VISUAL channel, you need to focus the signal so that it stimulates the visual senses. Use words like: 6'5" instead of tall; Fire engine red instead of bright red; "Can you see what I am saying?" instead of "does this make sense?" In essence, when communicating via the VISUAL channel use very vivid and visual words. As you talk or write your message you should paint a picture in the mind's eye of the recipient.

When you communicate to a visual person or through the VISUAL channel, you want to play off the eye. Incorporate more visual aids as you talk. Use charts, pictures, diagrams, documentation, write out key points as you talk them out, leave a visual reminder with people after you leave regarding what was discussed. This way, it can be seen later as a visual reminder.

With an AUDITORY person, utilize more words that play off the ear. Use more words which convey sound and noise to reinforce a message. For example: "Did you hear what I said?" "Does this sound like something that you would be interested in?" "It sounded like a window being shattered!" These words convey an image and that image is of sound. In AUDITORY channels of communication, you want to reinforce any VISUAL correspondence, for example, with a follow-up telephone call or leave a message in a voice mail or answering machine system so the receiver will hear as well as see the signal.

With the KINESTHETIC person, you want to adjust the signal to play off feelings and emotions as this channel conveys the feelings of the signal. You want to be more face-to-face interactive with this channel and with KINESTHETIC people. Use words like: "How do you feel about this idea?" "Does this sit well with you?" And make your statements flow like this: "The caller used a very soft and soothing tone of voice. It was like being in a doctor's office and having a very friendly mother figure assisting you for a nurse."

Becoming more effective as an interactive communicator in management (and in life overall) takes a systematic approach and quick intellect to make adjustments, as necessary, to attain desired results with each interaction!

To become more interactive, and a whole communicator, management must assume 100 percent accountability with respect to each of the three psychological steps of communication and in targeting each of the three levels of communication. To increase your effectiveness in communication, consider:

• First, reflect upon how your filters shape how you feel and think as you encode the signal.

• Second, reflect on how the other person's filters will shape how he feels or thinks as he decodes your signal(s).

• Third, with this reflective insight, consider which channel(s) would best transmit the signal from your brain to the receiver's brain.

• Fourth, once the signal has been sent, it is your responsibility (especially as a management player) to ensure that the signal has been received (level one), understood by the other party (level two) and that the receiver of the signal senses a degree of value attached to your message (level three)!

Loyola University conducted a study that reflects the accountability factor in communication. They solicited the quality or traits most sought in a good boss or organizational leader. The dominant response: Being a good listener! This is typically the same trait you seek in your best friend and closest relationships.

Improving interactive communication can have the single greatest impact upon increasing organizational efficiency and reducing player stress. By focusing energies on improving the listening activities within interactions, you will be able to improve the interactive communication of interactions. Interactive communication is your responsibility!

Chapter 11

Interviewing, Hiring And Promoting The Right Person: Eliminate The Number Of Nightmares Added To Teams

"Termination is the ultimate result of personal failure. In business, it's the result of failure of management in one fashion or another."
• Thomas Wratten
President, The Principal Group

Interviewing, Hiring And Promoting The Right Person: Eliminate The Number Of Nightmares Added To Teams

Each year organizations spend millions of dollars on the interview and hiring process associated with bringing a new player onto a team. And every year organizations experience new player trauma when they hire a person who develops a substantially different personality and work ethic than that projected in the initial interview phase. How do you counter this epidemic? Start by overhauling the interviewing and hiring process.

Keep in mind that in many places there are local, state and federal regulations which restrict a prospective employer from asking the types of questions necessary to find a peak performer. Many laws actually protect the mediocre individual at the expense of the organization. This chapter will focus on some ideas and strategies for countering the sea of rules and regulations which work against interviewing. This chapter will also focus on identifying some current interviewing behavioral patterns you have and ways to change self-defeating activities!

To maximize an interview session and increase the level of productive new hires, start by evaluating what you are really looking for in a successful candidate for your team - *develop a **people description**, rather than a job description*! Then measure that response against what you are presently doing in the interview process. You may determine that you are investing time in interviews asking the wrong questions or not listening effectively enough to all that is revealed by the candidate. These answers are the clues management needs to design and build cohesive, working, productive, winning teams for future growth and success.

Let's take the process one step at a time. Start by evaluating what you are looking for - *the people description via the **Winning Player Matrix**© model.*

WINNING PLAYER MATRIX

• **First:** If you were in an interview situation, list below all of the traits or characteristics that you would like to see in your ideal candidate/prospect.

Measuring Key: A=   **S=**

With the responses written down, go back and qualify or measure each response with this *"Measuring Key"* to determine what you are really looking for. From this collective answer you can then determine whether or not you have been asking questions to determine the "A" trait/

characteristic or the "S" trait/characteristic in your interviews and hiring procedures. Most organizations have been conditioned to invest disproportionate amounts of time asking questions to determine all about the "S" factor and completely overlooking the "A" factor. However, from the previous chart you more than likely have listed significantly more "A" traits/characteristics as characteristics of an ideal new employee for your team!

So, what do the "A" and the "S" represent? On the previous chart, go back and put either an "A" or an "S" next to each entry. Each entry can have only one letter beside it, so make a judgment call for each entry. If it could only be described as one or the other, which one does it tend to be more so than the other. The:

- "A" represents "ATTITUDE" traits/characteristics!
- "S" represents "SKILL" traits/characteristics!

From your personal overview did you determine that "ATTITUDE" is more critical in a winning player than "SKILL?" Most management teams working through this exercise determine that to be so. From this brief overview you and your interviewing teams may want to have an in-house retreat and pursue this exercise in greater detail. The team's (or your) collective responses to this exercise will give you greater insight as to the questions to focus on in the interviewing process.

As you ask questions of candidates, listen to the response you get from the person. Each answer or response actually carries two answers with it. If you listen closely to every response, you will be able to measure the candidate's "ATTITUDE" and "SKILL" levels! How do you hear two answers to each response? Easy!

> • The "SKILL" portion of the response comes from what the candidate actually says (the 7 percent factor from Chapter 10 of the person's actual words).
> • The "ATTITUDE" portion of the response comes from how he responds (or the 38 percent factor) through his tone of voice, as outlined in Chapter Ten.

The "Winning Player Matrix" is one way to determine whether or not you have really been focused in your interviewing and hiring efforts. Many times have management teams realized that they have been so focused in pursuit of the right candidate - technically - that they overlook the fact that this person's personality (attitude) is the factor that will be interacting others. Hire or promote the technically (skill) qualified candidate with poor people ability (attitude) and there will be tension, frustration and anxiety within the organization!

Another way of looking at candidates in the interviewing process is for you (as the MANAGER and organization) to be selfish. Look at the present work load, work requirements, tasks that you would like to be able to delegate (but presently are not delegating) and determine the skills and attitudes needed. With this collective thought, set out to find candidates that will meet these needs!

Design a profile of what the ideal candidate would look like and what the minimum requirements you would be willing to accept are and don't accept anything less. Anything less will only serve as trouble in the future.

As you review candidates, consider whether that person has been a TRANSMITTER, TRANSFORMER or TERRORIST (Rule 80/10/10 in Chapter Two). Advancement should go to TRANSFORMERS and to TRANSMITTERS when there is a feeling that this person could become more assertive and proactive with the right training and conditioning. To advance or hire a TERRORIST or typical TRANSMITTER will only allow you to maintain status quo - at best!

The action of interviewing, hiring and promoting is a process. And as a process management should take a step-by-step approach to the activities associated with interviewing. Consider the following subsections as ideas to approach the process and to facilitate the process for win/win outcomes for management, the organization, present members of that organization and the new prospect to be added to the team!

Management techniques and strategies to consider in the hiring and interviewing process:

> • *Agenda* - Design your agenda so that you can mentally and physically see where you are and ensure that the key "SKILL" and "ATTITUDE" traits/characteristics are being sought.

> • *Location* - The physical environment has a lot to do with how the candidate acts, feels, reacts, and will respond (open up) to the process (questions and interactions). You may consider the first meeting in a neutral office (meeting room, break room, board room, someone else's office, off site at a restaurant, etc...).

> • *Logistics* - How the interview room is set up also impacts the interaction. Some people get into psychological games of setting up the room, to positioning chairs and people, etc... Don't invest much time in these games. Focus on the purpose of this first session or subsequent meeting and aim toward that!

The room should be relaxed and conducive for all parties to open up and for management to see the candidate physically and verbally. Look at the nonverbal signals being sent by the candidate as well as listen to the actual responses to questions.

> • *Time* - Decide how much time to allocate for the session prior to initiating it. Position a clock, watch or time keeper to ensure that you stay on time. Consider the best time of the day/week for the session, as people perform at different standards depending upon their inner energy cycles. Your time constraints will be impacted by what is happening in your environment. You don't want to schedule an interview and then have to compete with constant interruptions. This becomes very distracting to both you and the candidate!

• *People* - Consider who should participate in the initial and subsequent interviewing sessions. You may want to delegate the first screening session to another team player or a small controlled team. The key players of a team or department need to be involved in the interviewing session(s). It becomes hard for people to point fingers and blame management for hiring a Terrorist if they, too, were involved in the screening and decision process!

You may want to have specific groups, teams or departments go through the "Winning Player Matrix" exercise. From that group's analysis, you can develop your profile for interviews. If you hire a player who meets the team's designed profile for new members, and that player turns out to be negative, it becomes harder for the players on the team to blame management. This issue now becomes a team issue and all members can be utilized to either work with that difficult player, educate that difficult player or eliminate that difficult player altogether!

• *Feedback* - Ensure that you don't dominate the interview. Keep notes of what the candidate says during the session and make sure that you solicit feedback on what you discuss. Those notes will assist you in further analyzing candidates objectively. When the candidate talks, you listen. Try not to interrupt a person in an interviewing session. These sessions are typically uncomfortable and intimidating to some; if you interrupt them, they may not open up again.

• *Pose Situations* - Reflect on some realistic situations which have caused stress among the players and pose situation questions to candidates to solicit their responses to these situations. This will give you additional insight as to how candidates think, analyze and rationalize situations. Remember, this is a person that you are considering investing money in to hire, train, insure, etc...

• *Your Expectations* - Share with the candidates what the expectations are for a successful new member of the team. Management needs to establish what its expectations are and the MANAGER should also share his personal, professional expectations for a successful new member. From these expectations solicit the candidate's feelings. Eliminate misunderstanding of expectations in this initial interview, so all parties have the opportunity to have expanded dialogue here. In far too many cases, however, the misunderstanding of the expectations is not realized until the candidate is hired and on the team. In many cases it is more difficult to get rid of the player than it is to keep him and shuffle him from one team or department to another.

• *His Expectations* - You need to determine exactly what the candidate's expectations are. There are several expectations that you need to determine right in the beginning and make sure that you write each down. Those expectations are:

> 1) expectations of management.
> 2) expectations of you as MANAGER.
> 3) expectations of fellow team members.
> 4) expectations of where he wants to be within the organization in six months, one year, three years and five years.

If the candidate is hired, these statements will be measurement gauges during his six-month and subsequent reviews. Both of you will be able to see if you are on track or off track with respect to where you started in the initial interview session for hiring or promotion.

• *Job Sharing/Rotation* - This concept refers to moving team players from one position to another. Leaving each player in a position for a period of time and then advancing him to another helps a player gain a better understanding and respect for others' positions and responsibilities. By rotating players around, management can avoid stagnation, procrastination and burn-out! This movement stimulates productivity and ingenuity. By exposing players to a cross-section of job-related tasks, both the player and management can determine career direction better and thus both can work accordingly.

• *Commitment Level* - Ensure success for each interview or review session by having pre-written objectives and therefore, specific commitments that you and the organization are prepared to make or offer. Don't allow the energy or emotion of the session to force you to make further commitments. Defer those additional decisions or commitments to a later call (via the telephone) or subsequent session.

Any commitments made in a session need to be written down and signed by all parties involved. This avoids either party having a misunderstanding of the offer or agreement.

• *Worse Case Scenario* - Always discuss with the other party what the recourse would be if the new candidate is hired and things don't work out. This provides management with unique perspectives about the candidate's mind-set. If there are no recourse perspectives to your "what if" questions, then give additional consideration to whether you will be in a positive or negative position should you hire this candidate and then have to terminate the player for some unforeseen issue!

• *Ultimate Measurement Assessment* - Prior to the session design objective ways (measurement models) to identify the candidate's abilities and capabilities. From these answers you can measure whether or not the candidate will be able to meet the needs of management. Refer to Chapter Six for several measuring models which should be aggressively used in interview sessions!

• *Profile Comparison* - In the interview session you can measure a candidate's potential and fitness for your organizational and management needs by profiling the most positive "Winning Player" already on the team.

Go over the member(s) of your team who are ideal team members and draft a description of what makes each such a winning player. In essence, develop a *"Winning Player Matrix"* of the traits and characteristics of that member. As you observe what makes that player such a positive contributor to your team, use that as a map to monitor whether or not your interview efforts, screening process or questions are allowing you to interview candidates. Utilize the opportunity to add new members to your team as both a luxury to fill a player ability level presently lacking and also as an opportunity to add to your TRANSFORMER base!

• *Gaps and Cracks* - Look for inconsistencies on resumes, chronological gaps and candidates' previous experience.

Gaining a better understanding of current team members and prospective new members through interviews and on-the-job rotations helps to decrease employee turnover and increase team unity and individual player productivity. Player profiles need to be designed and developed for each player to determine his abilities and potentials before placing a player in a position and then finding out that a player lacks the ability, skill, education, determination or desire to perform as management needs.

The combination of placing and promoting existing players into positions and the addition of new players is an art that needs to be undertaken with great consideration for future gains and advancements. The promotion or addition of the wrong player into the wrong position can spell disaster for players, management and the organization overall. The interaction of formal or informal questioning in the interview process has to be planned and carefully tracked.

The interview process should allow you to determine perfect (or near perfect) fits between organizational needs for present and future growth and candidates' ability levels (whether or not that candidate is already on staff or is to be brought in from outside sourcing). When it comes to hires, the typical mis-hires can be traced to one of or a combination of eight key factors, according to Mr. Martin Yates, former National Director of Training for Dunhill Personnel Systems, Inc. in his classic book, *Hiring the Best: How to Staff Your Department Right the First Time.*

Consider these eight factors as you design or re-design your interview process from start to finish. Mis-hire factors are:

- poor analysis of job functions.
- poor analysis of necessary personality-skill profile.
- inadequate initial screening.
- inadequate *interviewing* techniques.
- inadequate *questioning* techniques.
- poor utilization of "second opinions."
- company and career/money expectations over or inappropriately sold.
- references not checked!

Your face-to-face time (the informal or formal interview), therefore, needs be strategically designed to afford you maximum productivity. While it can become intimidating for some in the interview process or even easy to get off track from your objective, the interview session has to accomplish certain objectives. Those objectives may vary depending upon the position you're interviewing for. Therefore, script critical data needed via questions for the interview.

　• *Questions* - Develop minimum questions for each candidate to consider and respond to based upon the position you are interviewing for. The more technical the position, the more technical the questions should be. The more consumer or customer-service oriented the position, the more customer focused the questions should be, and so forth. There are four categories of questions to be asked, and you can expand to any degree necessary. They are: *Professionally* oriented questions to find out about their work background. *Personally* oriented questions to gain a perspective about the person you're hiring and how his personality will impact his performance on the job. *Business* oriented questions to determine his specific experience and background as it specifically relates to the position you're interviewing for and your organization. *Pressure* oriented questions to determine your candidate's ability on the spot. Present your candidate or prospect with situational questions or a mock situation and ask him to explain to you what he would do. Watch his body language and listen to what he says. You can gain true insight to who you are interviewing and thus who you would have on your team if hired.

MOCK POWER QUESTIONS

- **Why do you want this position?**
- **What should we know about you that we haven't discussed?**
- **What do you like the most about the organization? The department? The offer?**
- **What interests you the least about the organization? The department? The offer?**
- **How do you see yourself assisting us in saving money if you are hired?**
- **How do you see yourself increasing revenue if we hire you?**
- **What special and unique characteristics and strengths can you bring to the team?**
- **What weaknesses would you be bringing to the team?**
- **Why should we offer the position to you right now?**

In Chapter Six several models for player analysis were presented and those models should be utilized in the interview stages for new candidates and in the promotion interviews with players you don't really know. Consider whether a new player is really necessary for team development and advancement or whether or not the responsibilities of a former player can be spread laterally among other players, without overstressing the environment. With added responsibility, the new players will become more energized.

The critical factor in successful interviewing is to interview to determine if a candidate possesses the competencies necessary to fulfill the job description.

Chapter 12

Developing A Winning
Habit Paradigm:
Systems Of Measurement

" The future belongs to those who believe in the beauty
of their dreams...those who know where they have been
and can measure how to get to where they desire to go."
• Eleanor Roosevelt, American stateswoman

"If you can't measure it, you can't manage it.
If you can't manage it, you can't change,
fix or improve it!"
• Anonymous

Developing A Winning
Habit Paradigm:
Systems Of Measurement

In the face of market chaos and competition and in the face of the internal changes and challenges which players and management alike encounter, the ability to systematically measure work, activities, projects and progress is critical for success and growth. The ability to make these changes or shifts in performance and behavior for greater effectiveness and efficiency is the focus of this chapter - *Developing A Winning Habit Paradigm.*

The need for these paradigms (maps) and the need to change some paradigms is great. Organizations and management can no longer operate from the perspective that *bigger is better* and *technology alone is the secret weapon.* Some of the greatest failures in the this century come from looking at the back rooms of the leading Fortune 500 organizations who violated the people factor. Even though they dominated their fields through most of the 1900s, it is in the 1990s that these organizations started falling apart in unison. Why? Violation of the people factor and avoidance of **Yield Management** ideology and methodologies are the explanation.

Investing in your people and listening to each other, matched with systems of measurement leads to great levels of success!

In 1990 the *Harvard Business Review* published an article by professors and writers Michael Beer, Russell Eisenstat and Bert Spector on the need for measurement and the alternatives for management success in the coming decades. Their collective work was entitled the, *"Six Commandments For Team-Oriented Change"* and parallels the ideas and techniques laid forth in **Yield Management.** Consider the following chart as one winning habit paradigm.

SIX COMMANDMENTS FOR
TEAM-ORIENTED CHANGE

I.   *MOBILIZE COMMITMENT* through joint diagnosis of business problems.

II.   *DEVELOP A SHARED VISION* of how to organize and mobilize to increase unit effectiveness.

III.   *FOSTER CONSENSUS* for the new vision, *COMPETENCE* to enact it and *COHESION* to move it along.

IV.   *ENLIST SUPPORT* from all functional and staff units who will interact with the new team.

V.   *MAKE FORMAL CHANGES* in systems, structures and personnel *AFTER* the team is clear about its needs.

VI.   *MONITOR* and *ADJUST STRATEGIES* in response to problems in the teambuilding effort.

Team-oriented change can occur with the utilization of the ideas presented in *Yield Management* and with a management commitment. Players on the team always look toward management for the lead. If management is committed and walks the line they talk, then players will fall in line as well. However, if management is not 100 percent committed, players will sense this and their level of commitment to the team will be reflective of management's!

Systems of measurement deal with personal and organizational assessments. This chapter will center on measuring systems, how to design them, when to use them, where to implement them and who should be involved in them. *One general rule of management is that what gets measured gets dealt with.* Measure it and then you can deal effectively with it. Therefore, in management everything needs to be measured!

The fundamentals of a quality measurement system start with an understanding of what it is that you, the players within an organization, the senior management team of the organization and the organization itself, want and need in order to sustain life and ensure growth.

Before approaching the measurement instruments and tools that are available to management, consider your point of professional reference in conjunction with some national and international statistics. How you rate yourself against your own potential and how you rate in contrast with these statistics may also give some perspective to why your organization experiences its unique level of successes and failures. Consider some international levels of excellence and measures of achievement:

> • According to a CNN/Gallup Survey (1995), workers in Europe and Japan spend on average 22 percent of the work time each year engaged in some sort of on-the-job or off-site educational activities, while the working counter-part in America spends on average 2 percent of his annual work time engaged in educational training programs.

> • Harvard University polled Fortune 500 firms for the inner organizational traits and characteristics which led to their success. The dominant response was *attitude*!

> • In 1981, when management and employees bought back the ailing Harley Davidson Motorcycle from AMF, it had an exceedingly high default rate on the product its factories produced - some estimate as high as 50 percent. By 1987 when the Company opened on the New York Stock Exchange, that rate had declined substantially and by 1991 to what some industry analysts estimated to be below seven percent!

> How? The new team (made up of the employees/workers from the immediately previous team) realized that they were all a part of the same team and it was in their best interest to operate from a position of ownership, mutual respect and from a need to interact. All members took on roles of leadership and teaming!

• In 1993 a Butterball Turkey Company plant was experiencing a 158 percent employee turnover. Within one year that rate had fallen by more than 50 percent and the management measurement tools being applied were allowing MANAGERS to continue to bring about an organizational cultural change and further turnover declines.

How do you rate in comparison to other organizations and management challenges nationally? Consider the available management and organizational measurement instruments for analysis (ENDING) for increased management level interaction and increased effectiveness.

> **"Quality is not only right, it is free. And it is**
> **not only free, it is the most profitable**
> **product line we have."**
> • **Philip B. Crosby, Sr.**

As you consider the following measurement tools and their application to your organization and your management style, there are what Crosby calls, *"The Four Absolutes of Quality Management:"*

- **First**, quality means conformance to the requirements.
- **Second**, quality comes from prevention.
- **Third**, quality performance standard is Zero Defects.
- **Fourth**, quality measurement is the Price of Nonconformance.

This last absolute is powerful with respect to what this chapter is addressing. As you work toward quality, ultimate quality management and a quality organization, measurement is necessary. Ultimately, an organization will move to an environment where quality is built into every phase and each individual step. Quality is also inspected into each step by each player and the ultimate need for quality measurement and inspection will not be needed.

An immediate assessment tool that can be utilized at any time and within any level of organizational dynamics is surveys. Surveys are fast ways to obtain feedback for immediate course corrections or to confirm that your present management actions are strategically on track! For your

SURVEYS to be most effective, consider the following guide lines:

• Start with a clear understanding of what the vision or goal is (the first two mission statements   presented in Chapter Two).

• Solicit feedback from only the *vital few* in your internal or external business circle. The *vital few* is defined as those individuals who are vital to your business and without whom you would experience significant pain. Many times surveys fall flat because management solicits feedback from the *useful many*. The *useful many* are those around you who may be involved in your business but are not critical or vital to your success! Solicit feedback via surveys from those who have a direct impact on your mission!

• There are four ways to move organizations forward and maintain market advantage. Surveys can assist management to assess how to meet and exceed expectations of others' perspectives. There are four ways to distinguish yourself from others and surveys will assist in identifying where you are. You either have to give others *more*, do it *better*, do it *faster* or significantly *different* than others to win.

• There should never be more than three questions (or three sections of questions) on a survey to obtain the highest response rate. Make the questions positive in nature to obtain maximum response of positive and negative feedback; otherwise the questions will draw a response from the most negative and upset of players.

• Ideal questions a survey may present are: (1) "What am I doing well?" (2) "What could I do better?" (3) "What should I consider doing, that I am not presently doing or offering?"

• Measure what needs improvement and what is new.

• Design a response mechanism for the survey respondent to utilize that will make it easy for him to return your survey.

Consider making the response a fax number, a voice mail system (so he doesn't have to talk with a live person), a survey response card that can be mailed back, or a letter survey that can be filled out and placed into an enclosed, stamped, self-addressed envelope.

• You can obtain higher response rates from individuals by tailoring the response vehicle to be used. For women, provide a return envelope for the survey versus a simple response card that is filled out and mailed back. Women are more private than men when it comes to survey responses!

For measuring on-going projects and for measuring involved and complex projects, consider using a **GROWTH WHEEL** © note-taking technique. This technique allows you to place more notes and data in one place with less writing. Consider how the technique works:

• Take a piece of paper and draw a circle in the middle of the page. Inside the circle write down the main issue or topic (like the traditional note-taking formula that uses a Roman Numeral "I" to indicate the main point) that you are dealing with.

• From the circle draw lines outward. Upon each primary axis line, write down each point or issue which needs to be addressed to facilitate the main point within the circle. (This would be like writing a large capital letter "A" and subsequent letters to indicate a supporting point to the "I".)

• Any points, data, information or specifics that relate to any primary axis line point can be attached to the axis line via sub-axis lines to each (this would be like the traditional note-taking formula that calls for the letters 1, 2, 3, etc... that follow each large letter A, B, C, etc.).

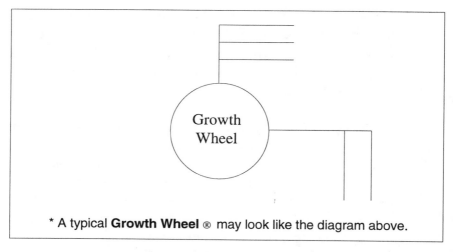

* A typical **Growth Wheel** ® may look like the diagram above.

• From a measurement perspective, this technique allows you to identify the individual elements of a project being monitored. Write them out and assess each at any point to determine present status. This technique also allows for synergy and ensures against hindsight management. This also works well as a "*Cause and Effect*" diagram.

When it comes to tracking entire processes, the involvement of individual players and where possible problems may lie, consider traditional **FLOW CHARTS.** There are some basic guidelines to consider for maximum benefit from **FLOW CHARTS**.

• Never plot more than one major issue. If there is more than one issue, then break each out on separate charts.

• Never have more than three to five major subpoints to a flow chart. The more subpoints there are, the more likely you are to overlook something. In the process stage of a FLOW CHART, if there are more than three to five points, break the additional points out into their own task, chart and responsibility.

• This chart allows you to graph the actual steps being followed. And this type of chart allows you to chart the steps which should be followed in an ideal situation. The comparison allows for adjustments and measurements for improvement and greater levels of success!

• This chart allows you to create a pictorial of what is happening and what needs to take place, what the flow is and who is involved, at what levels, and to what degree. This allows management at least one more tool in assuring productivity at an effective and efficient level.

• A FLOW CHART could look like this:

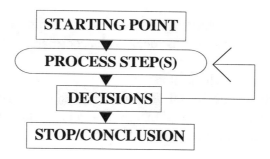

• With a FLOW CHART you need to analyze decisions and their impact on the process and actions. The *DECISION* step of the chart therefore is a never-ending step in the process.

If you're looking at the organization from an historical perspective, consider **HISTOGRAMS**. This tool compares consistent variables from the past with what you are doing now for the future.

• This chart allows you to plot classes of data and to determine if there are similarities in what happened before with what is taking place presently.

• You can easily see patterns in process and player participation with HISTOGRAMS. A typical chart may resemble a bar graph.

The most widely utilized management measurement tool is the **CHECK SHEET**. With a CHECK SHEET, you graph data to determine an answer posed from a challenge or problem management faces. Consider these steps:

• Through observations you can detect specific activities which may or may not be impacting an outcome which you may view as a positive or a negative.

• Through observation on a CHECK SHEET, you identify the categories of data needed and identify how many times something happens or how many of something you may have.

• This technique gives you a brief snapshot observation of an issue and should be dealt with accordingly.

• The issue to be plotted or observed needs to be representative of what typically takes place. If your observations are directed toward something that is not representative of the NORM, then the results will be skewed.

• In making your observation, ensure that you or the players conducting the observations have adequate time to accomplish a thorough analysis and data-gathering search!

• A CHECK SHEET diagram may look like this:

Problem	Time Period		
	month one	month two	total
1			
2			
3			
Total			

In developing a winning habit and identifying the models which work for you and others you may want to modify and adopt; the ultimate position is that the measuring system used be realistic and applicable. One of the major destructive points for business and MANAGERS is when they force themselves into a measuring system which doesn't take the specific environment into consideration.

When you are measuring factors - for change, improvement, modification, or elimination, consider the impact of the measuring system upon:

- Your people
- Your financial capabilities
- Your structures
- Your product or service

As you measure these factors, make sure that the point that you are measuring is comprised of equal variables of *'then'* and *'now'*. All factors must be equal for the measurement to deliver accurate data and findings. If the data are not equal, then build in allowances for the variances.

The continued growth of an organizational operation is dependent upon someone taking the responsibility to measure, analyze, monitor and offer modifications for future efforts. Forecasting future needs is based upon current activities, customer demands, market trends from the past, organizational capacity and abilities, along with management abilities and commitment which all impact life within the organization. Another measurement factor deals with the performance of the players in an organization.

PERFORMANCE OUTCOME POSITION© STATEMENT (P.O.P.) is a positive focus on what traditional management would refer to as *job descriptions,* although *job descriptions* can become counter-productive and limit participants' involvement and participation. In some environments *job descriptions* even become instruments from which management works against the players or players position themselves against management; and in either case, the outcome is stress, conflict and organizational confrontations! There is another alternative or option.

P.O.P. © is not a job description for players on the team. Instead it is a tool that management can utilize with players within an organization to non-confrontationally interact. It tells players what the scope of job responsibilities is and more. It focuses, one step at a time, on four core aspects to enable all parties to measure and progress with mutual understandings. An effective **P.O.P.** © spells out clearly for all parties ahead of time *the situation or condition which will exist when this part of the job is WELL done*. The criteria here subscribes to the *SMART* © formula presented in Chapter Nine.

An effective **P.O.P.** © sets out what the bottom line is regardless of the player. It is what is needed for that organization to function at peak performance and for that player to focus upon as his map. An effective **P.O.P.** © therefore incorporates *four* critical elements:

- **One**, what should be **DONE**.
- **Two**, what **RESULTS** should be achieved.
- **Three**, **HOW WELL** it should be done.
- **Four**, **WHEN** it should be done.

When drafted, an effective **P.O.P.** © statement may start off by saying something to the effect of: "Resulting in ..." or "So that ..." or "Therefore ..." or "We will be left with ...!"

The ability as a key management player to develop the players on your team is number one for success of the team. A powerful tool for this development is to move away from *job descriptions* and *performance evaluations* (which typically are argumentative, confrontational, emotional or vague and not developmental in nature) and toward a developmentally powerful **PERFORMANCE OUTCOME POSITION STATEMENT** ©.

On the following page is an example of a **P.O.P.** © statement and format which you can utilize in future employee/player development sessions or situations. Consider completing the following statement (as an ACTION PLAN) prior to your next encounter and then watch the performance outcomes from this systematic measurement tool.

PERFORMANCE OUTCOME POSITION ©
STATEMENT

Participant Name: _____

Position/Role: _____

Organization/Team/Dep't: _____

Date Of Measurement (from when to when): _____

Primary Goal/Objective: _____

_____

_____

_____

_____

_____**!**

Four Measuring Factors (DONE/RESULTS/HOW WELL/WHEN):

DONE = _____

_____

_____

_____

_____

_____

_____

RESULTS = _____

_____

_____

_____

_____

_____

_____

HOW WELL (the minimum level of acceptance, access to, authorization for, checking with, within what parameters/factors/values/costs/percentages, etc...) = _____

_____

_____

_____

_____

_____

WHEN = _____

_____

PERFORMANCE OUTCOME POSITION © STATEMENT

Participant Name: _____

Position/Role: _____

Organization/Team/Dep't: _____

Date Of Measurement (from when to when): _____

Primary Goal/Objective: _____

_____

_____

_____

_____

_____ **!**

Four Measuring Factors (DONE / RESULTS / HOW WELL / WHEN):

DONE = _____

_____

_____

_____

_____

_____

_____

RESULTS = _____

_____

_____

_____

_____

_____

_____

HOW WELL (the minimum level of acceptance, access to, authorization for, checking with, within what parameters/factors/values/costs/percentages, etc...) = _____

_____

_____

_____

_____

_____

WHEN = _____

_____

PERFORMANCE OUTCOME POSITION © STATEMENT

Participant Name: _____

Position/Role: _____

Organization/Team/Dep't: _____

Date Of Measurement (from when to when): _____

Primary Goal/Objective: _____

_____

_____

_____

_____

_____ !

Four Measuring Factors (DONE / RESULTS / HOW WELL / WHEN):

DONE = _____

_____

_____

_____

_____

_____

_____

_____

RESULTS = _____

_____

_____

_____

_____

_____

_____

HOW WELL (the minimum level of acceptance, access to, authorization for, checking with, within what parameters/factors/values/costs/percentages, etc...) = _____

_____

_____

_____

_____

_____

WHEN = _____

_____

_____

The critical factor about the **PERFORMANCE OUTCOME POSI-TION STATEMENT** © is that it focuses interaction energies upon the performance and not the performer. This takes the emotional factors out of employee and management player development and puts the logic track back into interactions, discussions and performance appraisals!

In using the **P.O.P.** © tracks with players as outlined on the previous pages, fill them out completely prior to interacting one-on-one with a player and then make copies. One copy goes with the player, one copy you refer to throughout performance and one copy goes into the player's performance file for future review or evaluation updates (build the player's file as activities develop instead of waiting until time to have that dreaded annual review and then trying to rebuild what that player has been doing for the previous extended period of time) and allow yourself to be objective in your employee performance evaluations!

Integrating these systems of measurement can serve as a mapping strategy to mark where you are, what you are doing, and thus serve to guide your actions toward where you need to be. Designing a winning habit paradigm starts by analysis and continues by designing safeguards against paralysis of analysis!

Measuring your progress, activities and net results against what the market, an organization or customers need is critical to organizational dynamics. In management a powerful tool for measurement in tracking the growth and development of a player, a system, machines, groups of people, products or services is to **BENCHMARK** you against another tangible statistic!

BENCHMARKING is merely a tool of measurement whereby one identifies what is perceived to be the best in a market (whether it is a product, service, employee performance, etc.) and then those data are used to gauge one's own performance and thus enables management to determine many important factors. Consider:

> • Measuring your reputation against others in similar positions. Gather data on other factors or competitors and then you can begin to determine any gaps which you can play against and improve

upon for marketable advantages and team development.

• To effectively BENCHMARK consider the following three steps: (1) Collect data and information, (2) Convert that data and information to systems of measurement between you and the other party, and (3) Look for those areas where you can improve and look for areas of uniqueness - customer expectations met.

• BENCHMARKING allows you to determine where others and your organization may be meeting or exceeding customer needs and, therefore, where and how you can compete - *Reverse Engineering*. Start with someone else's known success story or industry standard setter and break it down into component parts and analyze what it is that has lead to their success and then improve upon it with your efforts (see Chapter Fifteen, subsection "Creating Re-Engineering Laboratories").

• Data have to be written down to be measured and to measure against. Data and information gathered on perceived "bests" in industry are what you always measure against.

One of the most comprehensive and systematic approaches to analysis is the application of the "S.T.O.P." © Formula (as presented in Chapter Nine) to a four-step "Analysis Identification Matrix/AIM" © diagram. The power of this combined technique - the **"S.T.O.P. & AIM"** © **DIAGRAM** - is that it serves as another self-management tool either as an individual model for developing winning habits or as an interactive team tool for systematically and nonconfrontationally reaching positive outcomes!

This technique incorporates a four-step decision/analysis model and allows the user to plot out in minimal words the four critical elements in reaching positive and productive outcomes. To use the following "S.T.O.P. & AIM" © DIAGRAMS, merely follow the sequence mapped out within the inner circle (designated by numeral "I") and in the outer rings ("II" and "III") by writing in the called-for response. Take the diagram one step at a time.

S.T.O.P. Analysis Identification Matrix©

Theory Meets Reality Quadrant

In Reality Quadrant

III.

II.

I.

Pick, Plan, Prepare and **Proceed:**

S.T.O.P. and See: idenification of issue/cause/ task/project/person

P S
O T

Target: analysis & observation

Organize: options to move forward with...

In Reality Quadrant

In Theory Quadrant

JEFF MAGEE INTERNATIONAL®

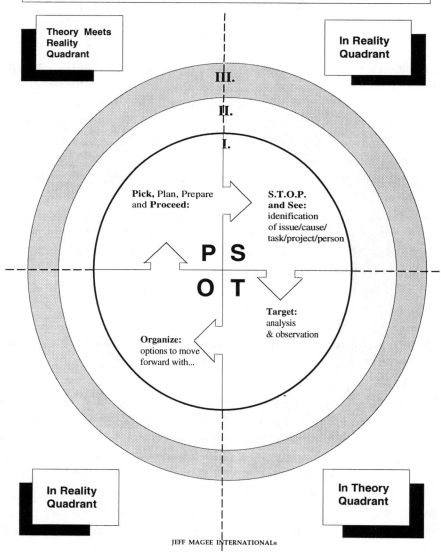

S.T.O.P. Analysis Identification Matrix©

Theory Meets Reality Quadrant

In Reality Quadrant

III.

II.

I.

Pick, Plan, Prepare and **Proceed:**

S.T.O.P. and See: idenification of issue/cause/ task/project/person

P S

O T

Target: analysis & observation

Organize: options to move forward with...

In Reality Quadrant

In Theory Quadrant

JEFF MAGEE INTERNATIONAL®

Designing Employee/Team Performance Appraisals

Expanded systems of measurement also include objective and consistent systems from which management and leaders can measure the development and grow of the players on the teams they are accountable for. Along with the *"Performance Outcome Positions Statements"©* presented earlier in this section, management personnel and team leaders also have to move away from traditional employee evaluation or annual appraisal systems and move toward regular and immediate systems of appraisal.

To maximize human growth and organizational development, players need immediate feedback on what they do or where they participate - good or bad. Tracking tools need to be easily used by management for both the documentation process for such appraisal meetings and for the issue development and personal feelings avoidance capabilities among players - management and employees.

There is a psychology to appraisals that needs to take on a paradigm shift itself!

Management and employees alike typically have a negative predisposition toward appraisals and appraisal meetings. This predisposition is based upon many factors which have been allowed to grow and persist over years within an organization. There are negative feelings based upon what the other party will think if critical elements are raised in a session, what legal ramifications can occur from these sessions, how one's confidence or lack of confidence plays into how the session is conducted and what real issues are addressed. These are just some of the factors impacting the negative fallout of what should otherwise be a positive and productive opportunity. To maximize the appraisal process, manage your actions and lead the other player toward growth and success.

To maximize your time and the players involved when it comes to appraisals and the appraisal meeting, break down the employee development cycle into three distinct phases - *Before The Session/During The Appraisal Period-Cycle/During The Session.* Appraisal sessions need to be held as a minimum, on a quarterly basis (monthly if possible), to ensure mutual participation by management and employees. **The sole purpose of an appraisal/appraisal tool is for player development and growth,** and not as an instrument to invoke pain, conflict and confrontations.

Before the Appraisal: Management and organizational leaders need to ensure that they are using consistent and objective tracking and measurement systems or tools for the entire team. For this matter, documentation is critical to ensure that personal feelings don't cloud the management of the interactions and the overall development of the player in question!

Collection of data as it happens throughout the cycle and before the scheduled and impromptu sessions can be accomplished in the following manner:

> • Maintain a log book for each player in their personnel file and as events happen (good or bad) log in a short note to that effect (with the specifics, date and time and outcome of that action). These are the events that are observed and documented throughout a cycle.

> • Scan the *"Performance Outcome Position Statements"*© prior to a session to determine if players are on course or off course in relation to the initial objective.

> • Break the player's performance down into manageable categories for measurement. Some of those categories should reflect: Assignments/Tasks assigned, Self-Management, Vertical relationships, Peer relationships, Management abilities, Leadership Initiative Abilities, Communication abilities.

> Each of the above main categories may then reflect multiple subcategories for each, as it relates to your environment and organizational dynamics and protocol!

• Prior to interaction, scan over previous documentation (from personnel file/folder) and review sessions for inconsistencies or consistencies in behavior, behavior changes and improvements or recurring problem areas.

• Visit with any colleagues, peers or superiors on issues to be discussed to gain a greater perspective on both issues and ways to improve and enhance the player's abilities.

• In final preparation for the review, you should draft the key issues to be discussed with key incident or fact points to each. These items can be drafted on an *"Agenda Manager"* © (as presented in Chapter Nine, "Counseling The Difficult Player" section).

This system will assist you in guiding the conversation from point to point or issue to issue. As the parties involved in the appraisal session address and resolve each issue, that issue on the *"Agenda Manager"* © can be initialed by each party involved. This documentation system is also effective because you can manage the conversation and avoid any confrontations or insinuations of personality differences.

• Design a few suggestions for "how-to" improve upon the present situation or behavior as a back-up for conversation, should the other person become silent in the appraisal and review session.

• Review what you have drafted as the issues to be addressed in the appraisal session; any concern areas and supporting documentations and associated solutions, as well as all positive areas for praise and continued improvements.

• Schedule adequate time for the appraisal session (on average at least one hour per player), in a suitable environment, with ample time for self-preparation prior to the session with the player in question.

During The Cycle: Between traditional and/or scheduled organizational appraisal or review sessions, it is critical for management and effective leaders to maintain a positive rapport with the players in the organization. As players interact with one another and as players perform their primary responsibilities during this time period, management is given multiple opportunities to track, trace and record player performance.

Impromptu appraisal sessions are also a valuable tool for employee development and team growth. Management and effective leaders draw upon every opportunity afforded to them by a player to interact and share guidelines and suggestions for peak performance. Whenever a player does something which warrants a positive word of praise, management needs to pursue that interchange as aggressively as one would when a player causes a problem or has a difficulty.

There are two easy ways to approach tracking player performance between sessions, so that when it is time for a scheduled organizational appraisal session, the review session itself will be more meaningful and easier for management to facilitate.

> • An *"Action Memo"* © (as presented in Chapter Nine, "Delegation Dynamics" section) is a very fast tool for documenting a player's actions of either accomplishments or problems throughout a cycle. Merely take a piece of paper and write down two items: First, what the issue or topic is; Second, what they did that was positive or what they could have done to avoid a problem. Then place this piece of paper in their file or on a *"Player Analysis Log"* © (PAL) sheet.

> • *"Player Analysis Log"* © sheet is a formal tracking device that management can keep in every player's personnel file. Team leaders can access the file and utilize it accordingly as well. This log allows management to formally track key incidents, issues and actions as witnessed by management and leaders throughout a recording period.

Player Analysis Log

Name: _____

Appraisal Sequence: _____/_____/_____ to _____/_____/_____

DATE	ISSUE/INCIDENT/TOPIC

During The (appraisal) Session: Maintaining positive conversation and energy flow during the appraisal session is a must for effective management between the player and leader. There are several key factors to keep in mind. Consider:

• Review the *"Player Analysis Log"* © prior to the session to familiarize yourself with the player's performance and the specific areas of interest for this session/review. This will allow you to mentally prepare.

• Prepare a copy of the appraisal session agenda (*"Agenda Manager"*©) and give it to the player at least 24 to 48 hours in advance so the player has time to review his record (i.e., strengths and weaknesses/growth and development areas/ areas for continued growth/concern areas/what he does best) and the appraisal session objectives before arriving.

The purpose of the appraisal session is to serve as a developmental tool to review the player's performance and outline the next best courses of action for either performance improvement or ways to maintain effective and successful performance!

• Engage in dialogue with the player to obtain his feelings and views on your agenda. Practice active listening while he responds to your questions and the items on your appraisal.

• Explain your position, your research, observations and how you have arrived at your impressions and or conclusions. Express your willingness to listen to his views as well and that the appraisal session is a give-and-take situation. Should a critical position that you have presented be inaccurate, you must convey to the player that you are prepared to revise your position based upon tangible evidence that he may present.

• Establish with one another and mutually agree to the time for the next scheduled appraisal or review session at the conclusion of this session and leave on a positive note!

The employee appraisal or performance review is the single most problematic area within American business. It is either not done or is not done as effectively as it should be, according to management guru Edwards Deming. An ancillary problem to an improper review is that it takes an employee as much as six months to recover from his annual review. This impacts behaviors, attitudes and ultimately performance and productivity of both players and organizations.

The appraisal review is a critical aspect of the MANAGER role of a leader (given the four alternative management roles or hats which can be used in leading and guiding the people on one's team).

An effective appraisal system allows management to monitor a player's performance and exert precise advice, guidance, or counseling as necessary to attain peak player performance for the immediate as well as for the long term needs of both the player and the organization!

The appraisal tool also allows management to *leverage* its position with the employee or player on its team to obtain higher levels of participation and commitment toward: Training purposes; Promotion opportunities; Professional development needs; Pay raise opportunities; And, the overall development from an Human Resource Development perspective for the employee. The appraisal allows management and the player to draft an *action plan* for future activity!

▼

**Nine Steps To
A Win/Win
"Appraisal"
Tool:**

1=Easy To Utilize
2=Accurate
3=Systematic
4=Objective
5=Validated
6=Meets "EEOC"
 Guidelines
7=Documentable
8=Focuses on Positive
 & Negative Areas
 Equally
9=Growth Oriented

In designing your next player performance appraisal, address the activity as a directional interaction opportunity afforded to both management and employee - become a leader of your team by utilizing the appraisal process as an instrument for growth and positive feedback. In essence the appraisal system allows management to become effective MENTORS in guiding both the individual player and organization alike!

The Ultimate Leadership Directed Appraisal System: A combination of the power of the most effective player development appraisal systems can actually be tied together in today's fast-paced and high-demand environments. Consider combining three appraisal systems into one joint effort for maximum player, management and thus organizational development.

First, start by requesting that the employee or player to be appraised conduct a *"Self-Analysis"* and submit that personal analysis, in writing, to management 48 hours prior to the scheduled face-to-face review. The areas of interest which you should direct the player to respond to might be questions like:

> • What are your three most powerful strengths within this position?
> • Your three greatest (personal) challenges within this position/ organization? Areas for concentrated improvement could be?
> • Your greatest accomplishment or contribution within this past appraisal cycle (period)?
> • And, where do you see yourself growing in the next appraisal cycle (period)?

Second, request a *"Peer Review"* from those players who have the most direct interaction with the player (vertically or horizontally) on a regular basis (within or outside of his specific area/department/divisions/etc.), to be submitted 48 hours prior to the scheduled session. This *"Peer Review"* can address the same sequence of observational questions presented above (or others) and should be submitted to management, with a copy to the player in question. Each colleague participating should schedule a few minutes within that 48-hour window to review his perspectives with the player, prior to his meeting with management.

Third, with this added perspective and teaming, effective leaders then conduct the *"Organizational Appraisal"* and review session. The combination of the three culminates in an organization's positive and constructive approach to player development. This will bring people together instead of polarizing individuals within an organization!

The Appraisal Instrument: The success and effectiveness of the entire appraisal process comes down to how effective the appraisal instrument is at addressing the core trait and behavior issues needed in your specific environment for ultimate success. How often the official appraisals and impromptu appraisals occur also impacts the effectiveness of the appraisal process. All of this impacts how effective the appraisal tool and appraiser will be at addressing successful habits and at addressing those areas which may be causing some difficulties for a player (employee).

From this instrument, managers and leaders can develop players' potentials for greater success and protect an organization against Terrorists! Before you engage in your next appraisal process, evaluate the instrument that you utilize to determine if it is a positive, focused tool or if it sounds hard and negative.

For an instrument to be effective it should contain three primary sections for management and the player (employee) to focus energies upon.

> • **First -** A general ratings section where core performance issues can numerically be addressed and rated. This section should have primary sections like (and then further broken down as applicable for your environment into subsections): General Performance, Job Performance and Knowledge, Adaptability and Initiative, Interpersonal Relationships, Communication Skills, and Supervisory Factors (for management staff).

> • **Second -** An employee development action sequence plan where positives and areas for improvement can be addressed in an essay/editorial format. This section can be broken down into subsections as well to address specifics in your environment.

> • **Third -** A signature or sign-off section with all appropriate players' signatures indicating that the review has been conducted.

On the following pages is an example of an effective employee performance appraisal form that incorporates the tenets presented in this section. You may want to make a copy of this form and utilize it directly with your team for developmental purposes!

• EMPLOYEE'S PERFORMANCE APPRAISAL •

Name Of Employee

Appraisal Period

Job Title

Evaluator / Title

RATINGS

Exceeds Expectations
Meets Expectations
Needs Improvement

1.0 GENERAL PERFORMANCE

❏ ❏ ❏ 1.1 MAINTAINS PUNCTUALITY. Employee observes assigned work hours in a punctual manner.

❏ ❏ ❏ 1.2 MAINTAINS REGULAR ATTENDANCE. Employee can be depended on to report to work regularly with few unplanned absences. Provides proper notification when absent.

❏ ❏ ❏ 1.3 COMPLIANCE WITH DEPARTMENT POLICIES AND PROCEDURES. Understands and follows department policies and procedures.

❏ ❏ ❏ 1.4 JUDGMENT AND DECISION MAKING. Demonstrates ability to make sound judgments; makes appropriate and effective decisions in carrying out duties.

❏ ❏ ❏ 1.5 DEPENDABILITY. Extent to which you can depend on employee to apply himself/herself to task, use time correctly, carry out instructions, and follow assignments through to completion.

❏ ❏ ❏ 1.6 PROFESSIONALISM AND WORK HABITS. Demonstrates pride in the job and conducts self in a professional manner in the performance of job duties; identifies with the purpose of the department.

❏ ❏ ❏ 1.7 ASSUMES EXTRA RESPONSIBILITIES. Employee accepts and/or volunteers for extra responsibilities beyond normal job duties in order to improve self and the services provided by the department.

RATINGS

Exceeds Expectations
Meets Expectations
Needs Improvement

2.0 JOB PERFORMANCE AND KNOWLEDGE

❏ ❏ ❏ 2.1 QUALITY OF WORK. Demonstrates accuracy, neatness, and thoroughness in performing job duties.

❏ ❏ ❏ 2.2 QUANTITY OF WORK. Demonstrates ability to meet required work output; performs the required volume of work without sacrificing quality.

❏ ❏ ❏ 2.3 JOB KNOWLEDGE. Possesses and demonstrates necessary knowledge and skills to accomplish job duties and responsibilities. Uses experience effectively to enhance work performance.

❏ ❏ ❏ 2.4 TIME MANAGEMENT AND ORGANIZATIONAL SKILLS. Demonstrates ability to effectively plan and organize work; demonstrates effective use of time management practices; completes tasks on a timely basis.

❏ ❏ ❏ 2.5 TRAINING AND SELF-IMPROVEMENT. Utilizes effectively what is learned in training; makes effort to obtain on-the-job training and to improve skills and knowledge for advancement and improved job performance.

3.0 ADAPTABILITY AND INITIATIVE

❏ ❏ ❏ 3.1 PROBLEM SOLVING. Demonstrates ability to solve problems effectively.

❏ ❏ ❏ 3.2 ADAPTABILITY. Adapts well to changes in job and in the work environment, and adjusts well to new situations.

❏ ❏ ❏ 3.3 INITIATIVE. Demonstrates ability to motivate self in attaining work objectives, with little or no supervision needed.

❏ ❏ ❏ 3.4 CREATIVITY/INNOVATION. Employee demonstrates new and creative ideas in carrying out job duties and makes constructive suggestions for seeking new and improved procedures.

❏ ❏ ❏ 3.5 PERFORMANCE UNDER STRESS. Demonstrates the ability to perform well in stressful situations, prioritize effectively, and meet deadlines without sacrificing quality of work.

RATINGS

Exceeds Expectations | Meets Expectations | Needs Improvement

4.0 INTERPERSONAL RELATIONSHIPS

❏ ❏ ❏   4.1   ATTITUDE. Demonstrates cooperative attitude with fellow employees and willingness to share responsibilities as part of the work team; displays positive attitude towards work and fellow employees.

❏ ❏ ❏   4.2   RELATIONSHIP WITH SUPERVISORS. Employee responds positively to supervision, direction, and constructive criticism.

❏ ❏ ❏   4.3   DEALING WITH PUBLIC. Employee demonstrates tact and patience in dealing with others; promotes good public relations and effective working relationships with others.

❏ ❏ ❏   4.4   DEALING WITH CLIENTS. Relationship with clients is firm but fair; demonstrates positive regard towards clients, and treats them with decency and respect.

5.0 COMMUNICATION SKILLS

❏ ❏ ❏   5.1   WRITTEN COMMUNICATION SKILLS. Demonstrates high level of competency in written expression, including written reports and correspondence; uses grammar and syntax correctly and expresses ideas clearly and succinctly.

❏ ❏ ❏   5.2   VERBAL COMMUNICATION SKILLS. Demonstrates competency in oral expression and listening; expresses thoughts clearly; listens and understands oral instructions and information so that actions reflect that understanding.

❏ ❏ ❏   5.3   CONTRIBUTES TO OPEN COMMUNICATION WITHIN DEPARTMENT. Interacts with peers and supervisors in such a manner that good rapport is maintained within the department; follows the established chain-of-command.

6.0 SUPERVISORY FACTORS

This section is to be completed only for those employees who perform supervisory functions as part of their job duties with the department. Supervisory personnel are to be evaluated in Section 6.0 as well as all previous sections.

RATINGS

Exceeds Expectations

Meets Expectations

Needs Improvement

❑ ❑ ❑   6.1   UNDERSTANDING OF DUTIES. Understands the duties, functions, and responsibilities of the supervisory position and the proper role of a supervisor; understands mission of department and adequately represents position of management.

❑ ❑ ❑   6.2   LEADERSHIP SKILLS. Demonstrates leadership qualities by setting an example of excellence and dedication for subordinates to follow; motivates subordinates to perform duties to optimum level of abilities.

❑ ❑ ❑   6.3   EFFECTIVE SUPERVISION. Supervises subordinates effectively in order to maximize their performance and produce the desired quantity and quality of work; exerts authority when necessary.

❑ ❑ ❑   6.4   ORGANIZATIONAL SKILLS. Demonstrates effective use of organizational skills in order to keep section & subordinates working in a cohesive and organized manner; good knowledge of all aspects of work of section.

❑ ❑ ❑   6.5   RELATIONSHIP WITH SUBORDINATES. Encourages "open-door" policy with subordinates; deals with all subordinates in a fair and impartial manner.

❑ ❑ ❑   6.6   INTERPERSONAL SUPERVISORY SKILLS. Demonstrates effective interpersonal relationship practices with peers, subordinates, and management, so as to foster good communications within the department; effectively and properly uses the chain-of-command.

❑ ❑ ❑   6.7   STAFF DEVELOPMENT. Effectively promotes the improvement and development of staff and subordinates; contributes to the overall staff development of the department through formal training sessions and other activities.

❑ ❑ ❑   6.8   COMPLIANCE WITH FEDERAL GUIDELINES. Supervisor is aware of and performs duties in compliance with FLSA, EEOC, ADA, and other applicable federal guidelines regarding personnel matter.

EMPLOYEE DEVELOPMENT PLAN

a.   Discuss areas of exceptional and noteworthy performance:

_____

_____

_____

_____

_____

_____

b.   Outline and describe specific areas needing improvement and designate areas where employee can develop additional skills. (NOTE: Ratings of "Needs Improvement" must be explained.)

_____

_____

_____

_____

_____

_____

c.   Describe projected goals for employee. Provide plan for implementation of goals and dates for follow-up:

_____

_____

_____

_____

_____

_____

d.   Recommended training to enhance employee's plan of action:

_____

_____

_____

_____

EMPLOYEE'S COMMENTS: (Additional sheets may be attached)

_____

_____

_____

_____

_____

_____

_____

_____

_____

_____

_____

_____

_____

_____

SIGNATURES: By my signature below, I hereby acknowledge that my supervisor/team leader has reviewed this evaluation with me and I acknowledge receipt of same. My signature does not necessarily imply my agreement with this evaluation.

_____   _____

EMPLOYEE   DATE

_____   _____

EVALUATOR / SUPERVISOR   DATE

REVIEWER'S OR DIRECTOR'S COMMENTS:

_____

_____

_____

_____

_____

REVIEWER'S SIGNATURE:_____DATE: _____

Upward Feedback: Accelerate the growth and development of not only the team player, but also the leader of the team (whether that is the manager, supervisor, team leader, boss, etc.) through some sort of upward feedback system! This can be accomplished by allowing, or even expecting, that all members of a work group (team, department organization, etc.) that are direct responsibilities or reports to manager level personnel be allowed to utilize the same appraisal system to regularly evaluate and appraise the management team!

This process can be very discomforting to some people and can actually lead to destructive behaviors and attitudes if not constructed in a positive productive manner. There are some safe guards which should be considered to ensure peak performance here. Consider:

> • **First** - Each member of a team has the opportunity to participate in upward feedback sessions on a regular basis (just as often as *Self-Analysis, Peer Reviews*, and *Organizational Appraisals* occur).

> • **Second** - All members must sign the upward feedback instrument; if they don't sign it, the appraisal is void. It is easy to criticize another person anonymously.

> • **Third** - Just as with the other appraisal systems, areas noted as challenges and difficulties for a person must be followed by the appraiser's notations for suggested *action plans* for future growth and desired success behaviors. The intent of this tool is for the development and growth of the leadership team, just as the other tools are designed to develop the player.

> • **Fourth** - The upward feedback can be delivered in person or tendered as a stack for review by the party in question. The management player can then meet one-on-one or as a group to brainstorm how to become more effective as a team and the team leader!

Chapter 13

Powerful Steps To Convert Negativity To Positive Outcomes: 22 Conversion Strategies For Changing A Negative Person Or Situation Into A Positive Outcome

"Difficulty and negativity is perception of a reality. How you view a reality impacts what you will experience emotionally, psychologically and physically. And it is how you respond (not react) that determines your effectiveness and happiness!"
• Jeffrey L. Magee

Powerful Steps To Convert Negativity To Positive Outcomes: 22 Conversion Strategies For Changing A Negative Person Or Situation Into A Positive Outcome

Challenge, change, conflict, confusion, communication cracks and confrontation can all contribute to levels of tension, frustration, difficulty and bottom-line negativity in a professional environment. When negativity develops in a professional environment it can lead to paralysis and stagnation of an otherwise effective team. Working to counter and even eliminate negativity in the professional environment, or being able to control and effectively deal with negative stimulants when they do arise is necessary for both management personnel and players alike.

Think about it. How many times have you heard negative comments or voices? How many times have you heard a negative voice in your own mind talking to you about something or someone which led to inner stress and anxiety for you? When this happens, reflect upon how much time is being distracted from productive causes and inwardly manifesting additional negative thoughts. All the while productivity suffers and personal health pays the price!

If you find yourself in similar situations or you observe that members of your team become unfocused due to challenging or negative stimulants, then as the lead player on the team, accountability has to start with you to stimulate some positives. Consider how negativity in most forms can impact a player's and, thus, an organization's performance and proactiveness. A few recent case studies have shown that:

> • A 1980s Gallup Study commissioned by Rev. Robert Schuller indicated that roughly 80 percent of adults in America viewed

themselves as having "low self-esteem!" The more one is subjected to negativity and stimulants which do not reinforce one's positives, the lower one's self-esteem factor may be. The lower the self-esteem factor, the lower one's peak performance factor is (see Chapter Nine)!

• How you view stimulants directly impacts individual and team interaction effectiveness. Harvard University reports from a 1990s study that an immigrant to America in the 1990s (specifically) has 4:1 greater odds of becoming a millionaire in their life time than does a person born and raised in America all of their life! Why?

The answer is easy. It is reflected in how a person views stimulants. Are they roadblocks and challenges or are they opportunities and fortunes. It lies in the eyes of the experienced participant!

So how does management focus energies on a negative situation or person and work to convert that unpleasantness to a positive situation or person. The process of stimulating a change in behaviors follows a *three-step interaction process*. You can accomplish these three conditioning steps in a number of ways (we will present 22 strategies and techniques), it does not really matter which. What does matter is that whatever course of action you pursue, you first reflect upon these three steps and accomplish each, one at a time, before progressing to the next and subsequent step.

A violation of any one of the three basic and primary conditioning steps will impact each outcome and could lead toward greater negativity and frustration!

Before you can convert a negative to a positive, there is a three-step sequence or formula that should be followed for lasting impact and results. Each step can be very involved or very simple, it is a subjective response depending upon what it is that management is faced with and which management alternatives are being exercised as one's management style at a given point in time. Consider:

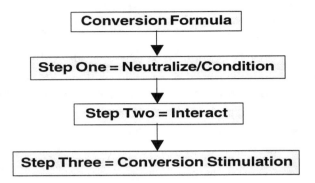

There are going to be times when you have authority and control powers to stimulate positive change through the utilization of some of these strategies and techniques and there will also be times when you cannot stimulate the change you desire. In those situations the best course of action will be to manage the challenge. There are more than 22 powerful conversion strategies, here are just some.

> • *Avoidance* - When you feel a negative situation about to develop or a negative conversation about to start (based upon prior experience and knowledge), then simply walk away from that negative. If you are not a willing participant with a negative person and don't take part in the interaction, there can be no negative encounter. Don't get sucked into negative zones.

> • *Don't Argue* - It takes two to debate and argue and if you're not a willing, active participant it becomes difficult for the other party to continue his disruptive behavior. When a conversation moves from issues and performance toward people and person-alities, it is time to end a conversation as an individual's emotions when they are wounded lead to significant tensions in professional environments. Convert these situations (oral conversation) into both an oral and visual conversation by immediately writing the issues down on paper so that you can navigate the conversa-

tion and other parties toward the black and white issues and not the side-bar argumentative topics.

• *Isolation* - There are two ways this can be interpreted. First, you can maintain your distance from those people or situations over which you have no control and which you know to be negative. Keep yourself isolated from them and focused upon other activities. (Idle time gets everyone into trouble in the face of negativity.) Second, there are times when a person may be negative, have a bad attitude or pose difficulty in certain situations, yet his presence is needed for other reasons. Then isolate them from other players. Keep him focused and busy at what he does best and don't allow him to have idle time to interact with other players on a team. Remember that negative people can become very toxic to a productive organization and you may need to interact as both MANAGER and COUNSELOR with these people should the negativity in them persist.

• *Garner Prior Support* - Identify your positive support network, those that will benefit from change or something new or different which you are enacting and interact with them prior to interfacing with the entire team. Gain support from your TRANSFORMERS (see Chapter Two) and strategically utilize them to motivate others.

• *Seek Linkage* - Identify key factors in your position and in that of the other party and link an aspect of the two together to establish common ground and linkage of the two positions. This tends to diffuse otherwise seemingly differing views and positions held by individuals and will stimulate a higher degree of interaction for a mutually desirable outcome. It becomes difficult for a combative or negative person to remain so on a winning team when you are tying elements from everyone's positions together. It also becomes very difficult to keep pointing the finger of blame or guilt at other people when there are at least minimal elements of linkage among the parties' positions. Linkage is a powerful diffusing strategy which allows you to interact successfully with others.

• *Double Standards* - By utilizing double standards, you can sometimes illustrate hyprocrisy and present an alternative point of view. For example, consider the double standard society has with regard to actions exhibited by men and women.

A man, can be assertive in a professional environment and be viewed as assertive. Perhaps if overly assertive he may be viewed as aggressive, pushy or even overbearing. Yet, if a woman is assertive in a professional environment, there is a very good likelihood that she would be seen as not aggressive, pushy or overbearing. She would be viewed when overassertive as a B _ _ _ _ (double standard)! By illustrating your position through a double standard you can assist the other party in non-confrontationally seeing another view-point!

• *Assign 100 Percent Accountability* - An explosive strategy for converting a consistently negative stimulant (your TERRORIST from Chapter Two) into a more participatory player on the team is to prepare your actions ahead of time so that the next time a player challenges your positions, merely allow him the pleasure of assuming 100 percent accountability for that task or project that he professes to be the expert on and on which he has been challenging you or other players. Assign 100 percent accountability, with no strings attached, and walk away.

• *Visualized Statements Required* - Another powerful technique for diffusing a negative person is to request or recommend that when he challenges a position or statement you have asserted, he, in turn, take his perspectives and ideas and write each down on paper with the associated rationale. Once written down, then the two parties should get back together to discuss them logically and calmly. A player that merely likes to challenge others will quickly back off from instigating negativity and tension if he learns that in response the other party is not going to participate in a verbal bashing match, but will engage in dialogue once he has written everything down!

• *Cost-Benefit Analysis* - Conduct a survey or study to illustrate in black and white the costs and benefits associated with a position, task or project which may cause controversy so that all parties will have documentation and not allegations on which to base decisions. Costs can be measured in player, environmental and physical factors.

• *Identify Distortion(s) And Immediately Examine* - When a negative statement, distortion or embellished statement is made that is misleading and which may cause further negativity, immediately stop an interaction and examine that individual factor - to determine and educate all parties as to reality and factuality. If you ignore a misstatement and allow it to go on and on, there will have been far too many misstatements made to be able to effectively go back and sort through and deal with each. Take each as it comes and as you first hear it. If you are consistent in your behavior here, the negative person will eventually learn that his behavior doesn't work with you and you will see a change in him.

• *Have Most Vocal Objector State His Position In Advance* - If you know that there may be a colleague present at a meeting who is opposed to you or your position and that he will eventually challenge you, put him on notice and turn the environmental conditioning factors around.

For example, immediately after presenting your idea turn toward your perceived negativist and ask him for feedback in terms of what his feelings are with regard to what you have just said. At this point you have merely asked a nonconfrontational question and peer pressure is on your side because, as you ask the question, everyone in the room will be looking toward the colleague to whom you have asked the question.

• *Breathing Pattern Adjustment* - When confronted with a challenging and/or negative situation or person you may experience a change in your breathing patterns. You may feel a shortness of breath, tight shoulders, tense limbs and a tight forehead resulting in a headache. Whether this happens while in a meeting situation, while on the telephone, in traffic or after leaving a face-to-face encounter, take a couple of minutes (two to three minutes will work) to control and adjust your breathing patterns. First, force yourself to inhale through your nose every breath for this period. Second, exhale each breath in this time period through your mouth. By changing your normal breathing pattern to this sequence for a period of a few minutes, you will relax psychologically because this breathing pattern relaxes you physiologically.

With a relaxed physical state you can regain control of your emotions and stimulate your logic track.

• *Avoid Challenge Words* - Work to remove words which may stimulate additional anger or negativity with combative or negative people. Words that cause confrontation with others are words like: however, you, but, opinion, think, and, ...

• *Utilize Ownership Words* - In dealing with people, whether you know them or not, replace challenge words with ownership words. These are words that don't stimulate any negativity or challenge when heard by others. In essence these are words that make it appear that you are pointing fingers at yourself and not another person. They are words like: we, us, team, I, feel, ...

• *Go One-On-One In Private* - With persistent, challenging players in an organization, you may choose to meet with them one-on-one in private (see Chapter Nine for COUNSELING ideas) to address the differing positions which you and the other parties have. This may be uncomfortable for you as a management player, but this may be a very educational experience for both you and the other person involved.

• *Stimulate A Conversation* - There are six very effective and quick ways to initiate a conversation with another person in a non-confrontational manner. There is an adage which says, "the one doing the talking and the one who talks first loses." This could lead to a confrontation with another person if you are face-to-face and no one wants to talk first for fear of losing. However, you can control a conversation while at the same time not dominating it.

The six fastest ways to motivate the other party to open up and talk so that you can direct the interaction toward agreement and proactiveness among the players involved is to start off your statement with: WHO, WHAT, WHEN, WHERE, WHY, and HOW. These six words alone are powerful openers. Remember: W, W, W, W, W, H!

• *Three Up* - When someone disagrees with you or another player, don't argue and don't defend your position (that is what he has come to expect and leads to confrontation). Request that the challenging player provide three alternatives to what he disagrees with. You may find a new and more effective solution or you may nonconfrontationally communicate to the other players - put up or shut up!

• *Demand An Alternative: Three Times* - Another very explosive technique to convert a routine negativist into either a TRANS-MITTER or TRANSFORMER is to halt conversations when someone else disagrees with you and move the conversation in a new direction using the six words presented above to gain another alternative or a nonresponse. Demand this alternative at least three times before you allow the conversation to proceed and before you let the other player off the hook.

For example: "What do you feel we should do?" If they have a nonresponse, don't proceed. Stay right on that question for a second try. "Really, what do you feel we could do, if this idea isn't realistic?" Another nonresponse, ask one final or third time, "No, really what do you feel we could do?"

• *Relocate* - Remove the task or issue at hand that causes the tension. If giving XYZ to player "A" will cause trauma and it will cause trauma every time, then remove that item to another player. In essence, relocate the negativity to another player where it will not be seen as a negative. Or relocate the issue and challenge from your accountability to another player or team/committee to deal with. Relocate it entirely (see additional examples and strategies as outlined in Chapter Nine in the *Delegation Dynamics* sub-section).

• *Empathy* - Another powerful diffusing strategy for increased interaction effectiveness is to acknowledge the other person's position. Empathy means acknowledgment, it does not mean that you agree or disagree with another person's position. Most challenging or negative people on your teams have learned throughout life that in order to get acknowledged, they have to be difficult for a prolonged period of time. If you acknowledge them immediately, it throws them off their mental track and puts you directly into control.

• *Blend With Them* - Look for a position that a challenging player has asserted that you can live with and join up with him. Your merging with him is least expected and also serves to neutralize him for successful interaction and subsequent conversion.

• *Increase Your "VAK" Communications* - As you interact with players in stressed environments or challenging and unpleasant situations, you should work to communicate each message through all three channels (see Chapter Ten) to eliminate any misunderstanding. Communicate each thought and signal through Visual, Auditory and Kinesthetic channels.

Converting negatives to positives is possible. Don't run or hide from negativity - face it head on for success!

Chapter 14

Principle-Centered Negotiation: Leveraging For Win / Win Outcomes

"In life you get what you negotiate for,
not what you want or deserve."
• Dr. Chester L. Karrass

"God's gift to us is life. Our gift back is
how we live that life. So ask yourself,
what am I giving?"
• Les Brown, Jr.

Principle-Centered Negotiation: Leveraging For Win / Win Outcomes

To effectively pull together resources and lead people of differing need levels and perspectives, effective management personnel need to possess or understand the tenets of power negotiation. Your ability to practice, in essence, negotiation jujitsu becomes critical to leadership effectiveness.

View negotiation as the art of interacting with differing need levels and interests of individuals who, for the most part, have similar end goals, merely differing views on how to obtain those results. You have to navigate those differences to attain organizational and personal net results. So what is negotiation? Think of negotiation in the following terms:

> • It is a process.
> • It involves posturing and positioning.
> • It is a well planned out series of events, actions, strategies and tactics!
> • It is a learned skill level.
> • It involves artfully designed questions.
> • It is verbal and nonverbal language/powerful body language.
> • It is a psychological process.
> • It involves give-and-take (gambits) actions!

The key factors of an effective negotiation process involve and focus efforts on four key elements. Consider:

> • Attack the *issues or problem* and never the people representing them.
> • Handle *interests* and not positions.
> • Brainstorm mutual *options*.
> • Rely upon *objective* standards and criteria to be used.

Setting a solid foundation from which to negotiate is critical to effective negotiation and successful outcomes. The power of your negotiation process comes down to two approaches. What you do before the negotiation process - or strategy - and what you then become capable of doing during the negotiation - tactics - dictate your negotiation strength, position, insight, and ability to finesse the interaction towards mutually acceptable outcomes, which address each party's true *need levels*!

Start by asking yourself what the attitude is among the players involved in the negotiation process. If the attitudes are neutral to positive, then you can expect healthy productive interactions and dialogue. However, if some of the players entering into this process have negative attitudes, then effective leadership would suggest that the initial focus needs to be either on neutralizing (conditioning) that negative player's attitude or eliminating that player from the dynamics of the interaction or group - they can easily become *Terrorists* (see Chapter Two for more on the subgroups in life) and thus sabotage your efforts and plans.

Before the negotiation process. Consider the following points and how they relate to you and your positioning. Each of the following subsections has a powerful impact on your planning processes and thus impacts your ultimate effectiveness once face-to-face in the negotiation process.

There are specific traits of effective negotiators and many experts believe that some commonly shared traits of successful negotiators are:

- Ability to plan and organize the process effectively.
- Realization that negotiation is always interactive and incorporates give-and-take situations.
- Ability to think clearly under pressure.
- Desire to acquire additional knowledge and skills.
- Commands good verbal ability and listening skills.
- Understanding of how "gambits" work.
- Has personal power and practices the skills everywhere.
- Studies the process continually.
- Ability to perceive and exploit power points.
- Ability to be persistent and maintain patience.

There are multiple need levels that all parties involved in a negotiation are seeking to have addressed and met. These need levels can be broken down into two categories and an effective negotiator attempts to identify these two need levels before entering into a negotiation process with another party. The two need levels are: Minimum Acceptable Needs and Maximum Desired Needs.

By identifying your Minimum Need level you will be able to focus your efforts on when it is best for you to walk away from the negotiation process and not be taken advantage of. And in reverse, if you can identify what the Minimum Need level of the other party is prior to a negotiation process, then you will know how much bargaining room or leverage you have and, therefore, what the other party's walk-away point will be.

These two need levels allow you to measure the negotiation and bargaining process. Remember, knowledge and information are critical to a negotiation process and the more you have prior to the actual interactions the better you will be able to prepare and strategize your moves, presentation, offer and tactics!

In preparing your negotiation and positioning yourself for maximum interaction and leadership, consider the entire negotiation process in three basic modules: Before, During, and After. Also, realize that there are three primary components which will impact your negotiation: The Situation, The Timing, and, the Players or people involved. I call this simply the *"STP Factor"* © of the Negotiation process.

The more you know and understand the *"STP Factor"* ©, the better off you will be in the actual negotiation process!

These elements will all assist you in preparing your *Best Course of Actions* (BCOA ©) and your *Best Course of Interactions* (BCOI ©) in the negotiation process - turn traditional hindsight into desired foresight!

Along with this prenegotiation activity effective leaders also identify the dynamics of the personalities who will be participating in the negotiation process and play to each specific personality's requirements.

There are endless ways to measure and determine a personality style or type and the number of personality measuring models and instruments available to management and organizational leaders seems endless. Given your own abilities in determining a personality style, the following matrix is merely another tool you can reference in determining one's personality style at a given point in time.

Therefore, the answer from this personality matrix and the acknowledgment will further assist you in preparing your interactions and will also have a great impact on how you may or may not approach and interact with another individual. Make allowances and adjustments to your interaction style based upon what another personality style would indicate you need to do to maximize your efforts with them!

Basically, personality will fall into one of four primary personality zones based on environmental factors and one's beliefs at any given time. Change the factors and a person's primary personality may also temporarily change. In plotting a person on the following matrix to determine his personality, always plot the vertical axis first and then the horizontal axis. From those two plot marks bisect the two and determine in which of the four zones the person would fall - and to what degree. You can then determine what adjustments you need to make to move from your personality style toward his for best interaction effectiveness.

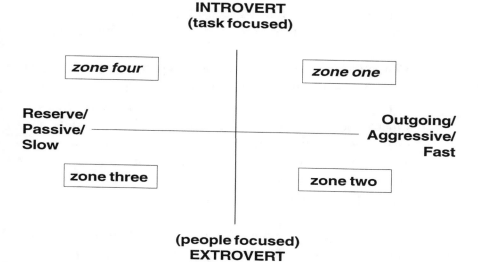

INTROVERT
(task focused)

zone four   zone one

Reserve/   Outgoing/
Passive/   Aggressive/
Slow   Fast

zone three   zone two

(people focused)
EXTROVERT

As you identify your or another person's personality style based on the previous chart, you will note that it falls into one of the four personality zones (one, two, three, and/or four). A person's personality style will give you tremendous insight to how a person may think and feel given your interactions and the negotiation process.

The personality styles for each zone can take on many names or titles, you may gauge each zone in the following categories.

> • **Zone One = the Driver** or Type "A" personality style. This person is typically very driven and energized, fast-paced and bottom-line oriented. They tend to be at peak performance when by themselves and not held accountable for others' actions and productivity. They focus on what things mean to them and how they will impact their fast-paced plans toward their goals. Get directly to the point with these people! Change doesn't always bother them and they are fast to adapt to new environments or needs. They tend to be <u>Auditory</u> communicators!

> • **Zone Two = the Coach or Performer** personality style. This person adapts quickly to new environments, tends to be focused toward others' needs levels and seeks action, fun, and interaction with others. They tend to focus on getting others involved and don't mind being held accountable for others' actions. They don't mind group activities and will consider how things impact others decision making. They tend to be <u>Kinesthetic</u> communicators!

> • **Zone Three = the Amiable or Blender** personality style. Tends to be involved with those around them. They don't like the spotlight placed on them and are very sensitive about the needs of others. They tend to be cautious and reserved about change and adapt very slowly to changing environmental concerns. These people can be very productive players, and for the most part, will blend into the environment about them and follow the flow set by others. They tend to be <u>Kinesthetic</u> communicators!

> • **Zone Four = the Critical Thinker or Analytical** personality style may (not always) pose the greatest challenge in an interac-

tion. This personality needs significant data and facts to support any change or new position/proposal. In the negotiation process, keep the presentation and conversation focused on issues and not on feelings or personalities. This player tends to focus in great detail on the status quo and will analyze how the norms of the right now meet needs. Therefore, he will scrutinize any suggestion of change for how it will impact people or organizational dynamics. These players tend to be at peak performance when left alone and don't like the spotlight or having to participate in large situations. They tend to be <u>Visual</u> communicators!

By identifying your personality style and those of the other people that you will encounter in interactions or in negotiation cycles, you can gain a better understanding of how to manage behaviors for desired outcomes. Management will attempt to control personality styles and behaviors, while effective leaders will utilize this new information concerning personalities and lead the interactions and players to desired outcomes - by first managing one's own behavior to interact with others from their perspectives.

Understanding one's personality will assist in the negotiation process in other ways as well. Body language is critical to gaining additional insight in the negotiation process. Each signal is another in a series of subtle clues that will further assist you in directing the interactions toward your desired Minimum and Maximum Need levels. Having determined what another person's personality style is or may be in that given environment, you can then identify more efficiently their non-verbal signals and body language and gauge what those signals may mean to you as you interact, speak, etc. in the negotiation process. Therefore, preparation now meets interaction.

During the negotiation process. Consider all of the advance work and how it can come together for a successful interaction. Whether you are going one-on-one or you are going to engage in a negotiation process consisting of multiple individuals, the effort placed in advance of negotiation will directly impact one's performance during the actual negotiation process. The negotiation process is similar in structure to that of the evolving organizational structure outlined in Chapter Five.

The negotiation process is a cycle and has to managed, while the personalities need to be led through this maze. To minimize the time spent in level or cycle two, prepare effectively for level one and this will enable you to effectively interact in levels three and four. After every negotiation action, invest time in level five to ensure future successes. The negotiation levels or cycles are:

- **Cycle One = Begin**, the start-up stage activities.
- **Cycle Two = Defend**, conflicts and confrontations arise.
- **Cycle Three = Blend**, status quo time and typically where most time is spent maintaining the norms.
- **Cycle Four = Transcend**, where peak performance and significant progress takes place.
- **Cycle Five = End**, or wrap up and final analysis takes place effectively here.

(Refer to Chapter Five for a greater explanation of the five cycles.)

To maintain control during the negotiation process, design and follow an agenda of key or core issues and points which need to be addressed to maintain and attain your Minimum and Maximum Need levels. You can utilize an agenda like the *"Agenda Manager"* ©, as presented in Chapter Nine. This agenda system will allow you to focus on the purpose of the negotiation during the process, focus on attaining that objective(s) in the amount of time allotted, and further assist you in maintaining your negotiation power positions.

During the negotiation process maintain a position of power over and among the other players involved. There are a number of positions which afford you the necessary power to maintain the leverage advantage and authority in the interaction. Consider throughout the process (before and during) what type of power you hold in comparison to the other participants in the negotiation. The more power positions you hold, the more likely you will be to command respect and authority throughout the interaction. Successful leadership and management of the negotiation process incorporates multiple positions of power.

There are eleven core positions of power in a negotiation process. Reflect upon each and identify among the players involved in the negotiation process (the four core personality types/personality zones), which powers are held by which personalities. Work to maintain your power positions and definitely draw upon them during your interaction to maintain control and to enable yourself to work toward your Minimum and Maximum Need levels.

Power positioning can be attained in many ways. An effective negotiator maintains and grows power in both traditional and nontraditional ways. Consider your position of power and how you can attain additional powers. Power sources come from:

- Personal Power
- Professional Power
- Influence Power
- Legitimacy or Reputation Power
- Commitment Power
- Aggression & Patience Power
- Knowledge Power
- Experience Power
- Competition Power
- Courage Power
- Bargaining Power
- Time & Effort Power
- Age/Background Power

These are just some of the sources of power that can be drawn upon to navigate your interactions. The actual interaction activities of the nego- tiation process - referred to as *tactics* - draw from your position of strength (power). Consider some of the following *tactics* for utilization in interacting with others to manage the interaction and to enable you to obtain a successful outcome.

- **Fractionate** - Take the core issue and break it down into individual and smaller component parts for discussion and agreement. Take the negotiation process one step at a time. This is an especially effective technique when disagreements arise. This technique also helps in moving the conversation forward one manageable step at a time.

• **Nibbling** - When an ambitious agenda is placed before you, take one piece at a time and work on it. Address and resolve one issue or point at a time and then move onward to the next. Nibbling can also be used when you are wanting to attain more than your Minimum Need level. You can nibble your way through the agenda and toward your Maximum Need levels and wants.

• **Mini-Agreements** - Work toward attaining as quickly as possible as many mini-agreements from the agenda issues as possible. From these mini-agreements you can then successfully work your way toward desired outcomes. The more mini-agreements attained, the more options afforded to you. Should your interaction reach a point of difference of position or opinion - back up to your last place of agreement.

• **Linkage** - Work to tie parts of your positions into parts of the other parties' positions. This linkage works to reduce tensions and positions of opposition.

• **Walk-Away Zone** - By pre-identifying that point in the negotiation where you are better served by walking away than staying engaged in the conversation, the other party many times will make significant concessions to get you back to the negotiation table.

• **Ask For Higher Authority** - When you reach a stalemate in the negotiation process with the other player, you may be able to instill life back into the process by asking to continue the negotiation process with a different person of higher authority. Change the players and sometimes you can change the situation!

• **Utilize Provoking Questions** - Rely upon open-ended and strategically designed questions to get the other party talking and working toward your desired directions in the negotiation process. The fastest questions that can lead toward this result are: Who, What, When, Where, Why, and, How.

• **Invent Options** - When there seems to be a breakdown in the discussion and negotiation points, make up alternatives or options with which the parties involved can work.

• **Qualify Concessions** - Should you desire to concede a position or point to the other party, always make sure that you qualify the concession so that the other party realizes that you are offering something. Only then can you utilize that concession strategically later in the relationship or negotiation process.

• **Stall** - Sometimes the other party may be pushing for a decision or commitment. A little stall for time may make the other party a little uncomfortable, and, their discomfort may give you further indication as to what their position is. Don't offer up a decision quickly, utilize the stall to reinforce your position or your last statement/offer.

• **Use A "Bogey"** - A trial offer or idea can also afford you insight to the other person and his need levels. At periodical intervals in the negotiation process, offer up to the other party some little bogeys or offers to gauge his position and receptiveness.

The negotiation process is a series of interactions and decisions, all of which impact the next interaction and decision (reference the *"Anatomy Of A Negotiation"* © diagram on the following page). Managed correctly, the negotiation process can always be a win / win, fair / fair outcome.

After the negotiation process. Invest private time after every negotiation to determine what took place before and during which impacted the outcome. Mentally and, if appropriate, physically make notes (reflect upon your agenda, the players involved, etc.) as to the entire interaction, so that future interactions of a similar nature will be managed even more efficiently!

Consider the following diagram as a negotiation facilitation tool (face-to-face, via telecommunications or through correspondence negotiation), as you plan your interaction - Before/During/After the process.

There are three distinct phases to the tool and you should utilize it as a reference for questions to be asked in search of data and answers to fit into each appropriate part of the diagram. The party with the answers to each part is in the position to initiate and facilitate the conversation toward a positive resolution. What is powerful about the *"Anatomy Of A Negotiation"*© is that it enables the user to see exactly what information is known and what is needed. The tool also allows the user to focus the conversation on quadrants three and four, as that is where common points of interest will be found and from which a nonconfrontational conversation can be developed.

Anatomy Of A Negotiation©

- minimum need level
- maximum need level

- minimum need level
- maximum need level

Player/Party One	**Player/Party Two**
Position = WHAT this side wants!	**Position = WHAT** this side wants!
1	2
3	4
Interest = WHY this side wants *what* they want!	**Interest = WHY** this side wants *what* they want!

Points of Linkage = **Common Ground**

Reminder: *How to use this tool.* **First** - engage in a dialogue to identify the answers to quadrants one through four. If you already know an answer then move forward to the quadrants where there are unknown variables. **Second** - identify both parties' need levels (minimum being worse acceptable case scenario and maximum being best possible case scenario). This can be determined through questions, observations, referencing previous interactions, etc. **Third** - you now begin your negotiation interaction by identifying mutual points of interest and work from quadrants three and four only! Quadrants one and two will never yield resolutions, as both parties are busy protecting their territory - Position. The *WHY* factors typically yield Common Ground!

Effective leaders and managers in today's workplace need to be effective negotiators to maintain forward focus for solutions among players!

Chapter 15

The Leadership Advantage: Putting Together A Winning Management Game Plan

"If you're not fired with enthusiasm,
you will be fired with enthusiasm!"
• Vince Lombardi

"When a mind is allowed to wonder and wander,
creativity is allowed to grow and alas anything
is possible.

Be open, don't self-restrict and allow
yourself to grow with and for others ..."
• Jeff Magee

The Leadership Advantage: Putting Together A Winning Management Game Plan

The management advantage for future success starts with the understanding and utilization of techniques designed in *The Leadership Alternative*!

Management effectiveness is both an art and a science. There are three key characteristics which must be present for effective management players to develop into effective leaders. The Gallup Poll organization in 1992 conducted a study of key factors sought in management and by leaders positioned to guide others. The poll determined that three factors were universally sought:

> • First, *Likability* in the person must be present.
> • Second, *Believability* in the person and his position.
> • Third, *Persuasive Skills* in interacting, communicating and managing others must be present.

Consider how you measure up to these national benchmarks for management excellence. Ultimately management and leadership must:

> ... realize that it is a ***process***, whereby (you, I, we)
> attempt to ***influence the behaviors*** of others. Once you
> start the process there is no stopping or turning back.
> The commitment moves you forward!

As you measure your self-development and management growth with the ideas mapped here, consider this book to be a resource for present and future interactions. Consider the following page as a map of the management alternative process to organizational success. You can adopt these steps in your present management paradigm and use them to assist you in making appropriate management paradigm shifts for greater success and productivity!

THE LEADERSHIP ALTERNATIVE!

4 Core Alternate Management Styles

5 Constantly Fluctuating Organizational Levels Of Operation

5 Critical Mission Statements For Operational Success

Your FIST Factor ® Influences Your And Others Actions

Objectively Analyze Your Players For A Winning Team

Organize Yourself To Sustain Your Success Quotient

Empowering Others: Each Subgroup Member Individually

Improving Interactive Communication: VAK System

Interview, Hire And Promote Efficiently

On-Going Systems Of Measurement And Analysis

Repeat Process And Reflect Upon Success Stories Around You

This map can be applied to your working environment and to the specific players on your team in many ways. Sometimes management finds that it is easier to manage in the same traditional ways, regardless of effectiveness. Managing is not a matter of right or wrong, good or bad. It is a matter of effectively utilizing yourself and the resources around you in the wisest fashion. Once a resource is utilized it cannot be retracted.

For others in the management level of an organization, putting together a gameplan for action or response to a concern is also a difficult matter. Putting a game plan together should not be difficult, merely a step-by-step encounter. Consider the following game plan as an example of action to stimulate productivity.

SIX-STEP GAME PLAN

Step One: Identify the person in question: _____

Step Two: Identify the issue in question: _____
_____

Step Three: Identify through the *"SA Model"* © which management style to utilize for your next interaction with this player: _____

Step Four: Identify what your *best course of action (BCOA)* could be with at least one back-up plan: _____
_____
_____
_____

Step Five: Identify the best time and location for this encounter: ___
_____

Step Six: Identify and mutually agree to a follow-up plan to ensure the integrity and success of this interaction: _____
_____!

Management is not an exacting science, yet all around the professional market there are examples of successful management players and leaders, as well as ample examples of walking nightmares in management. Remember, there are always alternatives to how one manages people for increased success and persuasion!

With the ability to interact with, manage and inspire others to greater levels of accomplishment, management players evolve into the fifth management style - leader! Consider what your management alternatives can be and how you can best interact and inspire others.

To gain *"The Leadership Advantage,"* you must realize that all four of the management styles detailed in this text, in part, make up the effective leadership qualities and attributes of a winning leader. The ability to put a workable management game plan before others and see it through to completion also incorporates leadership abilities. Leaders are not born, nor are they created by someone else. Leadership comes from inside a person when that person understands the five different mission statements, has solid values and strongly believes in something - then the leadership and take-initiative abilities come to the surface. For some, these leadership *flashes* are irregular events, while for others these leadership *flashes* are channeled, harnessed and directed in a systematic direction for success on a regular basis.

"The Leadership Advantage" comes from the ability to recognize that all four of the management styles (**MANAGER, MENTOR, COUNSELOR, COACH**) comprise the differing attributes of a successful leader. A leader has to realize the time and place to utilize a specific management style (or in essence when to wear which management hat) and whether or not a capable player exists on a team. Take this leadership style one step further.

A leader must know when to interact with a player or group to encourage, inspire, adjust attitudes and push others (**COACH**); when to strategically and surgically interact with a challenge or threat and deal positively with or remove others from the environment (**COUNSELOR**); how to establish a framework, set foundations, design structure, initiate training and educational systems and establish protocol (**MANAGER**); and when to guide, encourage, share with others and subtly motivate (**MENTOR**) others to successful outcomes!

Leadership involves having and understanding the mission vision of that organization's purpose and understanding the holistic picture and how everything comes together for the ultimate needs, desires and expectations of an organization and the overall good of the players. The inward *flashes* and core flame that burn toward leadership are rooted in something more significant than words, desires, mission statements and visions - it is rooted within one's unique and individual spirit and spirituality.

Leaders are guided by an inward energy and cause (spirit) and it is this energy which propels one toward greatness. Vaclav Havel (playright, dissident, prisoner and president of Czechoslovakia) as he was speaking before the United States Congress reflected upon democracy and leadership:

> "As long as people are people, democracy, in the full sense of the word, will always be no more than an ideal. In this sense, you, too, are merely approaching democracy uninterruptedly for more than 200 years, and your journey toward the horizon has never been disrupted by a totalitarian system...
>
> We must all learn many things from you, from how to educate our offspring, how to elect our representatives, all the way to how to organize our economic life so that it will lead to prosperity and not to poverty...
>
> The salvation of this human world lies nowhere else than in the human heart, in the human power to reflect, in human meekness and in human responsibility. Without a global revolution in the sphere of human consciousness, nothing will change for the better in the sphere of our being as humans...
>
> It is the fundamental factor in the movement of history. Spirit is. Consciousness is. Human awareness is. Thought is. Spirituality is. Those are the deep sources of freedom and power with which leaders rise and people can be led to move boulders and create change!"

A leader is a person who recognizes that consciousness precedes being. A leader is a person who holds the unusual power and ability to project his view and shadow, in essence, on others. A leader takes responsibility for establishing and creating the conditions from which people operate and live. These conditions start first from what is going on within the leader and his consciousness. This inward activity guides the leader's actions outward. How a person manages the inward forces impacts how the leader utilizes the four management styles and comes across to others. This impacts how others will, therefore, follow a leader or whether the people will conspire and work toward the downfall of a leader.

There are warning points to effective leadership as well, and they validate the need for effective leaders to aggressively utilize the four core management styles outlined. Parker J. Palmer, noted writer, lecturer and doctor of sociology, in his work, *LEADING FROM WITHIN: Reflections On Spirituality and Leadership,* outlines five shadows that follow some leaders and lead (or can lead) to their downfall. Palmer cautions leaders about the five shadows of leadership. They are:

- **First Shadow:** deep *insecurity* about one's own identity, one's own worth. It is hard to see in most leaders' outward extroverted identity.

- **Second Shadow:** the *perception* that the universe is essentially hostile to human interests and that life is basically a battleground.

- **Third Shadow:** *functional atheism* - the basic belief that ultimate responsibility for everything rests with *me*. This is an unconscious belief that leads toward workaholic behavior, stress, burn-out, broken relationships and unhealthy priorities.

- **Fourth Shadow:** among leaders, typically, *fear*. The most basic fear in the chaos of life.

- **Fifth Shadow:** the denial of death - the inability to accept reality and the end of something when it is no longer needed, required, necessary or even breathing. Leaders can't accept the end of some things and work to artificially maintain things that aren't alive any more!

It could be said that leaders exist only to serve their followers. In the 1970s Robert K. Greenleaf, a former management researcher for AT & T and management philosopher of the twenty-first century, introduced a concept that has been slow to catch on, but in today's business climate evidence abounds of its actuality - like it or not!

Greenleaf and the Robert K. Greenleaf Center for Servant-Leadership in Indianapolis, Indiana offered an essay titled *The Servant Leader*. The premise of the essay is that leaders exist to serve their followers and that the followers grant their leader their power and allegiance in response to their servant nature.

Servant leaders embody unique traits and qualities. Among them are seven core characteristics according to Greenleaf:

> • **First:** Leaders are servants first to the team and assist it to attain its true peak performance levels.

> • **Second:** Leaders articulate goals to all players within and outside of the organization.

> • **Third:** Leaders inspire trust among and with others.

> • **Fourth:** Leaders know how and why to listen to others, internally and externally.

> • **Fifth:** Leaders are masters of positive feedback in directing and counseling others to greater accomplishments.

> • **Sixth:** Leaders rely on foresight and allow themselves time to counsel and coach themselves to greater actions.

> • **Seventh:** Leaders emphasize personal development and that external problems must first be solved inwardly. It is the inward that leaders have one hundred percent control over and merely influence the external forces. Deal with, manage and change one's self first to stimulate positive changes with the others around you.

Given these seven guideposts for leadership and a leader as servant, leaders must also realize that philosophies must be subjective to the environment. Adjustments are always necessary for success. Practitioners of Greenleaf's ideologies abound. Consider two in the 1990s alone!

Herman Miller Chairman Max DePree successfully followed the Greenleaf plan and led that organization to remarkable successes. Chief Executive Officer Jack Welch of General Electric rescued a national giant from the brink of destruction and near bankruptcy and back to an international giant and leader. Noted by *Fortune* magazine as one of America's 10 toughest bosses, he turned General Electric into the world's most powerful corporation.

The General Electric storyline is not pleasant, but it did stay the almost certain death of a giant. Welch led the sale of $11 billion worth of existing General Electric business, the buying of another $26 billion of new business, strategically reduced manpower by nearly 300,000 people worldwide and invested in his people by doubling, and, in some cases, tripling, the managerial span of controls. Welch aggressively utilizes himself and encourages his players at all levels to utilize interactive managerial styles of leadership (MANAGER, MENTOR, COUNSELOR, and COACH) at all times and in all situations (management or organizational levels of operation).

Leadership among others and within yourself is the embodiment of following the four core management styles. There are times when you will need to be a MANAGER of actions, a MENTOR to yourself and others, a COUNSELOR of difficulties and challenges, and a COACH of encouragement and attitude adjustments to attain success, happiness and harmony.

Leaders and management players like these executives also realize that the players on their teams today and those added in the future, come already designed and, for the most part, perfected with personalities, attitudes and behavioral patterns (habits). As effective managers and leaders today, one has to rely on alternative techniques for managing interactions at different times with these different people for success. As discussed earlier, management also has to realize that every management action and decision impacts people in both immediate and future time frames. Every action, in essence, conditions those around you positively or negatively.

Authors David Sadker, M.D. and Myra Sadker, Ph.D. studied the conditioning factors of people from the earliest formal settings and found that many leaders unknowingly condition negatively. The Sadkers, in their book, *Failing At Fairness*, studied school-age children from first grade through graduation and found that early interactions with a person can impact long-term performance. For example:

> • Children measured for self-esteem factors in first grade measured differently by graduation. First-grade boys measured themselves 80 percent positive overall. Girls measured themselves overall 67 percent positive. By graduation, high-school boys measured themselves 74 percent positive, while high-school girls measured themselves 32 percent positive!

> • This early stage conditioning impacts self-view and performance at later dates. How do you condition people now for later performance?

Teachers in the national study identified how they conditioned boys positively and girls negatively, without realizing they were even doing so. For example:

> • Little boys receive more positive feedback and stroking for participation and responses in classes than girls.

> • There is greater male recognition than female acknowledgments in interaction situations.

> • Seating arrangements and leadership positions favored boys over girls in early years - not because boys were more often correct, but more so because boys answered faster than girls, and, in our fast conditioning as a society, we play into the speed trap.

Gaining *"The Leadership Advantage"* requires an ability to alternate management techniques and strategies just as the teachers in the Sadker study realized that they (and you) can fall victim to habits that can ultimately prove devastating to an organization and player development. For an organization to develop, player focus must continually be on the people equation for ultimate results to be positive.

Management's thrust is to solicit and stimulate the ability of its players to **willingly** cooperate with **one another** (people factors - "P") to attain desired **results** ("R"). People participation leads to greater commitment. Commitment leads to success!

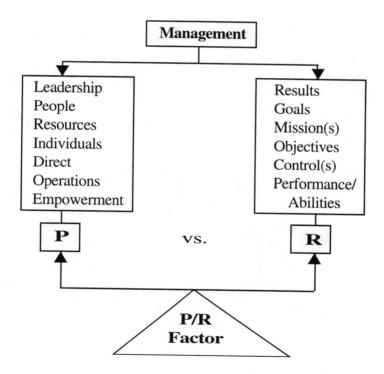

Management needs to maintain focus and practical balance between the people factor ("P" resource) and the results (outcomes or "R" factors) needed. Management personnel has to be able to intertwine these two factors for organizational effectiveness and ultimate efficiency of all resources. Traditional management can obtain compliance from the players within it, and not obtain commitment! With the management alternatives outlined in *Yield Management*, management personnel can now work to attain commitment and not just compliance from players. The balance of the two main factors (People and Results) coincides with the seven key factors that the Greenleaf Center sets forth for effective leadership and management!

Yield Management is a subjective plan of action with personal and professional models for guidance. Internalize those points which can help and adopt them into your life style(s). Those points which are not relevant at the present time in your life can be set aside for possible future consideration. Lead yourself to success!

Self-Illustration One: Consider the following activity to enable one to internalize the forces working with you and against you to align vision, mission, available resources and energy to attain organizational and self-development and growth. The key points within *Yield Management* can be best illustrated as follows:

- Materials required for activity include: (1) One pencil, (2) Two rubber bands, (3) One flat surface.
- Directions: Utilizing your individual effort, take the pencil and work the two rubber bands around the pencil at either end. Then by holding onto the rubber bands only, move the pencil to an upright position and hold firmly by the ends of the rubber band.
- Analysis: This can be accomplished, but the activity requires patience, thought and understanding of what forces are at work with you and against you. Again, effective management of the resources leads to successful leadership in unknown situations!

Team-Illustration Two: Same exercise as above, only now the players have one rubber band each, and the objective is the same!

Creating Re-Engineering Laboratories

In this state of constant change, flux, chaos (for some) and rapid-fire innovation the ability of leaders and management personnel to explore ideas, test techniques, and liberate fellow colleagues is critical to overall development (key *Organizational Development* principles - **OD**) and long-term success actions (key *Strategic Planning* processes - **SP**)!

Re-engineering suggests that individuals and groups take a new look, a fresh look, a different look, an alternate look at what needs to be done or what a group is missioned to be doing - not from a perspective of right or wrong - but from a perspective of determining if what is being done is still needed. This observation, analysis and interactive group discussion is based on the notion of whether or not there may a more strategic approach to one's *Mission Statements* and what an objective look would provide. In order for re-engineering to exist and have any degree of success, senior management must authorize and give ownership to the ideas and objectives.

The creation of a re-engineering laboratory suggests that a group of people such as an individual department, organizational division, a specific government agency, etc., be tasked with a very specific objective and empowered to address the task/challenge and attain results. From these results measurement can then take place and from the final analysis objective decisions can be made for the *Best Course Of Action* (BCOA) of entire organizations.

To create a re-engineering or experiment laboratory within an organization, a few common denominators need to be present:

  • All participating members/players must have a vested interest in the objectives and be held mutually accountable.
  • All members/participants must have a common sense of being together.

• All participants/members need to want to be a part of this new group endeavor.

• All participants/members need to be willing to put forth the efforts required in this new and different endeavor.

• All participants/members need to have access to the resources required to fulfill their challenge or task.

• Models for successful interaction and decision making need to be provided to participants in the beginning, along with any tools that can enhance their interactions for greater success.

• Participants brought together to interact within this special function should also be a cross mixture of players from that organization, department or agency.

In initiating an environment for creation and re-creation, laboratories need to be lead by visionaries and sustained with energies and support mechanisms. Laboratories need to be measured by accomplishing or working toward the initial objectives and goals and not measured by existing standards and measurements utilized within an organization, department or agency. Laboratories also should be free of the threats and challenges being faced by everyday employees and management personnel.

Laboratories for re-engineering can be applied along *Human Resource Department/Development* (**HRD**) traditional organizational lines of growth - that of being tasked as *Organizational Development* (**OD**), *Strategic Planning* (**SP**) or *Changing Culture* (**CC**).

Laboratories, in essence, become zones of experimentation and challenge. Participants tasked with specific objectives should be free from traditional organizational hierarchy and protocol to explore any and all realistic and viable options to attain desired outcomes within these test environment zones. Participants start at ground zero and explore both the status quo and alternate options or routes to greater levels of success through new ways and means. When a laboratory concludes its initial tasked assignment, the players should be able to communicate to participants within and out of the larger associated group, organization, department or agency exactly what took place within the laboratory setting.

Sustained organizational success depends upon an organization's ability to meet and beat market needs. An organization's ability to better predict how to meet those needs and be in an action mode and not a reaction mode puts it in a better position for success. That level of success can be attained through effective utilization of re-engineering laboratories, whereby senior management is always tasking the laboratories to inwardly reflect upon what is presently being done and to play with present procedures, machinery, systems, technology, people abilities, people dynamics and attempting to see if there are ways to tweek existing structures and people for greater efficient use of valuable resources.

Taking the concept of the re-engineering laboratory one step further or closer into the implementation phase, would include an atmosphere whereby managers can maintain a constant and never-ending laboratory experiments. Players should be charged with an ability to consistently be looking at what is being done and exploring ways by which efforts can be better directed and resources can more efficiently be used toward goals and objectives.

An alternative to traditional organizational dynamics and management is to establish an environment whereby departments become re-engineering labs, where agencies become re-engineering labs, where organizations become complete multi-layered labs of constant experimentations with what does and does not work to always push the human factor and the non-human factors to peak performance and whereby all participants are held accountable for their actions and results and whereby those players hold one another accountable for participation and results. This multi-layered laboratory experimentation approach causes growth, success and opportunity.

In establishing your laboratory environment consider what your team's objective is and what makes your team uniquely different from any competitive forces in your marketplace. Focus on your competitive advantages and in your laboratories of re-engineering ensure that your competitive advantages are not lost or watered down to a minimum!

Consider the following matrix as a model for re-engineering success within your organization and with your players!

RE-ENGINEERING LABORATORY MODEL ✔

4 Psychological Decisions Labs Must Address
& Player(s) Must Be Assigned For Each:
- I - Technical/Analytical Decision:
- II - Financial/Costing Decision:
- III - User/Acceptance Decision:
- IV - Coach/"I Like" Decisions:

Player(s)

Time Must Be Provided For Players To Meet
& Fulfill Their Purpose Aside From Present
Work Requirements And Obligations:

Time = When?

Purpose Must Be Defined Prior To Beginning:

Objective

!

Strategies Needed To Be Designed To Meet
Target(s) And Address:
- I - Primary Strategies:
- II - Contingency Strategies:

Strategies

Resources Needed, Required Or Access Given
In Order To Meet Lab Experiement Demands:

Resources

!

Deadline By Which Player(s) Are To Report Back
To Team Leader Or Finish Initial *Purpose*/Task:

Deadline

Players To Be Assigned To This Re-Engineering Lab Team Experiment:

Players

In converting a department to a re-engineering lab or in establishing a special and strategic group of players to a specific cause and designing them into this re-engineering lab with the authorization to experiment for a better net result, consider the previous page and the **"RE-ENGINEER-ING LABORATORY MODEL"** ©. This model serves as a starting point or check list to ensure that the basic ingredients which can spell the difference between success and failure.

In following the principles of *The Leadership Alternative* this model allows for management to empower a team with the "what" and "why" of a cause or need, and instills into the participants the power to determine the best "how" to the game plan designed. When participants design their own "hows" it is the same as entrusting them to establish their newly designed *Best Course Of Actions* (BCOA) and greater results are always achieved when players are involved in the establishment of "how" to do things.

Why does his model serve as such a valuable part of the establishment of an effective re-engineering laboratory or team? Consider what each grid on the model represents:

> • *4 Psychological Decisions* - In every overall decision making process (for example, buying decisions that a person may make), the human brain processes data and directs final decisions to be made after processing four independent factors. Once the brain has resolved and answered the questions dealing with the *Technical* aspects of the topic (purpose) and the analysis is complete, it can process the second decision. The *financial* decision impact, what costs are associated with this decision. The third decision focuses upon the *user* and how this decision impacts those people directly associated with the outcome of the decisions. Will it be resisted? The final decision rests upon the decision-maker's approval of the overall idea or decisions. Will this person mentally cheerlead the decision and *coach* others through any potential problem areas within the decision process.

> • *Time* - There must be a time line or time frame established prior to initiation and all players must be aware of it. How much time

will be allowed for participation and when are these time blocks reserved?

• *Purpose* - The purpose or objective of this team's assignment needs to be clearly communicated at the beginning. Make sure that you or management has spelled out what this lab is to produce or explore.

• *Strategies* - Need to be outlined within the lab and the net result of the lab should be to present a (possibly new) primary strategy and always contingency (back-up) strategy plans.

• *Resources* - Should always be studied and allocated to the lab so that failure can not be attributed to lack of materials and resources in the lab environment. Whether the resources are people, monies, machinery, technology, etc... within reason, ensure that your lab is suitably equipped. Also make sure that players not directly involved with the lab experiment are aware that those players in the lab have authorization to said resources.

• *Deadline* - Needs to established at the beginning of the lab assignment so that all players are clear as to when their activities are to be concluded.

• *Players* - Make sure that when a re-engineering laboratory is being established the players coming together to make up the team are compatible and have a common reason to be there. Make sure that the players you choose are from the necessary cross-section of your team and organization to ensure the highest level of creativity and success while in the lab.

Re-engineering labs are a fact of the future of successful organizational dynamics and are a powerful way to ensure success and growth and to increase players' ownership and participation levels in the organization. By looking inward to your own players for answers, serious challenges and threats can be easily and cost effectively resolved for future power.

The concept of re-engineering laboratories for achievement and organizational advancement can be utilized in may ways. Management can create these labs within the overall organization, managers can create them within their own areas and departments and players can even utilize the re-engineering concept on specific projects for which alternative answers and solutions may be desired. The re-engineering labs are places from which creativity can grow and when a lab concept is being utilized by only one person, it therefore allows for inner synergy (of the two sides of a person's brain).

From a psychological perspective and powerful behavioral motivator basis, true re-engineering labs or these new-wave teams are peak performers and can thus be sustained if management and leaders focus upon nine intrinsic team motivator factors. *The factors from which participants within teams will assume ownership and increase their level of commitment and synergy are*:

> • **Choice** - Players must be able to choose what they do and participate in or on (i.e., "These three tasks need to be addressed and completed this week. Go for it." As opposed to: "These three tasks need to be taken care. Tom, you take number one. Susan, you have number two and you take number three!").

> • **Decisions** - Players must be free to evaluate and make their own decisions free of vertical approval before acting.

> • **Feedback** - Whether positive or negative, all feedback must be presented immediately in a positive manner and with a solution. Every decision, for example, that a player makes brings with it additional ramifications and decisions and thus feedback needs to be immediate every time and that feedback needs to be resolved mentally and agreed upon by all parties involved before any further actions take place. Feedback equals action plan.

> • **Challenge** - The activities and involvement which participants are faced with must always have some degree of challenge (personally or mentally). The human machine is motivated by

challenge and without challenges players become stagnant, procrastinate and are complacent.

• **Competition** - Must be a present and looming factor. Players can be motivated by three laws of nature: Law One, we compete against *something else*; Law Two, we compete against *someone else*; Law Three, we compete against *ourself.*

• **Creative Solutions** - Players must be given autonomy and held accountable for designing their own solutions. Players will assume greater ownership of their own ideas and solutions to tasks and thus pursue them with greater energy levels.

• **Ownership** - Players who own their work become motivated and energized toward their future and that of the group - whether that group is a re-engineered lab, team or anything else! Empowerment builds personal ownership.

• **Accountability** - Ultimately every player in these groups must be held 100 percent accountable for their actions, efforts and participation levels. Players are held accountable for their actions as well of the players around them - peer unity.

• **Education** - The turbocharger to intrinsic teaming. Continued hard and soft skill education development is the life blood to sustained growth and success.

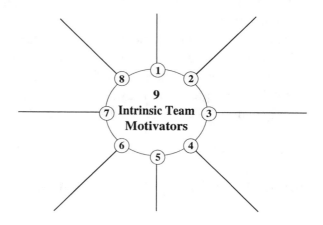

Re-engineering labs also allow people and organizations to look at and even consider testing ideas and actions which others may be using with success, but which at the present time are foreign to your organization. It also allows assigned players the opportunity to rethink what is going on and what you are all about to determine if any course corrections are necessary for survivability.

Management also draws upon all four management styles when interacting with re-engineering labs and the players within them. For the most part management will find themselves effectively operating as COACHES with this team of the future, as witnessed via the *"Management/Team Control Model"* © in Chapter Four and the relationship of the players' span of control - whether it lies with management or with the players on the team (or department of today).

The objective or purpose of **Yield Management** is to increase player participation and net results, while at the same time reducing the active role of management and management personnel in the traditional daily activities of the player(s) - turn traditional organizational layer bureaucracies where the *thinking* was reserved for upper management and the *action* was placed upon the lower levels (thus entry level, mid-management and the rank-and-file workers), into a new-age educational and empowered environment!

In this new environment, traditional management evolves into more of a leadership-management position and role. Vertical management is pushed to a state where each player is now accountable for his own level of *thinking* and *action*. Individual players and teams are now charged and allowed to learn (through both adaptive and survival based learning) and evolve via independent *thinking* and *acting* (if so desired). Management now assumes the appropriate position and management style (hat) necessary at any given time to attain peak performance!

As *Fortune* magazine recently said, "The most successful corporations of the 1990s will be something called a learning organization...The ability to learn faster than your competitors," and thus develop your people will be the net success factor. **Yield Management** is designed to enable managers and leaders of today to survive for tomorrow. These ideas are held as disciplines and maps which can allow for immediate application and results with other people. This is not a fad approach to management, as TQM was in the 1980s and early 1990s. Tom Peters and others reference the staggering high statistics attributed to the failure rates of organizations (large and small) that undergo TQM oriented management philosophies and changes.

Along with Peters' statistic that 1:10 organizations undergoing TQM will survive, the late W. Edwards Deming (perhaps the leading authority in the world on quality initiatives and management) felt that a major reason for this was due to a shift in management player thinking. Deming felt that nearly 98 percent of organizational success was centered upon basic changes on how people were treated and how people think. The focus must be upon the "systems" within organizations and allowing the thinking to take place at the proper level and that management must make a shift in how they operate from a straight MANAGER role to more of a leader manager.

"The Hotson Factor"
A True Leadership Alternative

Sometimes a MANAGER, supervisor or team leader has to manage within very rigid systems of rules, regulations and procedures and that can be very discouraging in one's attempt to execute the ideologies and methodologies presented herein. There is still a high level of success when one puts on the creativity cap and reflects on ways that can still accomplish the theme of *Yield Management.*

Recently, I had the opportunity to experience a Sunday Brunch at the Westin Hotel in downtown Kansas City, Missouri where there was a true visionary in management and a person who emulated a successful leader manager. *Benton's Restaurant* MANAGER, Mr. Melvin Hotson, who would customarily be seen greeting patrons as they came off the hotel elevator and/or interacting with patrons as they dined; on this Sunday he was in a Captain's uniform and serving tables. His explanation for his new role reversal was very shocking in today's traditional world of business!

As Mr. Hotson explained, today was the birthday of one of his wait team members and the hotel policy did not allow him to give that person a day off with pay. Nor could he give that person a special pay bonus for working on their birthday, nor could he reposition her to a special position for that day with a pay raise increase. So, his management and thus leadership alternative allowed for multiple gains. What did he do:

> • He changed jobs with her for the Sunday Brunch shift. She served as hostess and greeter (thus not having to wait on tables) and he assumed her wait responsibilities. She gets her normal hourly pay, he waits tables on this busiest day of the week.
> • He forwards all of the tips left by patrons at the end of the day to her.
> • He gets an opportunity to interact more directly with customers to learn how they view the services of the business and employees. He also gains a nonthreatening opportunity to show the team how to attain peak performance by doing it himself - lead by example!

Empowering oneself (granting oneself the qualified authority) to facilitate activities and grow the people around and within an organization is the thrust of *Yield Management* To finish your approach and strategically decide on your next *Best Course Of Action* (BCOA), reflect upon the players you have on your teams presently and the players which you may add in the future.

"The BETA © Factor"

The true test of *Yield Management* is that of enabling managers, leaders, followers and people to attain overall higher levels of performance and success in an ever-changing world. In order to attain this success a survey of business leaders of profit and not-for-profit organizations, from Fortune 500 executives to civic leaders and members of Boards of Directors was conducted. Each was asked to respond to one simple open-ended question: "If you were to add or hire another member to be among your team, what would a successful candidate look like?"

Among the multitude of responses, there developed a very definite category of responses and those have been converted into four areas! The four prerequisites of individuals: *Brains, Energy, Talent,* and *Attitude.*

Mr. Frank Sorrentino, senior vice president at vintage Guardian Life Insurance Corporation, paralleled the concept with more than 30 senior management leaders from among Fortune 500 organizations and said of **"The BETA © Factor,"** "to even be allowed to compete with successful people of tomorrow, a player must exhibit, truly exhibit, all three core factors. The fourth is the secret ingredient for ultimate and sustained life success!"

Entry into the level of tomorrow's successful professional world requires as a minimum: Brains, Energy and Talent. But you can *bet* that without the last component - a positive Attitude - true success and player empowerment will not occur!

"The BETA © Factor" requires all four for success and your *management alternative* is a powerful map for meeting that challenge! Ensure that no player be allowed to bluff his way through organizational dynamics on another player's B., E., T. or A. factors of **"The BETA © Factor!"**

All management and leadership strategic planning and actions must aim toward the support and growth of this factor. All interdepartmental or inter-team interactions should also support and reinforce both the individual's and group's development of said factor. Analyze the level of commitment that each has toward this factor and what each does to ensure planned and structured growth of each on a daily, weekly, monthly, quarterly and annual basis!

Think of this leadership alternative as, *"get out of their face management"* and *"get into increased net results management!"* What is the actual yield your present management and leadership styles (**Yield Management©**) produces and could some of these alternative ideas, strategies and tactics assist with your future growth and direction? This is the foundations of leadership today and for tomorrow!

SECTION THREE

Case Studies - How Organizations In Today's Market Emulate *THE LEADERSHIP ALTERNATIVE* Concepts

"The future is not a gift - it is an achievement."
• Harry Lauder, *Forbes* magazine

"It can be very difficult to make significant changes, especially when you have been in the habit of doing things differently for decades, and especially when the very success that brought you to the positions you now hold is rooted in doing some things, frankly, the wrong way."
• W. Edwards Deming

Case Studies - Case One:
It's A Big Wonder At SmallParts, Inc.

(600 Humphrey Street, Logansport, Indiana, 46947)

BACKGROUND: SmallParts, Inc. is in the very competitive machine parts industry as a provider of stamped metal parts and assemblies, and feeds a majority of its finished goods to the automotive, electrical and appliance industries. Like most businesses today and especially within the manufacturing industry, SmallParts has experienced a growth in business and a need to search out more efficient ways in which to meet those new business demands.

What compounds this growth and the way the company does business is an awakening they had in September of 1993. The aftermath of a tornado left SmallParts with the majority of its structure damaged and all of its finished goods inventory (to meet client orders) totally wiped out! This reality left SmallParts with a choice: Fold up the doors and close down their business; or, find an immediate answer to how to remain in business while fulfilling the orders with no inventory in hand!

SmallParts found that the realization of how to move forward after a tornado made it easier for all members of the SmallParts family to pull together and re-evaluate how they did business and how they could do it better.

The traditional work environment of management layers and rank-and-file workers (the old head-to-hands pyramid) would need to be eliminated and work teams with all members understanding how to act as both a member of the team and as a team leader would be required.

With the organization transition in place and the renewed attitude of the players on-line, there still was a need for focus and skill development among the players. The business data in 1993-94 indicated the business was in a growth mode, yet there were some serious warning signs for senior management that things were headed toward another disaster!

THE FACTS: While SmallParts' business has been in a continuous growth mode since 1985 (then at $14 million dollars in business) to nearly $36 million dollars in 1994, there were signs of problems. Some of those problems signs:

- Inventory was turning only 12 to 15 times per year.
- Machines were averaging 22.8 percent up-time (with all systems/machines on-line).
- The plant(s) were running behind (late) on nearly 300 jobs.
- The team was working a mandatory 6-day work week.
- Players were required/expected to put in a minimum 10-hour work day.
- The prevailing view of the employees was that of boredom, lack of ownership and commitment. Players would come to work, do their job and leave with no feeling or demonstration of accountability. If there were problems with a job, the marketing people would absorb the anger and stress from the client, while the person on the line responsible for the lack of quality control and care was exempt from accountability directly to or with the client.

Senior management, realizing that the team was working harder, yet the work was piling up and jobs were not getting out the door, needed to do something different - really different. One-by-one, each of the four primary shifts would undergo this something different. And in October 1994 the something different began!

REALITY CHECK: October 1994. The month that the something different arrived was October 1994. The first shift to undergo a management transformation attended a full day, comprehensive management/ team-building training session. Arriving on a Saturday, after their last work day of that week under the traditional management and worker departmental shift approach, what each member was about to experience would be by most accounts a radical undertaking. As the company president, Mr. Mike Jordan announced in the opening of this session,

"Yesterday you were a shift, today the "shift" is history as you sit here in this hotel conference room, and on Monday you will be a team. Listen up, take in the ideas and enjoy. Ask questions and challenge the program...On Monday you will have the opportunity to realize your every dream...if you have ever thought to yourself why it may be that management does the things they do and felt that you could do it more effectively, then now is your time. You will now have sole responsibility to do everything, from ordering the supplies you need through to setting your own work schedules and dealing with customer inquiries."

Six months after the first shift became the pilot team the results were staggering!

> • Inventory is turning at nearly 60 turns a year (based upon the pace set at the six-month point of the new teaming approach).
> • Machine up-time is now averaging 31.23 percent.
> • The team is now at about 27 jobs behind schedule at any given time!
> • The six-day work week is optional.
> • The day is now down to a 9 hours.
> • The team is averaging a 50 to 60 percent voluntary participation for the Saturday work schedule.
> • The team is clearing an average of five jobs more per week as opposed to the traditional work shift approach.
> • And the team has set as their ultimate goal to attain a 100 percent on-time and 100 percent defect-free parts objective.
> • The prevailing attitude on the teams (all four of the shifts have been converted to this team approach) now, is that of direct involvement. The Annual Management Meeting which traditionally would have been attended by about 46 core individuals, this year was attended by nearly 100 people. The meeting was more productive than ever before and the participants left with a powerful action plan for moving this company beyond the $40 million dollar point as a business!

How did all of this happen? Well, in part through a comprehensive educational program that armed each participant with the tools necessary to be able to effectively interact with their fellow team players and for the rotating team leader to be able to function effectively in this management leadership position - whether they had or lacked the typical and expected management training background. The system that this organization embraced and fully supported and supports in every way is that which has been outlined within this text - *Yield Management!*

Company President, Mr. Mike Jordan (with SmallParts since 1968) understands how to motivate a player and how to maintain organizational growth. Consider how many million dollar companies would undergo such a transformation of taking the scheduling, tracking, quality assurance and shipping out of the traditional management layer's hands and placing it directly into the hands of the players themselves and allowing them to make not just these decisions, but also decide on who their team leaders will be!

Consider one powerful measuring trend which indicates the increased production line with teams. The machine up-time has increased measurably in the past year and the radical up and down trends have leveled off and are becoming more even and are steadily increasing in a positive direction. Look at the following chart for an analysis of 1994 to 1995 machine up-time:

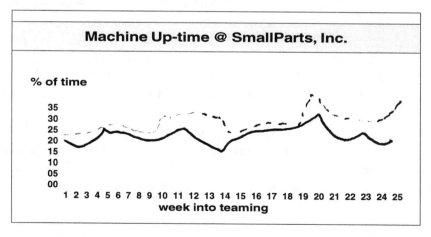

- 1994 average was 21 percent up-time
- 1995 average ytd was 23.7 percent
- Last 12 weeks of measurement, average up-time was running at 24.6 percent!

"Now as we explore this teaming approach and continue to learn how to better interact with each other and meet the customers' needs, senior management can focus on the long term of the organization in terms of exploring new markets and keeping the business in business for everyone's future... and the team will take care of the needs within," said Jordan.

In their classic *Harvard Business Review* article, "The House of Quality," authors John R. Hauser and Don Clausing assert that direct customer contact (with the external end-user customer) enables employees to shift their focus and energies away from the traditional internal concerns, thus allowing them to pay more attention to overall customers (external) needs. For organizations, employees (team players) and management (team leaders) to attain continued levels of success into the future, all will need to realize this mind-set transition and establish the right place within the system for each player - regardless of how a player has been utilized within an organization up to today!

For example, now if a customer calls into SmallParts with a problem, they may not end up talking with a marketing person about their concern (as they would have expected to based upon the previous way of doing business); they will talk directly with the person on the line that was involved with the customers product/issue - customer to player contact is critical for helping each player to understand both accountability and responsibility!"

Now, the team explores how to get more done with fewer people, attain higher levels of quality assurance by eliminating work efforts and ways to increase output while making it easier for the players and machines.

By evaluating players based upon objective criteria, players are exploring pay for performance issues, rewards for attaining greater production expectations than expected, and continual on-line educational opportunities to grow the players' and thus teams' ability levels.

To meet this need and the industry demands, SmallParts, like many other success-minded, team-driven organizations, is looking both inwardly at present members and identifying how to educate and train present members to meet their internal needs and thus allow them to fulfill the external customers' needs. To complement them, these organizations are also looking outwardly at better ways to attain the right-minded individuals to join their teams - no longer is the requirement for the manufacturing industry applicant be that they merely be breathing and have two hands. Now they must be able and willing to think independently on their feet.

One such program, for example, being explored by employers are cooperatives with educators and secondary education institutions to meet the employer-based needs. In Indiana, for example, employers are working jointly with the Technical Preparation Program (TechPrep) to grow and develop individuals within the present education system, who upon graduation are skilled in an immediately employing field!

It truly is a big wonder at SmallParts!!!

Case Studies - Case Two:
Teaming With The
Salty Iguana Restaurant

(8228 Mission Road, Prairie Village, Kansas)

BACKGROUND: Food service is an extremely volatile business market and one with exceedingly high employee turnover and bankruptcy statistics nationally. How many times have you thought about opening your own bar, neighborhood pub or restaurant? For most Americans, the conversation about opening one's own business of this sort has occurred at least once.

The Salty Iguana Restaurant is one of those businesses which came about due to some people coming together without really thinking. Add an autocratic form of management to this and you have a recipe for disaster!

In April 1992 the restaurant opened with sales of $102,000. The menu featured both traditional American cuisine and Southwest Mexican dishes. The menu was copied from another successful restaurant and the staff was very young. Meal portions were traditional and the menu pricing was consistent. By June of 1992 sales were down to $82,000 and by September of 1992 sales had fallen again to $52,000.

FACTS: Consider these problems experienced in the first year of the restaurant:

> • No market research for what the immediate neighborhood wanted in a restaurant (the immediate possible patrons).
> • Wrong menu for operation.
> • Wrong mixture of menu items.
> • Rigid autocratic management style made for difficult working environment, no flexibility.
> • Products ordered on credit and no ordering adjustments made when sales went down.

• Adversarial management roles.
• No restaurant theme or niche. Restaurant had a name but it didn't mean anything.
• Several owners operated with their own management styles and restaurant beliefs which led to more on-the-job confusion for players.

Changes and new management approach has lead to a new outlook. Consider:

• One partner bought out two other partners as business was financially on a downward turn.
• Member of staff who had restaurant experience was offered ownership option for dedicating himself to rebuilding restaurant with primary owner.
• Initial operational changes included assigning management responsibilities to the two primary partners - one partner serves as CFO and the second partner as the COO.
• All food and supplies were ordered C.O.D. as the business finances were aligned.
• The menu was redesigned to one theme and not a multitude of food options. The restaurant was focused solely as Southwest Mexican cuisine.
• Hard, expensive to prepare items were eliminated from the menu.
• The restaurant name was changed to something that employees and customers could relate to. Little iguanas appeared on shirts, hats, menus, and pictorials were painted on the walls throughout.
• Food portions were increased. Jokingly management says, "even if the meal isn't good, at least there is a lot of it!" However, the food is great, the portions are large, the price is very reasonable.
• Staff understands responsibilities and management serves in an advisory role now.
• Players are encouraged to interact with one another and hold each other accountable, thus reducing management's work.

• Base pay was increased for bus boys and kitchen staff which directly impacts attitudes and performance.

• Base pay for wait staff was decreased - commission opportunities were dramatically increased. Thus service increases, product movement increases and tables turn more times in a meal hour!

• New staff and management profiled customers coming in to determine who their present customers are and matched that with market research which outlined their potential customer. They found that the majority of their customers come from within a five-mile radius.

• Management learned from previous management players. New management never says "NO" autocratically. A "NO" now always comes with alternatives or questions.

The net result of the new management alternative is a revenue increase consistently each month for more than a year. Profitability increased each month. Positive attitudes increased. New customer business, and repeat customers increased. The work environment is seen by employees as a fun environment with colleagues and management and not an adversarial environment.

REALITY CHECK: One would expect this neighborhood place of business located in a shopping strip-center in an upscale part of the city to be decorated nicely with the traditional amenities of a hot new restaurant. One would also expect to be greeted by a nicely dressed host or hostess with quiet coves of seats, tables and booths. In the Salty Iguana Restaurant, you will experience the opposite.

When you enter you may find that your greeter will be whoever is free and open (that can be a waiter, waitress, the hostess for the evening, the bartender or a young guy in a T-shirt with little iguanas painted on it, a smile from ear to ear and a dirty apron about his waist - meet Steve Conrad the operational owner).

When you are seated you are immediately greeted by a young man or woman who serves you huge complimentary chips and salsa and takes your drink order. If you are a chip-aholic, this is the place for you. It would seem that there are invisible alarms in each chip basket as every time you eat the last chip, the basket is whisked away and a fresh basket appears with a smile from a member of the restaurant team. It may not even be a person you have seen thus far!

When your order is taken and filled, you will find the meal portions to be extremely large. As Steve joking tells customers, "Even if the food isn't good, there is a lot of it!" But the food is great and you regularly see customers leaving with portions of their meal boxed up for later.

As you have been sitting, relaxing and visiting with your colleagues, friends or family, you start to notice that everyone else seems to be relaxing and having fun as well. Upon further glance you notice that patrons are dressed in suits and casual clothes, exercise attire or summer shorts. At the Salty Iguana there is no dress code, only a code of relaxation and fun - instilled by Steve. You also notice that each room in the restaurant has iguanas painted with different themes. In the bar, it is local professional sports figures as iguanas, in the family portion of the diner it's "Little Lizard Land," and throughout the remaining restaurant it is iguana-land relaxed style.

As an owner, Steve is not what you would expect. He moves from table to table checking with customers, from the front door to the bar and to the kitchen and back, to a clean-up detail to fixing a broken cash register to laughing out loud with a colleague or with a customer - many of whom know him by first name! You can tell that Steve enjoys what he does and that is carried through to the other members of the group.

As you watch Steve interact with others you also witness the power that the workers in the restaurant are entrusted with. One employee asks to leave early, Steve responds that as long as he has cleared it with his colleagues he doesn't care - immediately putting the level of accountability back into the hands of the team's players.

Another player approaches Steve with an idea for solving a problem and is met with a big smile, a pat on the back and directed to follow through with his idea if he believes it will work. Steve turns and is off on another mission and the team becomes one level more effective.

Management has a unique perspective for its industry in terms of how to manage a successful team and operation. Find people that want to work, people that like the environment and understand what has to be done to be successful and give customers a good experience. Then give them the tools to do that and provide each with a compensation package that is directly linked to their performance.

The better each player is, the greater reward opportunities there will be for each, from the kitchen staff through the wait staff and clean-up detail. Each player is linked to the other for success. The more they assist one another in serving the customer, the more each table will turn and the greater the business transactions and tips each customer will leave the team. The more the tables turn with happy customers in the restaurant business, the more business you will have - for today and the future!

Case Studies - Case Three:
Flying High With Kimberly Clark/
KC Aviation, Inc.

(301 Discovery Drive, Appleton, Wisconsin)

BACKGROUND: The year was 1969 and the paper powerhouse Kimberly Clark was operating its own airline fleet and aviation department. Their service was so good that the company decided to subcontract their services for corporate jet maintenance and refurbishing to other corporations. From this a new business grew and KC Aviation was born. In the beginning the business had one building and hanger in Appleton, Wisconsin where the corporate headquarters were. Today KC Aviation has four facilities in four states.

A great example of what ideas and strategies like those outlined in *Yield Management* can do for you is displayed at the Appleton, Wisconsin location. Spend a day with Mr. John Rahilly, General Manager for the operation and you can quickly see why the organization has had back-to-back years of growth, profitability and success in an otherwise tough business market.

FACTS: KC Aviation posted more than $200 million in business in 1993 alone. The success can be traced to the overall alternative management styles its key leaders exhibit. Consider:

- Employees grew from 600 to in excess of 1,000 employees nationally.
- Planes arrive on the tarmac from across America and from foreign countries carrying an impressive list of other business leaders' names. Meeting the planes and coordinating overall activities for that jet isn't the operations manager for the facility - it may be a player who flew to the prospective client's operation last year and met with someone, or a technician in charge of specific areas who assumes responsibilities for fellow team players not present.

• Each department or major technical line is separate with a supervisor responsible for his own team. Team meetings initiate each day's activities and the meetings take place right on the spot where work takes place.

• Operations are set up in order of work, a systematic assembly-line-like environment which allows for work to take place without interruption of flow.

• Workers are empowered to make independent decisions within their realm of expertise.

• Special "hot teams" have been created to take care of work details that fall out of the realm of traditional work flow so that teams assigned to major tasks experience as few interruptions as possible.

• Operations have been set up so that every aspect required to facilitate a job is on-site. This eliminates the opportunity for work to get slowed down because a procedure or step is not complete due to subcontracting.

The net result is a high-growth operation setting world-class standards and maintaining a reputation that draws international attention to performance and work.

REALITY CHECK: As you approach the complex on the main airport highway, you notice the massive structure which has experienced three major construction additions. When you walk in the front door, you are made to feel as if you are at home (your home away from home).

The main lobby is designed with individual work rooms for clients to have a private escape space with work table, telephone and computer access. The open lobby area includes television, relaxing furniture, current newspapers and magazines and refreshments. An open staircase leads to the general manager's office upstairs, but you won't find him there. The GM can routinely be found walking the plant, interacting with team players from lead technicians and electronics team players to design, engineering, to interior design and layout players to support staff and clients. To say the GM works the building would be an understatement!

Other factors that tell you that you are in a unique operation include:

- As you tour the facility you notice other differences among the players. Everyone is on a first name basis and very approachable. The team here realizes that everyone makes for a successful outcome and likewise any one player can cause a failure if so desired. Players hold each other to high accountability and support one another in a professional manner!
- Another environmental factor you notice to be a little different here is that, while talking with members of a crew preparing a jet for exterior painting, there are a few members of the team outside (a mere fifty feet away) playing a quick game of basketball in the sun and on the side hanger deck. A physical on-the-job outlet!
- In the middle of all of this organized madness, a player reports that an unexpected client has called with a major job. The players immediately look at one another and, instead of falling victim to complaining, they come together as a team to design their plan of action.
- Again you witness what makes for an interactive team. As you look at the players, you realize another rarity in the 1990s work environment - player longevity.
- As you interact and meet the players on the team, it is a common variable among players to find players that have been on the KC Aviation team for 10, 15, or 20 years.
- Another factor that supports management's understanding of alternative management techniques comes when you recognize now that you have invested three hours in a very detailed tour of the KC Aviation operation, met with dozens of key players and team leaders and the person who has been guiding you through this one-on-one tour is the General Manager (the person responsible for the multi-million dollar operation) and not a support staffer!
- And you realize that while you have been touring, there have been no less than a dozen major interactions and decisions made on the run with players and no need for interruptions or "can you wait" statements.

Bibliography
And
Suggested Reading

Leaders are readers. The ***International Who's Who In Business*** estimates that the top business people in America read an estimated 21 books each year! How many books have you read this year?

Bennis, Warren and Nanus, Burt, <u>*Leaders*</u>, *The Strategies For Taking Charge*, Harper & Row, 1985

Canfield, Jack and Hansen, Mark Victor, *THE ALADDIN FACTOR*, Berkley Books, 1995

Creech, Bill, *THE FIVE PILLARS OF TQM: How To Make Total Quality Management Work For You*, New York, NY, Penguin Books, 1994

Drucker, Peter F., *Management, Tasks, Responsibilities, Practices,* Harper & Row, 1973

Fournies, Ferdinand, *Coaching For Improving Work Performance*, Liberty Hall Press, 1978

Francis, Dave and Young, Don, *Improving Work Groups*, Pfeiffer, 1992

Goldratt, Eliyahu M., *THE GOAL*, North River Press, 1984

Griffith, Samuel B., *SUN TZU: The Art Of War*, Oxford University Press, 1963

Katzenbach, Jon R. and Smith, Douglas K., *THE WISDOM OF TEAMS*, HarperBusiness, 1993

Kelly Francis J. and Mayfield, Kelly Heather, *What They Really Teach You At The Harvard Business School*, Warner Books, 1986

Kindler, Herbert, Ph.D., *RISK TAKING, A Guide for Decision Makers.* CRISP Publications, Inc., 1990

Kouzes, James M. and Posner, Barry Z., *THE LEADERSHIP CHALLENGE*, Jossey-Bass, 1987

Magee, Jeffrey L., *The "P" Factor*, Wee Print, Kansas City, MO 1994

Magee, Jeffrey L., *Power Charged For Life: Designing A Championship Attitude For Life!!!*, Wee Print, Kansas City, MO 1993

Merrill, David W., Ph.D., *Personal Styles & Effective Performance*, Chilton Book Company, 1981

Peters, Tom, *Thriving On Chaos*, Knopf, 1987

Peters, Tom, *Liberation Management*, Fawcett, 1992

Peters, Tom and Austin, Nancy, *A Passion For Excellence*, Warner Books, 1985

Poley, Michelle Fairfield. *A Winning Attitude, How To Develop Your Most Important Asset!*, Mission, KS, SkillPath Publications, Inc. 1992

Pryor, Fred, *The Energetic Manager*, New York, NY, Prentice Hall, 1987

Robbins, Anthony, *UNLIMITED POWER*, New York, NY, Simon & Schuster, 1986

Schmidt, Warren and Finnigan, Jerome, *THE RACE WITHOUT A FINISH LINE: AMERICA'S QUEST FOR TOTAL QUALITY*, Jossey-Bass, Inc., 1992

Seligman, Martin, Ph.D., *Learned Optimism,* New York, NY, Simon & Schuster, 1990

Senge, Peter M., *THE FIFTH DISCIPLINE: The Art & Science of The Learning Organization*, New York, NY, Doubleday, 1990

Tarkenton, Fran, *HOW TO MOTIVATE PEOPLE/ The Team Strategy for Success*, Harper & Row Publishers, 1986

Yate, Martin, *Hiring the Best*, Bob Adams, Inc., 1990

Yield Management:
The Leadership Alternative©

• Management / Leadership / Teaming Skills
Self-Assessment Inventory •

Name/Code: _____

Date: _____

❑ **Pre**-Reading Assessment
❑ **Post**-Reading Assessment

❏ Management / Leadership / Teaming Skills Self-Assessment Inventory ©

The following inventory is designed to assist you in assessing your skill level and knowledge base as a member of a (team-based) interactive collaboration-oriented work environment.

HOW TO UTILIZE THIS INVENTORY: Whether your capacity is as a member of the work unit, leader, facilitator or director, this inventory is designed to assist you in objectively evaluating your skill level and knowledge base **prior to** this workshop activity, **and,** then **at the end** of the workshop activity.

Mastery	Average	Needs Improvement, Learn More, Use More Frequently	Skill / Knowledge Assessment
❏	❏	❏	Connecting: Ability to connect with colleagues on what the core objective is of our work unit. I understand how to connect with others and work towards a common goal/objective.
❏	❏	❏	Connecting: Ability to gain commitment from others within my work unit to accomplish goals/objectives.
❏	❏	❏	Connecting: Ability to systematically make decisions by myself to avoid procrastination and paralysis-of-analysis. The science of management and psychology asserts that there are four basic steps in systematic decision making. Outline those four steps in the space below. _____ _____ _____ !
❏	❏	❏	Encouraging: I understand how my verbal and nonverbal signals impact how others will participate and interact with me and others.
❏	❏	❏	Encouraging: I understand how to gain agreement from individuals and groups that I interact with, for greater results.
❏	❏	❏	Questioning: I effectively use non-combative questions to gain a better understanding of the other person's perspectives and interpretations on items.
❏	❏	❏	Questioning: I understand the difference between internal and external questions; and the importance of each in collaborating with others.
❏	❏	❏	People: I understand the basic four personality types and how they integrate for effective teaming.

❑ Self-Assessment Inventory ©

Mastery	Average	Needs Improvement, Learn More, Use More Frequently	Skill/Knowledge Assessment
❑	❑	❑	People: When selecting people for a team (team activity) I understand how to objectively evaluate what that person's *skill ability* actually is and therefore how best to incorporate that individual into activities for maximum quality output.
❑	❑	❑	People: In selecting people for an activity, I understand how their diverse background can augment the efforts of the team overall to allow for greater results in a shorter period of time.
❑	❑	❑	People: I am capable of maintaining control in conflict and confrontational situations, thus attaining positive productive outcomes. The science of psychology has shown conclusively that people have 100 percent constant control over only one factor in life. That constant impacts all that we do. What is that single factor: _____ !
❑	❑	❑	Interaction: Conflicts appear within a team for basic reasons. I am capable of identifying what causes them; and how to analyze them.
❑	❑	❑	Interaction: I understand the difference between a traditional work unit and a team and collaborating group.
❑	❑	❑	Interaction: I understand the *span-of-control* philosophy and how to use and work within it.
❑	❑	❑	Interaction: I follow systematic (mental or physical) steps in generating ideas with others - idea fluency/brainstorming.
❑	❑	❑	Interaction: I know how to systematically identify problems and how to work through them to attain high impact decisions.
❑	❑	❑	Interaction: When interacting with groups of other people, I know that a group breaks down into three subgroups. And I know what those groups are and how to manage them independently to pull all members together for action.
❑	❑	❑	Celebration: I know how to reward and motivate myself and others.

❏ Self-Assessment Inventory ©

Mastery	Average	Needs Improvement, Learn More, Use More Frequently	Skill/Knowledge Assessment
❏	❏	❏	Tactics: In participating in or facilitating a meeting, there are three basic types of meetings that can be held to address items. I am effective at understanding them and using them. List the three types: (1) _____, (2) _____, (3) _____.
❏	❏	❏	Tactics: I am effective at being the delegator/delgatee and getting things done, with minimal distractions and miscommunication. There are five core steps to delegation. List the five steps to effective delegation: (1) _____, (2) _____, (3) _____,(4)_____,(5) _____.
❏	❏	❏	Focus: Define the basic components of what a *Mission Statement* must contain:_____ _____ _____ !
❏	❏	❏	Focus: I can identify what causes group conflict. What tends to be the source of group conflict (circle one): a. management styles b. operational structures c. power alignment/turf issues/territorial issues d. none of the above e. all of the above
❏	❏	❏	Focus: There are three basic ways to keep others informed as to what I am doing and to receive signals from others to make sure I am in sync with them. I understand those three channels for communication exchange and use them. The three channels are: (1) _____, (2) _____, (3) _____.
❏	❏	❏	Coping: I know how to best manage myself when interacting in an environment or with another person whom I would rather not be with at that moment in time, so as to remain focused and productive. Success: Define a professional application to this word. Success is _____ _____ _____ !

The Leadership Alternative
• Reader Survey Questionnaire •

You are important to us as our customer and business colleague. Would you please take a minute and share your reflective feelings about this innovative text. This survey should take you no more than five minutes to fill out. **P**lease read the statements below, select a numeric response and circle the number that best represents your position on that question.

Name_____

Title_____

Address_____

_____

Phone_____

1. I found ideas and techniques within this book to be helpful in my immediate professional interactions. (Circle One)

1	2	3	4	5	6	7	8	9
strongly disagree				neither agree nor disagree				strongly agree

2. The use of words, charts and tables within this book are easy to follow and understand.

1	2	3	4	5	6	7	8	9
strongly disagree				neither agree nor disagree				strongly agree

3. The book layout is easy to follow and it is easy to find key points when looking back through the text.

1	2	3	4	5	6	7	8	9
strongly disagree				neither agree nor disagree				strongly agree

4. This book includes information and techniques that are new to me.

1	2	3	4	5	6	7	8	9
strongly disagree				neither agree nor disagree				strongly agree

5. I expect to use this text as a reference tool and source for future ideas and methodologies.

1	2	3	4	5	6	7	8	9
strongly disagree				neither agree nor disagree				strongly agree

6.   Please note to what degree this book has met your expectations.

| 1 | 2 | 3 | 4 | 5 | 6 | 7 | 8 | 9 |

strongly disagree   neither agree   strongly
                                     nor disagree   agree

7.   This book was recommended to me by a colleague.

| 1 | 2 | 3 | 4 | 5 | 6 | 7 | 8 | 9 |

strongly disagree   neither agree   strongly
                                     nor disagree   agree

8.   I have recommended this text to another person.

| 1 | 2 | 3 | 4 | 5 | 6 | 7 | 8 | 9 |

strongly disagree   neither agree   strongly
                                     nor disagree   agree

9.   Please indicate briefly below how this information may be applied in your work environment.

10.   Please indicate what, if any, information you would like to see addressed or expanded upon in a future updated edition of *Yield Management: The Leadership Alternative for Performance and Net Profit Improvement©*.

Please Send Your Completed Survey To:
JEFF MAGEE INTERNATIONAL ®
P. O. Box 701918
Tulsa, OK
74170-1918

Index

Other Publications By Magee Include:

- **BOUNCEBACK SELF-MARKETING:** The "Cruise Missile" Marketer's Approach To Gaining The Winning Edge
- **YOUR NEXT MOVE:** Financial Aid Guide To Collegiate Alternatives
- **THE AMERICAN HERITAGE:** A Collection Of American Flags & American History
- **POWER CHARGED FOR LIFE:** Designing A Championship Attitude
- **THE "P" FACTOR:** The "Personality Jumpstart" Advantage
- **The Leadership Alternative!** Essential Skills For Emerging Leaders

Other Audio and Video Programs By Magee Include:

- **Coaching and Teambuilding Skills for Managers and Supervisors** (two audio cassettes)
- **Coaching and Teambuilding Skills for Managers and Supervisors** (two video training program)
- **Promoting Yourself In The Work place: How to quietly help yourself by helping others** (two audio cassettes)
- **Performance Driven Selling: The audio seminar** (three sudio cassettes program)

These titles are available through Jeff Magee International® at 918-495-3626.